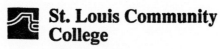

Seashore Paspalum
THE ENVIRONMENTAL TURFGRASS

R.R. DUNCAN
R.N. CARROW

ANN ARBOR PRESS
CHELSEA, MICHIGAN

Library of Congress Cataloging-in-Publication Data

Duncan, Ronald R.
    Seashore paspalum : the environmental turfgrass / by Ronald R. Duncan, Robert N. Carrow.
        p.   cm.
    Includes bibliographical references.
    ISBN 1-57504-141-3
    1. Paspalum vaginatum. 2. Turfgrasses—Effect of stress on. 3. Turf management. I. Carrow, Robert N. II. Title

SB615.P3 D86 2000
635.9′642—dc21   99-087984

ISBN 1-57504-141-3

© 2000 by Sleeping Bear Press
Ann Arbor Press is an imprint of Sleeping Bear Press

PRINTED IN THE UNITED STATES OF AMERICA
10 9 8 7 6 5 4 3 2 1

About the Authors

Dr. Robert N. Carrow is Professor of Turfgrass Stress Physiology and Soil Stresses, Crop and Soil Sciences Department, University of Georgia, Griffin. Research emphasis is on turfgrasses as affected by environmental, traffic (wear and soil compaction), and edaphic (soil chemical and physical) stresses. (E-mail: rcarrow@gaes.griffin.peachnet.edu)

Dr. Ron R. Duncan is Professor of Turfgrass Breeding (Paspalum, Tall Fescue) and Stress Physiology, Crop and Soil Sciences Department, University of Georgia, Griffin. Research emphasis on developing turfgrasses with enhanced tolerance to abiotic, edaphic, and biotic stresses, improved compatibility with the environment, and minimal requirements for maintenance. (E-mail: rduncan@gaes.griffin. peachnet. edu)

Acknowledgments

A comprehensive undertaking of this magnitude could not have been accomplished without the assistance of many, many people. Several of the direct and indirect contributors are listed below.

Universities
Dave Kopec (AZ)
J. Bryan Unruh (FL)
James Read (TX)
Jack Fry (KS)
Charles Taliaferro (OK)
Al Dudeck (FL)
Vic Gibeault (CA)
Ali Harivandi (CA)
Vance Baird (SC)
Terry Riordan (NE)
Bingru Huang (KS)
Bob Shearman (NE)
John Boyd (AR)
Fred Yelverton (NC)
Greg Wiecko (Guam)
Byron Burson (TX)
Laurie Trenholm (FL)
S. Kris Braman (GA)
W.W. Hanna (GA)
Gil Landry (GA)
B.J. Johnson (GA)
Tim Murphy (GA)
Joe Purser (GA)
Rodney Connell (GA)

USGA
Jim Snow
Mike Kenna
Kimberly Erusha
Pat O'Brian
Mike Huck
Larry Gilhuly
Pat Gross
Paul Vermeulen
Chris Hartwiger
Ron Reed
Jim Latham
Jim Moore

Georgia GCSA
Karen White

GCSAA
Jeff Nus

GC Architects
Pete Dye
Robin Nelson
Bobby Weed

International
Gary Beehag (Australia)
Gad Ron (Israel)
Neil Tainton (South Africa)
Geungjoo Lee (South Korea)
Phil Ryan (Australia)

Miscellaneous
Jim Watson (CO)
Tom Staton (HI)
J.B Beard (TX)
A. Baltensperger (NM)
J.K. Wipff (OR)

Litta Wei (P.R. China)

Turfgrass Producers Intl.
Ken Morrow (GA)
Mark/Jimmy/Keith Egan (GA)
David Doguet (TX)
Thomas Bros. (TX)
Steve Beeman (FL)
Don Roberts (AL)

Golf Course Superintendents
Ronny Mobley–Cherokee Rose (GA)
Mark Hoban–The Standard Club (GA)
Stewart Bennett–Alden Pines (FL)
Steve Swanhart–Kapolei (HI)
Brian Darrock–Fairbanks Ranch (CA)
Don Parsons–Old Ranch (CA)
David Stone–The Honors (TN)
Gary Grigg–Royal Poinciana (FL)
Tony Taylor–Thai GCC (Thailand)
Robert Volpe–Moss Creek (SC)
Gary Smither–Landfall Club (NC)

Gil Lovell (GA)
Larry Stowell (CA)
Wendy Gelernter (CA)
Mike Healy (AL)
Andree-Anne Couillard (OH)
Hank Obenauf (FL)
Frank Reed (FL)
Jesse Grimsley (GA)
Mark Prinster (GA)
Tom Burton (GA)

Ken Schwark–Tony Lema (CA)
Terry Vassey–Carolina National (NC)
Tim Cunningham–Atlanta National (GA)
Fred Flora–Hohenwald G. & Rec. (TN)
Carl Suding–Padre Isles (TX)
Craig Baker–Sailfish Point (FL)
George Mackanos–Hawks Nest (FL)
Lewis Lawrence–Berkeley Hills (GA)
Tom Davis–Bay Beach Club (FL)
Larry Garrett–Butternut Creek (GA)
Kyle Rushing–Kings Crossing (TX)

Special accolades to the funding agencies: U.S. Golf Association, Golf Course Superintendents Association of America, Turfgrass Producers International, Georgia Turfgrass Foundation Trust, Georgia Seed Development Commission, Potash & Phosphate Institute.

Special appreciation goes to Elaine Cooksey, who typed this manuscript initially and who traveled down the multiple-revision path many times with two individuals who always found ways to change things around.

To those individuals who might have been inadvertently left out, our humble apologies for failing to acknowledge your contribution.

Preface

A NEW GRASS FOR A NEW ERA

The twenty-first century will bring changes in the turf industry. Environmental regulations at the international, federal, state, and local levels will result in close scrutiny of pesticide, fertilizer, and irrigation applications. Water quality and quantity issues will result in major shifts in turf to *utilization of alternative water resources,* ranging from good to bad quality wastewater. Seashore paspalum provides an alternative grass of comparable texture and quality to the hybrid bermudagrasses that can tolerate effluent, brackish, and seawater blends, with some ecotypes tolerating straight seawater. Use of variable quality water resources subsequently changes management strategies. Choice of salt-tolerant grass cultivars becomes an increasingly important consideration, since selecting salt-sensitive species can double management costs compared to salt-tolerant species.

NEW MANAGEMENT PROTOCOLS

This reference book combines basic science, history, the global chronicles of seashore paspalum, and *comprehensive management protocols.* Management of seashore paspalum for turf is presented from three perspectives: (1) based on specific scheduling of regular maintenance practices (fertilization, irrigation, pest control, mowing); (2) based on specific industry use (golf courses, athletic fields, lawns and landscapes, sod production); and (3) based on specific environmental stress situations (use of effluent water, sites using seawater or those affected by salt water intrusion, acid soil complex soils, environmentally sensitive wetland sites).

A NEW PRECEDENT

The authors hope that this book will establish a precedent within the turf industry regarding information packaging and providing *an operational manual* for turf managers when new cultivars are released for industry use. Since turfgrass managers are faced with *site-specific multiple stress problems* and decision-making, a four-pronged approach to growing seashore paspalum has been developed.

The four components of communication and problem-solving are:

- A seashore paspalum operational manual combining science and specific management options.
- A book entitled *Salt-Affected Turfgrass Sites: Assessment and Management* (Ann Arbor Press, 1998) that covers soil, water, and turf management in saline-affected sites.
- A two-day advanced-level workshop sponsored by the Golf Course Superintendents Association of America on "Salt-Affected Turfgrass Sites: Assessment and Management."
- The development of new and improved seashore paspalum cultivars with multiple stress resistance (especially high salinity tolerance) and high turf quality and performance attributes.

A NEW ERA HAS BEGUN....

Table of Contents

Part IV. Basic Principles When Using Alternative Water Resources/Problem Sites

xiii

Seashore Paspalum
THE ENVIRONMENTAL TURFGRASS

Part I
Seashore Paspalum
Background and Description

CHAPTER 1

Introduction

Two domineering factors will significantly affect turfgrass management in the twenty-first century: **water quality** and **water quantity/ conservation**. These will dominate management decisions, since potable water use will shift primarily to human and industrial components while alternative water resources (recycled, gray, effluent, nonpotable, wastewater, brackish, and ocean water) will be used exclusively for irrigating turfgrass sites (golf courses, sports fields, lawn/landscape areas, parks, roadsides) (Carrow and Duncan, 1998; USGA, 1994). Concerns for the environment and federal, state, and local governmental regulations (particularly the Food Quality and Protection Act) mandating compliance will force major shifts in turfgrass management strategies. Turfgrasses will be required to have (1) multiple environmental stress tolerances, (2) improved nutrient uptake and utilization efficiency (require judicious applications of fertilizers), (3) more stable disease and insect resistance (require minimal pesticides), and (4) the capability to tolerate a wide range of alternative (variable quality, nonpotable) water resources. These more **environmentally compatible turfgrasses** will necessitate a change in philosophy on how they should be managed. Management protocols will change in comparison to current practices, because these grasses will be exposed to more than one abiotic (salt, drought, high/low temperatures, low light intensity/shade, extreme soil acidity or alkalinity, low soil oxygen), biotic (insects, diseases), or man-made stress (wear, traffic, compaction, mowing height). Successful turfgrass managers will adjust their management decisions without compromising turf quality, cosmetic appearance, or short- and long-term performance.

With the right choice of grass species and cultivars for their particular environment, turfgrass managers can have more flexibility in their management decisions. Well adapted grass species offer a better buffer to environmental extremes, a less radical response to those stresses, better persistence and long-term performance, lower overhead budgets, and easier and more flexible (a shift from micro- to macromanagement strategies) management decisions. Poorly adapted grass species exhibit rapid stress-related responses, have less persistence, have cyclic shifts in overall quality, traits, and performance, cost more to manage, and require enhanced monitoring with little margin for error. Management costs are greater and environmental extremes often cause a rapid and complete collapse in the turfgrass management system. Alternative turfgrass choices that are environmentally friendly will be needed. Or, currently used species will have to be improved in their multiple stress tolerances.

One grass that will play a dominant role in turf systems in the twenty-first century will be seashore paspalum (*Paspalum vaginatum* Swartz) (Duncan, 1999ab; Morton, 1973). This grass has multiple stress resistance: salinity tolerance (up to ocean water salt levels for some ecotypes: 54 dSm^{-1} or 34,400 ppm); pH range of 3.6 to 10.2; ecotypes with drought resistance equal to the best drought tolerant centipedegrass (*Eremochloa ophiuroides* Munro cv. TifBlair) and better than the best bermudagrasses (*Cynodon* spp.); waterlogging/low oxygen tolerances; and low light intensity tolerance when exposed to monsoonal or prolonged cloudy conditions, or reduced light in domed stadiums (not tree shade tolerance). Paspalum requires minimal pesticides and only judicious applications of fertilizers for long-term maintenance. It is very efficient in the uptake of critical fertilizer nutrients and can tolerate a wide range of recycled water resources. Turf quality traits and performance are equal to or better than most bermudagrasses, especially in environments subjected to multiple stresses and poor quality water. This grass can also be used for bioremediation (to clean up the environment via phytoaccumulation/hyperaccumulation of metals and organic chemicals or via rhizofiltration) (see Chapter 19).

CHAPTER 2

Nomenclature

Paspalum vaginatum O. Swartz is primarily known as seashore paspalum, or simply paspalum. Other less common names include siltgrass (Morton, 1973) or sand knotgrass. In Australia, it is traditionally referred to as saltwater couch. In Latin American countries, paspalum characteristically involves the words grama, gramon, or gramilla with additional localized phrases or words (Table 2.1).

2.1. SYNONYMY

A complex set of synonyms involving genera and species chronicles the progression of this grass in botanical literature (Table 2.2). These emerging synonyms can be used to track publications during the period from 1788 to 1901. Additional references include Acevedo de Vargas, 1944; Bosser, 1969; Loxton, 1977; Mejia, 1984; Schulz, 1962.

From the early 1900s to 1976, *Paspalum vaginatum* was the predominately used scientific name (Chase, 1929; Hitchcock, 1971). In 1976, taxonomists tried to switch the name to *Paspalum distichum* C. Linnaeus (Loxton, 1974; Guedes, 1976). The ensuing debate in the literature (Fosberg, 1977; Renvoize and Clayton, 1980; Guedes, 1981) lasted until 1983 (*Taxon* 32:281) when the nomenclature committee for Spermatophyta officially designated *Paspalum vaginatum* O. Swartz as the correct scientific name. The confusion in nomenclature is reflected in a number of publications where *P. distichum* is used in place of *P. vaginatum* and *P. paspaloides* is used for *P. distichum*:

1. Sleper, D.A., K.H. Asay, and J.F. Pedersen. 1989. *Contributions from Breeding Forage and Turf Grasses*. CSSA Spec. Pub. 15. Crop Sci. Soc. Amer., Madison, WI.
2. *Tropical Grasses* by Skerman and Riveros, 1990.
3. *Panicoid Grass Weeds* by Hafliger and Scholz, 1980.

Table 2.1. Common Names for *Paspalum vaginatum* Swartz

United States	seashore paspalum	bisquitgrass
	sand knotgrass	seaside millet
	siltgrass	sheathed paspalum
	saltwater grass	
Western Australia	seashore paspalum	
Eastern Australia	saltwater couch	
Malaysia	water couchgrass	
France	herbe rampante	
Peru	grama bobo	
	grama saluda	
Cuba	gramon	
	cambute	
	grama de mor	
Chile	chepica	
Columbia	grama bobo	grama cristovao pereira
	grama de mar	grama rateira
	hierba de aluvion	
Brazil	grama	
	capim de praia	
Argentina	chepica dulce	
	gramilla dulce	
Other Spanish	gramilla	
	gramilla blanca	
Java	asinan	
Philippines	pagetpet	
	panluilui	
Madagascar	herbe la mare	
	chiendent des marais	
South Africa	country club grass	

Sources: Bosser, 1969; Hafliger and Scholz, 1980; Mejia, 1984; Morton, 1973; Skerman and Riveros, 1990.

Correct nomenclature distinctions can be found in Webster, 1987; Echarte and Clausen, 1993; Alderson and Sharp, 1995; and Hitchcock, 1971.

Table 2.2. Published Synonyms for *Paspalum vaginatum* in Chronological Order

Year	Genus	Species	Authority	State or Country
1759	*Paspalum*	*distichum*	C. Linnaeus	Jamaica
1788	*Paspalum*	*vaginatum*	O. Swartz	Jamaica
1810	*Paspalum*	*littorale*	R. Brown	Australia
1816	*Digitaria*	*foliosa*	Lagasca Y. Segura	Cuba
1820	*Paspalum*	*tristachyum*	LeConte	Georgia
1824	*Digitaria*	*tristachya*	Schultes	—
1829	*Paspalum*	*brachiatum*	K. von Trin. ex Von Esenbeck	Martinique Nees
1829	*Paspalum*	*foliosum*	K. Kunth	—
1830	*Paspalum*	*kleineanum*	J.S. Presl.	Peru
1850	*Paspalum*	*inflatum*	A. Richard	Cuba
1854	*Paspalum*	*didactylum*	Salzm. ex Steudel	Brazil
1855	*Panicum*	*vaginatum*	Gren. & Godr.	France
1861	*Paspalum*	*distichum* var. *tristachyum*	Wood	—
1864	*Paspalum*	*distichum* var. *vaginatum*	Swartz ex Grisebach	British West Indies
1877	*Paspalum*	*reptans*	Poiret ex Doll	—
1877	*Paspalum*	*vaginatum* var. *nanum*	J. Doll	Brazil
1877	*Paspalum*	*vaginatum* var. *pubescens*	J. Doll	Brazil
1883	*Paspalum*	*reimarioides*	Chapm.	Florida
1897	*Paspalum*	*vaginatum* var. *reimarioides*	Chapm.	Florida
1898	*Paspalum*	*distichum* var. *nanum*	(Doll) O. Stapf	—
1901	*Sanguinaria*	*vaginata*	(Swartz) Bubani	Florida
1902	*Paspalum*	*distichum* var. *littorale*	R. Brown	Australia
1941	*Paspalum*	*distichum* subsp. *vaginatum*	(Swartz) Maire	Africa
1976	*Paspalum*	*distichum*	C. Linnaeus	United States
1977	*Paspalum*	*vaginatum* subsp. *nanum*	O. Swartz (Doll)	S. Africa
1983	*Paspalum*	*vaginatum*	O. Swartz	United States

Sources: Chase, 1929; Hitchcock, 1971; Hitchcock and Chase, 1917; Webster, 1987.

CHAPTER 3

Taxonomy

3.1. CLASSIFICATION

Family	Gramineae (Poaceae)
Subfamily	Panicoideae
Supertribe	Panicodae
Tribe	Paniceae
Subtribe	Setariinae
Genus	*Paspalum*
Group	Disticha
Species	*vaginatum*
Authority	Swartz

The Panicoideae includes a diverse group of grasses found primarily in tropical and subtropical latitudes (Chapman and Peat, 1992), but extending into temperate climates (Watson and Dallwitz, 1992). The supertribe Panicodae can be found in diverse pantropical to temperate habitats with widely variable rainfall requirements. Besides *Paspalum*, the tribe Paniceae also includes *Axonopus* (carpetgrass), *Digitaria* (crabgrass), *Panicum* (torpedograss), *Pennisetum* (kikuyugrass, fountaingrass, buffelgrass), *Setaria* (bristlegrass), and *Stenotaphrum* (St. Augustinegrass) (Watson and Dallwitz, 1992). Buffelgrass was formally listed in the genus *Cenchrus,* but is now considered a *Pennisetum* (Wipff, 1995). The subtribe Setariinae also includes *Paspalum, Panicum, Brachiaria* (signalgrass), *Echinochloa* (barnyardgrass), *Setaria,* and *Axonopus* (Chapman and Peat, 1992; Hafliger and Scholtz, 1980) as well as 60 additional genera. The group Disticha includes *P. vaginatum* that inherently colonizes saline ecosystems such as along seacoasts and on brackish sands, and *P. distichum* can be found dispersed over a wider geographical area away from coastal venues, but growing in freshwater, moist habitats (Silveus, 1933). Paspalum is thought to have evolved directly from *Pani-*

cum (Chapman, 1992). *Paspalum* and *Digitaria* have closely related spikelet inflorescence morphology (Hafliger and Scholtz, 1980).

3.2. BOTANICAL DESCRIPTION

Paspalum vaginatum is an ecologically aggressive, littoral warm-season perennial grass. The species is both rhizomatous and stoloniferous (Morton, 1973; Webster, 1987). Flowering culms are erect or basally decumbent, and vary in height from 8–60 cm with 5–13 glabrous (hairless) nodes. Stolon nodes are distinctly pubescent. Mid-culm leaves do not have sheath or blade auricles, are distinctly distichous, 50–220 mm long, 1–4 mm wide, are linear and glabrous, gradually tapering to a narrow apex. The prophyllum is 20–40 mm long. The 1 mm ligule is membraneous and truncate with a pubescent collar. The inflorescence is fully exserted at maturity, and is composed mainly of two primary branches (racemes) 20–60 mm in length, with 16–32 twin-rowed spikelets on the primary branch. Each spikelet is solitary, plano-convex, subsessile, elliptic, 2.5 to 4.5 mm long, and 0.9 to 1.5 mm wide. Anthers are 1.2 to 1.6 mm long. Caryopses (seeds) are 2.5 to 3.0 mm long and 1.5 mm wide, narrowly obovate, subacute, and slightly concavo-convex (Hafliger and Scholtz, 1980; Silveus, 1933; Vegetti, 1987; Webster, 1987). The range in leaf textures among *P. vaginatum* ecotypes includes: very coarse, ornamental types; coarse types (resembling St. Augustinegrass); intermediate types (resembling common bermudagrass); and fine-leaf types (resembling dwarf bermudagrass).

3.3. CHROMOSOME NUMBER/CYTOLOGY

The genus *Paspalum* contains either 320 species (Watson and Dallwitz, 1992), 330 (Clayton and Renvoize, 1986), or 400 species (Chase, 1929, 1951). Approximately 220 species can be found in practically all herbaceous communities within various ecosystems in Brazil (Valls, 1987). A substantial number of *Paspalum* species are characterized by an apomictic, autotetraploid race and a sexually reproducing self-incompatible diploid race (Quarin, 1992). Phenotypically, cospecific tetraploid and diploid biotypes do not normally differentiate and usually form sympatric populations in South America (Norrmann et al., 1989). Diploids provide the genetic variability during the evolution of apomictic tetraploid *Paspalum* species (Espinoza and Quarin, 1997). The diploid *Paspalums* are generally self-incompatible and nonapomictic (Bovo et al., 1988). The basic chromosome number for most *Paspalums* is x=10 (Bovo et al., 1988; Pitman et al., 1987).

Paspalum vaginatum is a sexually reproducing decumbent diploid species with some self-sterility and a propensity for cross-pollination between clones of diverse origin (Carpenter, 1958). The chromosome number for *P. vaginatum* O. Swartz is 2n=2x=20 (Echarte and Clausen, 1993; Fedorov, 1974; Llaurado, 1984; Okoli, 1982; Quarin and Burson, 1983). One report of a tetraploid (2n=4x=40; *Taxon* 25:155–164) and a hexaploid (2n=6x=60; *Taxon* 24:367–372) has been documented for *P. vaginatum*. This species has the **D** genome (Bashaw et al., 1970; Burson 1981a, 1983), which is unique among the diploid *Paspalums* (Table 3.1) with the exception of *P. indecorum* Mez. whose chromosomes exhibited partial homology with members of the **D** genome (Quarin and Burson, 1983). Interspecific hybridization using *P. vaginatum* has been difficult, but limited success in producing hybrids has been accomplished using *P. vaginatum* as the pollen parent and *not the female* parent (B.L. Burson, personal communication). All hybrids between *P. dilatatum* J. Poiret (2n=4x=40) and *P. vaginatum* were completely sterile (Burson et al., 1973). Five triploid hybrids (2n=3x=30) were produced between *P. urvillei* Steud. (2n=4x=40) and *P. vaginatum* (1.3% crossability) (Burson and Bennett, 1972). Twenty-eight diploid *P. jurgensii* Hackel x *P. vaginatum* hybrids have been produced (Burson, 1981b). Eight diploid hybrids were made between *Paspalum notatum* J. Flugge (2n=2x=20) and *P. vaginatum*, but no viable seed were produced (Burson, 1981b). Seven diploid *P. pumilum* Nees x *P. vaginatum* hybrids and two reciprocal hybrids have been produced (Burson, 1981b). Four *P. indecorum* x *P. vaginatum* diploid hybrids (2 had 2n=2x=20 and 2 had 2n=2x=21 chromosomes) revealed partial homology between these species (Quarin and Burson, 1983), but no hybrid produced viable seed. The unique **D** genome would account for this difficulty. Attempts to consistently produce viable seed of this species has not yet been successful.

Investigations into the self-incompatibility problem in the sexual diploids *P. simplex, P. chaseanum,* and *P. plicatulum* Michx. (Table 3.1) indicated that these species were highly self-sterile but cross fertile (Espinoza and Quarin, 1997). The low self-pollinated seed set was caused by failure of the pollen tube to reach the ovule. The pollen germinated and actually penetrated the stigma, but the pollen tube failed to grow in

Table 3.1. Additional *Paspalum* Diploid Species and Genome If Known

Species	Genome
vaginatum	DD
indecorum	DD (partial)
pumilum	NN
chromyorhyzon	NN
notatum var. *saurae*	NN
quadrifarium	II
intermedium	II
brunneum	II
haumanii	II
densum	II
jurgensii	JJ
paniculatum	JJ
setaceum var. *ciliatifolium*	SS
chacoense	
simplex	
plicatulum	
chaseanum	
thunbergii	

the style. With cross-pollination, the pollen tubes penetrated both the stigma and style, grew through the ovary, and reached the micropyle.

3.4. PROPAGATION

Paspalum vaginatum (hereafter referred to as paspalum) must be propagated from sprigs or sod, since seed production has not been reliable. Sprigging rates can vary from a minimum of 5 bushels per 1000 ft² (or 200 bushels per acre) to normal warm-season grass rates of 400–600 bushels per acre. Generally the finer-textured paspalum ecotypes establish better than the coarse-textured types because of a greater node volume (node ratio roughly 13: 5) (Webster, 1987).

In order to maintain genetic purity and prevent or minimize cross-contamination in the paspalum breeding program at the University of Georgia-Griffin, very strict protocols in handling vegetatively propagated material have been implemented. Following initial field evaluation, promising ecotypes are taken to the greenhouse where a single stolon is selected and planted in soilless media. This experimental ecotype is continually increased in the greenhouse and is eventually planted in advanced-stage evaluations on golf courses and in sports fields. A foundation field is subsequently planted in anticipation of possible release for commercial use, with the source vegetative material always tracing back to the single stolon breeder material.

3.5. DIFFERENTIATION FROM *Paspalum distichum* L.

Both *P. distichum* and *P. vaginatum* are members of the Disticha group, but can be differentiated by several key attributes. Botanically, both species have rhizomes and stolons, membraneous ligules, and rolled leaf buds (Beehag, 1986; Hitchcock, 1971; Hitchcock and Chase, 1917). *Paspalum distichum* has pubescent (hairy) glumes while *P. vaginatum* has glaborous (hairless) glumes. Both species inhabit aquatic biotopes, waste places, rotation crops, and perennial crops (Hafliger and Scholtz, 1980). However, *P. distichum* occurs primarily in freshwater habitats, i.e., swamps, irrigation canals, earthen dams, and drainage outlets, while *P. vaginatum* dominates saline soils and brackish swamps in esturine sands and marshy muds near the seashore (Barnard, 1969; Bor, 1960; Skerman and Riveros, 1990).

Common names for *P. distichum* include knotgrass, joint grass, eternity grass (United States), water couch, couch paspalum (Australia); mercer grass (New Zealand); chepica, grama colorada, grama de aqua, pasto dulce (Spanish); gramilla blanca, pata de gallina, salaillo (Peru); groffe doeba (Suriname); gharib (Iraq); and sacasebo (Cuba). This grass has a number of synonyms involving the scientific name (Table 3.2), but the dispute among taxonomists regarding *P. distichum* or *P. paspaloides* was finally resolved in 1983 (*Taxon* 32:281) when the nomenclature committee for Spermatophyta officially designated *Paspalum distichum* L. as the correct scientific name. However, confusion in the literature is reflected in Skerman and Riveros (1990), Hafliger and Scholtz (1980), and Sleper et al. (1989), where only *P. paspaloides* can be found. Correct nomenclature is used in Alderson and Sharp (1995), Echarte and Clausen (1993), and Webster (1987).

At least 20 morphological characteristics can be used to differentiate the two species (Echarte and Clausen, 1993; Ellis, 1974; Loxton, 1974) involving the inflorescence and leaves, with hairy (pubescent) glumes (*P. distichum*) and hairless (glabrous) glumes (*P. vaginatum*) being a primary distinction. Both *distichum* and *vaginatum* have two conjugate

Table 3.2. Synonyms for *Paspalum distichum*

Year	Genus	Species	Authority	State or Country
1759	*Paspalum*	*distichum*	C. Linnaeus	Jamaica
1803	*Digitaria*	*paspalodes*	A. Michaux	South Carolina
1816	*Paspalum*	*digitaria*	J. Poiret in Lam.	South Carolina
1816	*Milium*	*paspalodes*	S. Elliott	South Carolina
1817	*Milium*	*distichum* (L.)	G. Muhlenberg	—
1829	*Paspalum*	*michauxianum*	K. Kunth	—
1830	*Panicum*	*paspaliforme*	J.S. Presl.	Peru
1830	*Panicum*	*polyrrhizum*	J.S. Presl.	California
1830	*Paspalum*	*fernandezianum*	L. Colla	California
—	*Paspalum*	*polyrhizum*	J.S. Presl.	—
—	*Panicum*	*digitarioides*	Rasp. ex Kunth	—
1836	*Paspalum*	*fernandezianum*	L. Colla	Chile
1854	*Paspalum*	*chepica*	E. Von Steudel Chile	
1877	*Paspalum*	*vaginatum* var. *pubesens*	J. Doll	Brazil
1886	*Paspalum*	*schaffneri*	A. Grisebebach	Mexico
1890	*Paspalum*	*elliottii*	S. Watson	—
1894	*Paspalum*	*paspaloides*	(Michaux) Lamson-Scribner	—
1895	*Digitaria*	*disticha* (L.)	Fiori and G. Paoletti	Italy
1901	*Anastrophus*	*paspaloides*	G. Nash	—
1906	*Paspalum*	*distichum* var. *digitaria*	E. Hackel	Argentina
1912	*Paspalum*	*distichum* subsp. *paspalodes*	A. Thellung	—
1976	*Paspalum*	*paspaloides*	(Michx.) Lams.-Scribn.	United States
1983	*Paspalum*	*distichum*	C. Linnaeus	United States

Sources: Bor, 1960; Chase, 1929; Hitchcock, 1971; Hitchcock and Chase, 1917; Webster, 1987.

racemes in the inflorescence and are considered psammophilous species (Barreto, 1957). In comparing chromosome numbers, *P. vaginatum* is predominately diploid (2n=2x=20) (Bashaw et al., 1970; Burson et al., 1973; Echarte and Clausen, 1993; Fedorov, 1974; Llaurado, 1984; Okoli, 1982; Quarin and Burson, 1983). For *P. distichum,* two cytotypical groups have been documented: tetraploids (2n=40) in one group and pentaploids (2n=50), hiperpentaploids (2n=52,54,57,58), and hexaploids (2=60) in the other group (Echarte et al., 1992). Tetraploid and hexaploid cytotypes reproduce by aposporous apomixis (Quarin and Burson, 1991). The hexaploids are the dominate cytotype in Buenos Aires province, Argentina (Echarte et al., 1992). Phenograms indicate a distinct, nonintegrated clustering pattern between the two species and probable unique genomes (Echarte and Clausen, 1993). The genome designation for *P. distichum* is currently unknown.

P. *distichum* is used for levee bank stabilization purposes in the Sydney, Australia area. This species can be found in a similar role on earthen dams in moist nonsaline inland sites in the Americas.

CHAPTER 4

History

4.1. ADAPTATION ZONE

Paspalum vaginatum is a littoral, warm-season perennial grass found normally between 30–35° N–S latitudes near sea level in tropical and subtropical to warm temperate regions (Morton, 1973; Skerman and Riveros, 1990). The species is considered helophytic and mesophytic (Webster, 1987). This hydrophilous grass is suited to aquatic, semiaquatic, and moist environments (Skerman and Riveros, 1990). The grass will tolerate waterlogged conditions and periodic meso-haline flooding in salt swamps, coastal flats, and tidal marshes (Colman and Wilson, 1960). It is useful for erosion control on salinity-sensitive lands (soil stabilization) and areas subjected to tidal influences (sand-binder, beach protection) (Skerman and Riveros, 1990). Paspalum occurs wild on seacoasts of both hemispheres. In the Americas, it is found almost exclusively along the Atlantic coastal exposure in marshy, brackish ecosystems. It is considered the most salt-tolerant warm-season turfgrass (Carrow and Duncan, 1998), with ecotypes that are tolerant to ocean water (34,400 ppm or 54 dSm^{-1} salt) salinity levels.

Vegetation regions in Australia where *P. vaginatum* grows include tropical heaths, tropical and subtropical rainforests, tropical and subtropical wet sclerophyll forests, dry sclerophyll forests, tropical and subtropical subhumid wetlands, semiarid shrub woodlands, and acacia shrublands (Webster, 1987). It can also be found in mangrove swamps.

In southern Africa, *P. vaginatum* is found widely distributed in South Africa, Namibia, and Swaziland. In South Africa, it occurs mainly, but not exclusively, along the coast from the northwestern extremity of KwaZulu-Natal (abutting Mozambique) to the furthermost southwestern tip of the country (Cape Town vicinity). In the southwest, the ecotypes are very fine-leaf textured and have been referred to in *Flora capensis* as *P. distichum* L. var. *nanum* J. Doll Cape types (Chippendall, 1955, and Table 2.2). A different fine-leaved ecotype grows near a salt marsh behind the dunes near East London in the Eastern Cape. This ecotype does not appear along the western coastline of the country, but can be found in the vicinity of Swakopmund, Mariental, Free State, and southern Gauteng regions in Namibia. The distribution extends over much of the Mozambique coast and northward toward East Africa (Neil Tainton, personal communication).

Paspalum vaginatum occurs on sandy beaches, on the banks of estuaries frequently inundated by salt water, and along the banks of coastal rivers. It can be found inland near the edge of saline water on sandy soils.

4.2. CENTERS OF ORIGIN

Some botanists consider *P. vaginatum* indigenous to Asia, Africa, and Europe (Judd, 1979), while others consider it native to the New World but introduced and naturalized in the Old World (Bovo et al., 1988; Chase, 1929; Echarte et al., 1992; Morton, 1973). Based on ecotype collection of paspalums along the eastern coastal United States, coarse-, intermediate-, and fine-textured types are found primarily in Georgia and South Carolina at off-loading sites for slave boats from Africa that arrived during the 1700s and 1800s (Gray, 1933). Sites such as Sea Island and Ft. Pulaski, Georgia and Sullivan Island (Charleston area), South Carolina have provided diverse fine-textured genetic material. No paspalum accessions have been found at St. Augustine, Florida, which is the oldest settlement in the continental United States (Gray, 1933). Boat traffic to this latter site was mainly from Spanish America or Spain and not from Africa. Collection activity along the gulf coast has produced only scattered coarse or ornamental (extremely coarse) types that are supposedly indigenous to the region. Only introduced intermediate types have been found along the west coast in Southern California, reflecting the introduction of Adalayd and Futurf from Australia in the late 1960s. Most Caribbean islands have paspalums of varying textures, depending on boat movement via the trade winds from various African coastal countries. Some Central American countries have paspalums on their Atlantic coasts. Caye Chapel, an island near Belize City, Belize has both intermediate and fine-textured ecotypes on the island. Brazil and Argentina could be a possible secondary center of origin, since boat traffic between Africa and those countries was significant during the 1800s. A listing of coastal sites where paspalum has been found is provided in Table 4.1. Refer to Section 5.2 in the genomics sector for relationships among ecotypes collected from around the world.

Table 4.1. Sites Where *Paspalum vaginatum* of Varying Textures Have Been Found

United States

North Carolina	Georgia	Alabama	Arizona
South Carolina	Florida	Mississippi	
Louisiana	Texas	California	

Mexico (Baha: Vera Cruz, Tamalipas)

Central America
Belize (Corozal, Caye Chapel, Glover's Reef)
Costa Rica
Nicaragua

South America

Columbia	Bolivia
Venezuela	Ecuador (Balao)
Guyana	Peru (Lima, Callao)

Surinam (Paramaribo, Warappacreek, Lower Surinam River)
Chile (Valdivia)
Brazil (Pernambaco, Rio Grande do Sul, Boa Virgem)
Argentina (Buenos Aires, Brondsen, Vidal, Rosario, Brogado, Junin, Santa Fe)
French Guiana (Sarcelle Savannah, Mana)

Caribbean

Curacao	Dominica
Trinidad and Tobago	Martinique
Haiti (Cape Haitien, Jacmel, Tortuga)	Antigua
Dominican Republic (Higuey)	Barbados (Crane Beach)
Puerto Rico (Mona, Vieques)	Bermuda
Virgin Islands (St. Croix, Tortola)	Jamaica

Bahamas (New Providence, Watling's Island, Fortune Island, Inaqua, Long Cay)
Cuba (Havana, Oriente, Las Villas, Pinar del Rio)

Iberian Peninsula	**Asia**	
Spain	India	Japan
Portugal	China	Korea
	Ceylon	Surinam
	Pakistan	Tiawan
		(Tatu estuary)

Europe	**Middle East**
Italy	Saudi Arabia
France	North Yemen
Sardinia	South Yemen
Israel	Oman (Dhofar)
	Socotra

Table 4.1. Sites Where *Paspalum vaginatum* of Varying Textures Have Been Found (Continued)

Africa

South Africa (Durban, Cape Peninsula, Transvaal-Cullinan)
Senegal (Thiong Island, Djibonker, Casamance River Basin)
Nigeria (Lagos Lagoon, Port Harcourt)

Algeria (Hodna)	Cameron	Cape Verde Islands
Ghana (Elmira)	Zimbabwe	Mauritius
Tunisia (Gabes)	Tanzania	Seychelles
Sierra Leone	Kenya	Canary Islands (Tenerife)
Gabon	Sudan	
Angola	Reunion Island	

Pacific Rim

Malaysia	Malay peninsula
Tonga	Philippines (Luzon, Panay, Samar)
Java	Gilbert Islands (Butaritari/Makin, Marakei,
Modoera	Tarawa, Nikunau)
Halmahera	Caroline Islands (Palau-Babeldaob, Koror,
Samon (Upolu island)	Ngarakabesang, Peliliu, Angaur, Tobi, Yap,
Carolines (Peleliu)	Ulithi, Fais, Woleai, Ifaluk, Truk-Dublon,
Wake Island	Tol, Fefan, Param, Namoluk, Lukunor,
Indonesia	Satawan, Nukuoro, Kapingamarangi,
	Ponape, Mokil, Kusaie, Pingelap)

Marianas Island (Pagan, Anatahan, Saipan, Tinian, Guam)
Marshall Islands (Kwajalein, Ailuk, Likiep, Ailinglapalap, Majuro, Arno, Jaluit, Roi-Namur)

Australia	**Geobotanical Distribution—Australia**	
Queensland	Arnhem	Dawson
New South Wales	Carpentaria	Bencubbin
Victoria	Cape York	Nullarbor
Western Australia	Great Sandy Desert	Darling
Northern Territory	Burdekin	Nepean
South Australia	MacDonnell	

New Zealand

Sources: Bor, 1960; Cope, 1985; Fosberg et al., 1987; Hafliger and Scholz, 1980; Ibrahim and Kabuye, 1988; Lazarides, 1980; Morton, 1973; Roseveare, 1948; Webster, 1987.

4.3. DISPERSION

Chorology

The geographical distribution of the *Paspalum* genus is in tropical and subtropical venues and harsh, stressful environments. This large genus is ecologically aggressive and many species possess apomicts that may account for their evolutionary survival (Chapman, 1992). *Paspalum* has a C_4 NADP-ME biochemical type photosynthetic pathway, which is characteristic of malate-forming grasses that occur in moist ecosystems (Chapman and Peat, 1992). The NAD-ME malate formers are normally found in arid environments, while PEP-CK aspartate formers are intermediate (Hattersley, 1992).

$C_4 1$ (NADP-ME) types include *Axonopus* A. Palisot de Beauvois, *Stenotaphrum* K. von Trinius., *Eremochloa* L. Buse, *Digitaria* A. von Haller, and *Pennisetum* L.L. Richard. $C_4 2$ (NAD-ME) types include *Buchloe* G. Engelmann, *Bouteloua* M. Lagasca y Segura, *Cynodon* L.L. Richard, *Distichlis* C. Rafinesque-Schmaltz, *Sporobolus* R. Brown, and *Eragrostis* N.M. von Wolf. C_4 3 (PCK) types include *Spartina* J. von Schreber, *Sporobolus* R. Brown, *Eragrostis* N.M. Wolf, *Zoysia* C. Von Willdenow, and *Bouteloua* M. Lagasca y Segura among the warm season grasses (Chapman, 1992).

Paspalum vaginatum can be grouped into a specific phytochoria (ecological habitat) based on salt-affected and moist biotopes. It is the most salt-tolerant warm-season turfgrass that is known (Carrow and Duncan, 1998) with a salt tolerance at ocean water levels (54 dSm^{-1} or 34,400 ppm salt).

Movement

Paspalum vaginatum has been vegetatively transported around the world for two different reasons. First, the grass was used as bedding in the bottom of slave boats as they moved between Africa, North America, South America, Central America, and the Caribbean islands. This would account for the discovery of diverse paspalum ecotypes at key staging areas for unloading slaves along the Georgia (Sea Island, Ft. Pulaski) and South Carolina (Sullivan Island) coasts, (Gray, 1933) but not universally throughout eastern U.S. coastal venues and only on specific Caribbean islands where the ships happened to have docked (Table 4.1).

Secondly, the grass was introduced into salt-affected areas as the need for forages, land reclamation, and turf increased. Australia received their first saltwater couch from South Africa during 1935 (Beehag, 1986; McTaggart, 1940; Trumble, 1940) with an introduction into South Australia for use in soil stabilization and pasturage on saline soils. By 1951, the grass had migrated to Western Australia for similar uses, where it became widely used as a lawngrass in the Perth region on sandy soils. By 1954, it was being grown on a 10 ha sod farm for turf in South Australia, where in the late 1960s it was established on the bowling greens at Delungra Bowling Club in Adelaide. Eventually, over 30 bowling greens were initially planted with paspalum in South Australia (Beehag, 1986), but that number has diminished as new superdwarf bermudagrasses have been introduced into the country. Greenleaf Park bermudagrass (a selection from a bowling green of the same name in Sydney, Australia) is widely grown on bowling greens throughout Australia.

O. J. Noer (of Milorganite® fame) was responsible for early distributions of seashore paspalum in the southeastern United States, with his source material originating from the #13 fairway on the marsh course at the Sea Island Golf Club (Morton, 1973). The Sea Island course was built in 1925 and paspalum was already established along the fairways adjacent to the marsh. He sent some initial material to Vero Beach, Florida, and additional material to the Ornamental Horticulture Department at the University of Florida in Gainesville. Noer, as a consultant for Robert Trent Jones, Inc., took paspalum to Hawaii and established it on the Mauna Kea Country Club golf course (i.e., the Mauna Kea ecotype originated from Sea Island, Georgia material).

Dr. Horne at UFL-Gainesville supplied paspalum to Ralph White, Ousley Sod Company west of Deerfield, Florida. During 1961–1962, verticuttings were sold to Otto Schmeisser, superintendent at the Gulfstream Golf Club, Delray Beach, Florida for sequential planting on fairways #8, #5, and #10 (Morton, 1973). Dr. Evert O. Burt, turf specialist at the UFL Agriculture Research Center, Ft. Lauderdale, Florida also conducted some research on paspalum for home lawns (Burt, 1963). Other reports on *P. vaginatum* in Florida include Horn, 1963; Smalley, 1962; Busey, 1977; Rose and Lorber, 1976; and Craig, 1976.

O.J. Noer in about 1953 supplied paspalum to Mark Mahannah, golf course architect at the Riviera Country Club, Coral Gables, Florida where it was established in experimental plots. Mark and Charles Mahannah transplanted some of the material to a one-acre field, from which sprigs were established on the King's Bay Yacht and Country Club south of Miami about 1958.

During December 1969, Julia Morton arranged for Charles Mahannah to ship paspalum sod to Henry J. Riese at the Boca Patrick Estate near the village of Barber, Curacao, Netherlands Antilles (Morton, 1973). He established the paspalum in lawns at that site and at Spaanse Water, on the windward side, southeastern coast of Curacao. During April 1973, Julia Morton obtained additional paspalum sod from Charles Mahannah and shipped it to Dr. Humberto Belloso in Maracaibo, Venezuela for trials around Lake Maracaibo.

In 1972, Hugh Whiting introduced 'Futurf,' a selection from Torquay, Victoria, Australia, into California (Campbell, 1979; Henry, 1981; Henry et al., 1979). In 1975, he also introduced 'Adalayd' (also called 'Excalibur'), a selection from Adelaide, Australia, into California. Both selections were planted on plots at the San Jose Field Station in 1976 and in 1977 at the South Coast Field Station in El Toro, California on University of California property where V.B. Younger, Stan Spaulding, and Mark Mahady conducted initial research.

Intersol (Indio, California) began growing and distributing primarily Adalayd throughout California, Texas, and Florida. Early distributors included Burkhard Nurseries Inc., Pasadena, California; Clearwater Sod, Clearwater, Florida; and Glenn Oaks Turf, Camilla, Georgia. Coastal Turf, Bay City, Texas and Pacific Sod in Camarillo, California continue to sell the original Adalayd.

Research on paspalum salt tolerance was conducted in California during the 1980s (Gibeault et al., 1988, 1989; Harivandi and Gibeault, 1983; Harivandi et al., 1984, 1987; Henry, 1981; Henry et al., 1979); at the University of Florida–Gainesville during the 1980s (Dudeck and Peacock, 1985; Peacock and Dudeck, 1985); and in Hawaii during the early 1990s (Joy and Rotar, 1991; Marcum and Murdoch, 1994). J.B Beard at Texas A&M University–College Station also conducted some research on paspalum during the 1980s and early 1990s (Beard et al., 1991abc, 1982). The first breeding program on this turf grass was initiated by R.R. Duncan in 1993 at the University of Georgia–Griffin with core funding from the U.S. Golf Association.

Adalayd was established on Kings Crossing golf course (Duble, 1988) in Corpus Christi, Texas; Alden Pines golf course (Anonymous, 1982) on Pine Island, North Ft. Myers, Florida; and Fairbanks Ranch Country Club (Vermeulen, 1992) at Rancho Santa Fe, California during the 1980s.

Fairbanks Ranch was actually the equestrian venue for the 1988 Olympics in Los Angeles and was built on a salt lake bed and floodplain, on land previously owned by Douglas Fairbanks.

Paspalum from Sea Island, Georgia was introduced into Hawaii in the 1980s by Walter Nagorski. It was planted at Honolulu International Country Club on Oahu and eventually at the Mauna Lani Resort on the Big Island of Hawaii (Kona Coast) (Morey, 1994). A selection from this Sea Island introduction eventually became 'Salam' (Southern Turf Nurseries on Oahu).

Paspalum (probably Futurf) was first introduced into Israel during the early 1980s. In 1991, Adalayd was taken to Israel from California. No distinction was made between the two cultivars, except that Futurf was superior to Adalayd (Gad Ron, personal communication). In 1996, a special ecotype with short internodes was found at a remote oasis on the Sinai peninsula-Ein Khudra. This accession (Q36313) is in the U.S. collection (Table 5.1).

Paspalum has been used as a utility turf for erosion control and coastal environmental stabilization in South Africa, Australia, New Zealand, and the southeastern United States. The grass has been used for sand dune stabilization and revegetation in Florida (Craig, 1974, 1976; Rose and Lorber, 1976). It has been used for sports turf in Australia, Israel, Argentina, Brazil, and California. It has been used in residential, commercial, and park landscapes in the Middle East, Australia, California, Hawaii, and Argentina. Paspalum has been used on golf courses in California, Texas, Florida, the Middle East, South Africa, Argentina, China, Thailand, Indonesia, and the Philippines. It has also been used as the primary grass on a polo field in Rancho Santa Fe, California (adjacent to Fairbanks Ranch golf course) and on bowling greens in Australia.

Its use as a forage has been documented in Africa, Australia, South America, and the United States (Malcolm, 1962; O'Kelly and Reich, 1976; Theron et al., 1972; National Acad. Sci., 1975; Edwards and Ekundayo, 1981; Swaine et al., 1979; Facelli et al., 1989; Rinciman, 1986; Maddaloni, 1986; Fisher and Skerman, 1986; Dirven, 1963ab; Garland and Duff, 1981; Malcolm, 1986; Everist, 1974, 1975). Dry matter production can range from 1.3 to 7.0 T ha^{-1} yr^{-1} for the coarse types on saline fields (Malcolm, 1986). With fertilizer, dry matter yields have reached almost 23 T ha^{-1} (Hill, 1978ab).

CHAPTER 5

Genetics

5.1. WORLD COLLECTION OF ACCESSIONS

A small collection of 28 *Paspalum vaginatum* accessions from the province of Buenos Aires, Argentina was assembled from 1986–1988 (Clausen et al., 1989) and is maintained at the germ plasm bank of the Estacion Experimental Agropecuaria, INTA, Balcarce, Argentina. Ten accessions from primarily the southeastern United States were assembled at the Ft. Lauderdale, Florida agricultural center by 1977 (Busey, 1977). An unknown number of *P. vaginatum* accessions are located in the germ plasm collection of *Paspalums* in Brazil. A larger collection (Table 5.1) has been assembled at Griffin, Georgia involving coarse, intermediate (Adalayd types), and fine-textured accessions from nine countries and seven U.S. states.

Assembling a World Collection

The decision to initiate a breeding program on seashore paspalum was made in 1992 and was predicated on the fact that most other warm-season grasses had established breeding programs with historical funding. R.N. Carrow initially was interested in the potential for the grass. After conversations with Dr. Jim Watson, he and R.R. Duncan found that USGA agronomists had indicated a need for research on *Paspalum vaginatum* because of increasing development of golf courses in coastal venues and the escalating need for high quality turfgrasses that could tolerate poor effluent water quality or even brackish water for irrigation. After six months of intensive literature review by R.R. Duncan and the delivery of four-inch paspalum cores from Sea Island, Georgia by Tom Burton, R.R. Duncan began the task of assembling a world collection of paspalum.

The first collection trip was to Alden Pines Country Club on Pine Island near North Ft. Myers, Florida during July 1993. During 1993, David Kopec from the University of Arizona in Tucson provided several

Table 5.1. *Paspalum vaginatum* Collection Assembled at the University of Georgia, Agricultural Experiment Station, Griffin, Georgia from 1993–1999.

PI Number/Designation	Country/Location	Source/Collector
PI 299042	Rhodesia (Zimbabwe)	SRPIS
PI 364368	Mozamique	SRPIS
PI 364985	South Africa	SRPIS
PI 377709	South Africa	SRPIS
PI 509018	Argentina	B. Burson
PI 509020	Argentina	B. Burson
PI 509021	Argentina	B. Burson
PI 509022	Argentina	B. Burson
PI 505023	Argentina	B. Burson
SIPV 1 and 2	Sea Island, GA	T. Burton
HI-1 and 2[a]	Oahu, HI	T. Staton
Mauna Kea[a]	Hawaii	T. Staton
Tropic Shore	Hawaii	R.J. Joy
Temple 1	Miss. State via Auburn	B. Burson
Temple 2	TX Gulf Coast	B. Burson
310-79	Argentina	B. Burson
561-79	Argentina	B. Burson
Excalibur[b]	Australia	Hugh Whiting
PI 576136 (Q28959)[b]	Israel	Gad Ron
PI 576137 (Q28960)	Israel	Gad Ron
PI 576138 (Q29193)	Brazil	R. Pittman
PI 576139 (Q29194)	Brazil	R. Pittman
PI 576140 (Q29195)	Brazil	R. Pittman
Q 32710	Thailand	S. Rojawat
Q 37086	Guam (Mangilao GC)	Duncan
Q 37087	Guam (Leo Palace GC)	Duncan
Q 37089	Australia (Adelaide Oval)	Duncan
Q 37090	Australia (Adelaide)	Duncan
Q 37091	Australia (Brisbane-Golden Beach)	Duncan
Q 37092	Australia (Falcon Bay Beach-Manrah, WA)	Duncan
Q 36313	Israel (Ein Khundra-Negev desert oasis)	Gad Ron
Q 36314	Israel (Talmon-Tel Aviv)	Gad Ron
Q 36315	Israel (Rishon LeZion Stadium)	Gad Ron
Q 36316	Israel (Hatsor Kibutz)	Gad Ron
Q 36317	Israel (Caesarea Golf Club)	Gad Ron
K169[a]	Hawaii	D. Kopec
K10 → 13	Caribbean	D. Kopec
K16-17	Yuma, AZ (Desert Hills GC)	D. Kopec
Adalayd	TAMU, College Station, TX	R. Duncan

PI Number/Designation	Country/Location	Source/Collector
Adalayd	Camilla, GA (Glenn Oaks Turf)	R. Duncan
Adalayd	California (Riverside)	V. Gibeault
Taliaferro	Jupiter, FL (Loxahatchee GC)	C. Taliaferro
Parrish	Parrish, FL (Ornamental type-Horticulture Systems)	O. Bundy
AM 3554	Chatham Co., GA (old Ft. Screven, Tybee Island)	H.J. Haynsworth
Fidalayel[b]	California (Irvine)	V. Gibeault
AP-1 → -16[b]	Ft. Myers, FL (Alden Pines CC)	R. Duncan
GAL-1	Galveston, TX (west beach)	R. Duncan
GS-1[a]	Gulf Stream CC, FL	R. Duncan
FSP-1[a]	Gulf Stream CC, FL	A. Dudeck
FSP-2[a]	Gulf Stream CC, FL	A. Dudeck
FSP-3[a]	Sea Island—hotel putting green, GA	A. Dudeck
FR (4)[b]	Fairbanks Ranch CC, CA	R. Duncan
Salam[a]	Hawaii (Oahu)	Southern Turf
STN 1097[c]	Israel	Southern Turf
Variegated[a,d]	Hawaii (Oahu)	Southern Turf
TFP (30)[e]	Ft. Pulaski, GA	R. Duncan
SIPV (120)[e]	Sea Island, GA	R. Duncan
TI (5)[e]	Tybee Island, GA	R. Duncan
JI (2)[e]	Jekyll Island, GA	R. Duncan
HI (35)[a,e]	Hawaii (Oahu, Hawaii, Kauai, Lanai, Molokai)	R. Duncan
KC (9)[b,e]	Kings Crossing GC, Corpus Christi, TX	R. Duncan
PILA	Pecan Island, LA	R. Duncan
ET (5)[b,e,f]	Port Orange, FL	R. Duncan
Listed but not available:		
PI 299777	South Africa	SRPIS
PI 300080	South Africa	SRPIS
PI 404887	Uruguay	SRPIS
PI 9056602	Dublin Co., NC	SCS-NC

[a] Originated from Sea Island
[b] Derivatives of Adalayd
[c] Futurf or its derivative
[d] A chimera, useful for landscaping
[e] Multiple selections
[f] Selections from Alden Pines

SRPIS = Southern Regional Plant Introduction Station, Griffin, GA
SCS = Soil Conservation Service, North Carolina

ecotypes that he had assembled over the years from trips to Hawaii, the Caribbean, and in Arizona. His material was designated the "K" series for evaluation purposes. The second trip was to Hawaii during late January 1994 and with the assistance of Tom Staton at Quality Turf, Waimanalo, Oahu, all five major islands were visited and paspalum selections were collected. Two additional trips in 1997 and 1999 resulted in additional selections from the islands that were added to the collection. During May 1994, a comprehensive collection trip was made to the Georgia coast, including Sea Island/St. Simons Island, Jekyll Island, and Tybee Island/Ft. Pulaski in the Savannah area.

The Soil Conservation Service agronomists were contacted in Virginia, North Carolina, South Carolina, Georgia, and Florida. Only a couple of ecotypes were available through their plant materials center at Americus, Georgia. Charles Taliaferro at Oklahoma State University provided one ecotype that he had collected from a Jupiter, Florida golf course. A trip was made to St. Augustine, Florida during September 1995, but no ecotypes were found in the oldest city in the United States. An additional trip to Pensacola, Florida area revealed a similar lack of fine-textured ecotypes in that Gulf Coast region.

During January 1996, a collection trip was made to Fairbanks Ranch Country Club at Rancho Santa Fe, California, which is north of San Diego. In February 1996, Kings Crossing Country Club in Corpus Christi, Texas was collected. During April 1996, a second trip to Hawaii (Oahu) added to the collection.

During July 1997, R.R. Duncan visited Kwajalein Island (one of the Marshall Islands) and Guam (one of the Marianas Islands); then proceeded to Australia and stops in Sydney, Perth, Adalaide, and Brisbane. The Australian collection trip produced only three new accessions, mainly because only coarse and intermediate (Adalayd-type) ecotypes were found. The official herbarium collection in Perth revealed very little diversity among the Australian paspalum sources.

Through contacts around the world, additional accessions have been sent to quarantine grow-out in Glenn Dale, Maryland from Israel, Brazil, Greece, Peru, and Thailand. Additional prime sites for collection are Brazil-Argentina, South Africa, and the Caribbean Islands. In the U.S. Atlantic coast region, collection activities are being concentrated on sites for off-loading of slaves from Africa, mainly port sites near Charleston, South Carolina and Norfolk, Virginia. The priority is for fine-leaf textured ecotypes.

An additional 30 accessions of *Paspalum distichum* have been as-sembled. All are intermediate leaf texture and have better cold tolerance than *P. vaginatum,* but do not come close to the high turf quality traits of *P. vaginatum.* An additional accession, *P. hieronymii* Hack. cv. Lalo, was collected at the Molokai Plant Materials Center, Hawaii (Joy and Rotar, 1984). This species is an extremely prostrate-growing, stolonifer-ous grass with exceptional wear/traffic tolerance and natural resistance to Round Up® (glyphosate). However, this species has very little cold hardiness.

Breeding Approach: Creating Additional Diversity

Seashore paspalum is a self-incompatible, sexual diploid. Cross-fer-tilization is difficult because its genome (**D**) is different from most other paspalum species (Table 3.1). Cross-pollination is accomplished at 18–21°C (mid 60s°F) during early morning hours (0500–0730) just prior to sunrise (Burson, 1985).

Several hybrids with other *Paspalum* species have been made (Burson, 1981; Quarin and Burson, 1983), but most hybrids did not produce viable seed. Viable seed production is extremely low (Carpenter, 1958; Malcolm, 1983) due to sterility, ergot (Raynal, 1996), and the self-in-compatibility problem. No research on *P. vaginatum* has been conducted to determine if the incompatibility problem is sporophytic, gametophytic, or a combination of the two.

Seed viability studies at Griffin, Georgia (200 m elevation) and Blairsville (510 m elevation) in the north Georgia Appalachian moun-tains revealed variability among ecotypes for potential seed production and location x germination interactions (Duncan, 1999). Among six ecotypes grown at both locations, mean germination was 10.1% (range 2.3 to 20.5%) at Blairsville and 2.9% (range 0.5 to 7.4%) at Griffin. Among 28 ecotypes grown at Blairsville, the mean germination was 11.9% (range 0 to 45%); at Griffin, 4.9% (0 to 12.2%). The cooler nighttime tempera-tures at the higher elevation were instrumental in achieving a higher vi-ability and germination percentage. Seed germination occurs at temperatures >20°C or >68°F (optimum 25–30°C) preceded by a cold vernalization treatment (Carpenter, 1958; Skerman and Riveros, 1990). Even though commercial seed is not available (Malcolm and Liang, 1969), seed production is possible in swards of mixed genetic backgrounds when conditions are favorable for cross-pollination. Dual spikes in the raceme can range from 10 to 65 mm in length, with the coarse types having the longest spike length (Duncan, 1999). Consequently, the potential for economical seed production is available, but problems associated with (1) locating the best environment for maximum seed production, (2) finding the best parental combinations for effective cross-pollination, and (3) mechanical harvesting challenges in field situations, will govern the eventual success of marketing seed of this species. Promising environments for seed production in preliminary studies include Blairsville, Georgia, Las Cruces, New Mexico, and Hubbard, Oregon.

One published report (Ramirez and Romero, 1978) indicated seed of seashore paspalum was deposited on a beach at Playa Grande, Mehuin, Valdavia province in Chile. A small amount of hybrid seed from Argentina accessions (Table 5.1) was initially available from the Plant Introduction Station at Griffin, Georgia. Selections have been made from the hybrid grow-outs for further turf evaluations.

As the world collection of *P. vaginatum* accessions was being assembled between 1992 and 1996, mixed plantings of ecotypes differing in country of origin were planted in polycross blocks at Griffin and Blairsville, Georgia. Seed harvest was normally by hand during the fall months of October–November. Seed were air-dried, placed in a plastic bag with holes, and placed at 0°F in a cold chamber for three months. Previous attempts to break seed dormancy with 40°F temperatures for 1–3 months was unsuccessful. Scarification and treatment with 5% potassium nitrate or weak acids did not enhance germination. Only the prolonged exposure to subfreezing temperatures effectively enhanced germination. Current research is focused on natural environmental exposure, involving ocean water, to break seed dormancy and enhance germination.

Approximately 1,000 viable hybrid seeds have been germinated; the seedlings were transplanted to small pots in the greenhouse for increase, and subsequently were transplanted to turf field plots. These new hybrids were immediately subjected to close mowing stress (<13 mm cutting height) with judicious applications of fertilizer and water. Only one hybrid—HYB5—a greens type, has emerged from the hybrid evaluation program for advanced testing.

Additional variability was created by subjecting paspalum to *in vitro* propagation (Cardona, 1996; Cardona and Duncan, 1997ab, 1998) using nine different ecotypes—PI 509021 (Argentina); HI-1, Mauna Kea, K-3, K-7 (Hawaii); Adalayd (Australia); PI 299042 (Zimbabwe); SIPV-1

(Sea Island, Georgia); AP-6 (Florida). Over 5,500 tissue culture regenerated plants were planted in turf field plots and subjected to mowing stress (3–16 mm). Approximately 100 selections were made of "improved" plants with turf traits that appeared to be superior to the donor parents. Subsequent evaluations produced four superior types for additional evaluations on greens, tees, or fairways (TCR 1, 3, 4, 6). Additional trait information is provided in Section 6.2.

The philosophy of the evaluation program is to subject the ecotypes to real world conditions as fast as possible: (1) mowing at 3 mm in 3 × 3 m plots on a USGA-specification green, (2) mowing at 15–16 mm on a fairway, (3) mowing at 4 mm on a push-up tee, or (4) mowing at 13 mm on a native, heavy clay soil. The promising ecotypes are expanded to larger areas and also are subjected to multiple stresses: drought, soil acidity, minimal fertility, cold stress, salt stress, and multiple insects. The best ecotypes overall are increased in the greenhouse and field; then shipped to collaborating golf courses across the southern United States where they are exposed to high salinity or poor recycled water quality environments. The golf courses or sports field serve as the final exam prior to release. Depending on the number and expertise of specific collaborators, data are accumulated from the evaluations to justify release of new cultivars. Additionally, collaboration with private sod companies provides the best management information for sod and stolon (sprig) production prior to release. Operational management manuals are developed for each new cultivar based on use (golf courses, sports fields, landscapes) and are available at the time of release.

5.2. GENETIC ANALYSIS

An RFLP analysis of 51 accessions from 29 *Paspalum* species has revealed six cluster groups (Jarret et al., 1998) (Figure 5.1). Cluster group 5 includes *P. distichum, P. unispicatum, P. conjugatum* Berg., and *P. vaginatum*. RAPD profiles for selected *P. vaginatum* ecotypes revealed seven groups within *P. vaginatum* (Liu et al., 1994, Figure 5.2).

Simple sequence repeat (SSR) analysis of (GA)n and (CA)n repeats (Figure 5.3) using five primers produced 47 loci with repeats of n≥3. The number of alleles resolved per locus ranged from 6 to 16, with an average of 14 (Liu et al., 1995). The SSR dendrogram for the 46 ecotypes (Figure 5.5) was similar to the RAPD (Figure 5.4) profiles (Liu et al., 1994). No (AT)n, (ATT)n, (CTT)n, or (GATA)n repeats were detected.

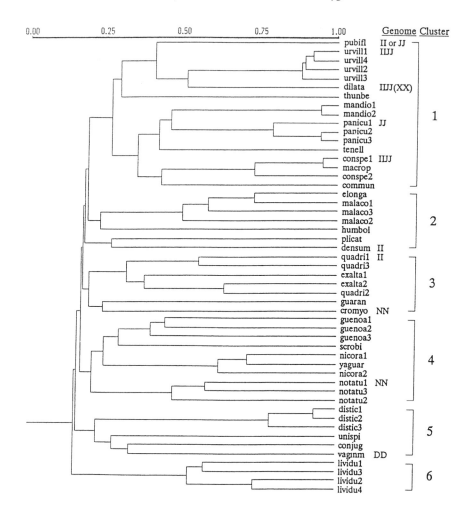

Figure 5.1. RFLP *Paspalum* species dendogram.

Specific SSR analysis using five markers (Brown et al., 1998) and 10 accessions (50 electropherograms) detected an average of 8.4 fragments and had a diversity index of 0.79 for each primer pair (Figure 5.6). Overall fragment similarity for the SSRs varied from 0.16 to 0.26. The dendogram depicting the genetic relationship among the 10 ecotypes revealed Excalibur, Fidalayel, and FR-1 (Fairbanks Ranch) had identical DNA profiles, and all three had an 85% similarity to Adalayd (Figure 5.6). PI 509018-1 (Sea Isle 1) and AP-14 had a 55% similarity to each

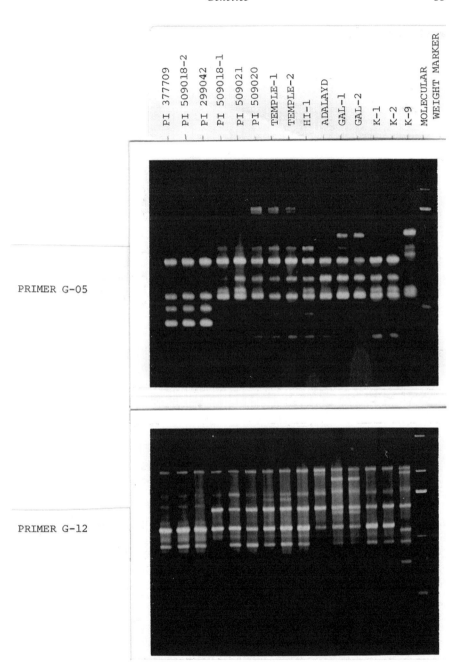

Figure 5.2. RAPD profiles of *P. vaginatum* ecotypes.

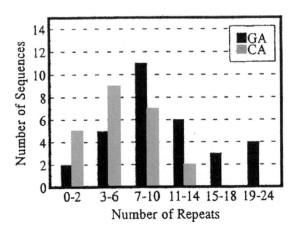

Figure 5.3. Comparison of number sequence repeats in paspalum.

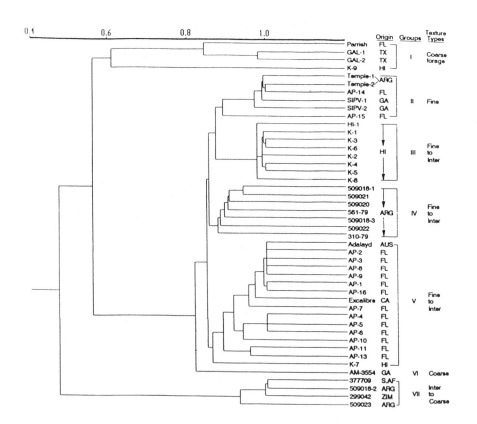

Figure 5.4. RAPD dendogram of *Paspalum vaginatum* ecotypes (Liu et al., 1994).

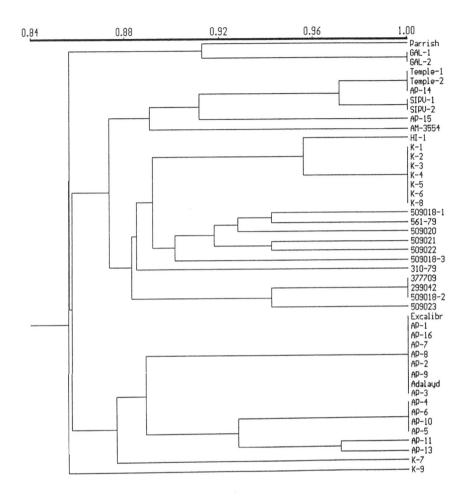

Figure 5.5. SSR dendogram of *Paspalum vaginatum* ecotypes (Liu et al., 1995).

other, and PI 509018-1 and AP-10 had a 45% genetic similarity to each other. AP-10 (Sea Isle 2000) and AP-14 were supposedly Adalayd derivatives, but their genetic similarities were 35% and 30%, respectively, probably revealing significant genetic mutations toward finer-textured ecotypes and away from the intermediate-textured parental Adalayd. AP-10 and AP-14 were only 30% genetically similar and morphological traits plus turf performance had revealed their differences in research plots. Directional mutation in *P. vaginatum* has supposedly been coarse → intermediate → fine leaf texture. Field observations within fine-textured

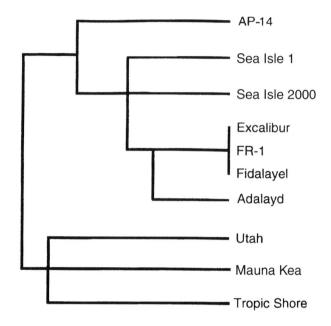

Figure 5.6. Dendogram exhibiting the genetic relationship among ten paspalum accessions (Brown et al., 1998).

ecotypes and regenerated plants from tissue culture of fine-textured types has not produced any additional mutations. The diploid genome apparently is quite stable at that point (fine-textured status) of evolution.

Genetic analysis of *Paspalum* species is listed chronologically to date in Table 5.2.

Ecotype Relationships

RAPD (Figure 5.4) and SSR analyses (Figure 5.5) were similar for the 46 paspalum ecotypes. Using the grouping format for RAPDs, the following conclusions can be drawn:

1. The coarse forage types are apparently unique to each continent, with the North American group closely related and possibly indigenous to that country. The close relationship between African and Argentinean coarse types indicates introgression, probably from Africa to Argentina; e.g., PI 377709

Table 5.2. Genetic Analysis of *Paspalum* spp.

Species	Analysis	Source
vaginatum	RAPDs	Liu et al., 1994
vaginatum	SSRs	Liu et al., 1995
multiple	flow cytometry	Jarret et al., 1995
scrobiculatum	RAPDs	M'Ribu and Hilu, 1996
notatum	RFLPs/RAPDs	Ortiz et al., 1997
simplex	RFLPs	Pupilli et al., 1997
vaginatum	SSRs	Brown et al., 1998

RAPD = Random Amplified Polymorphic DNA
SSR = Simple Sequence Repeat (microsatellites)
RFLP = Restriction Fragment Length Polymorphism

and PI 509018-2 have a similarity coefficient of 1 (Groups I, VI, VII).

2. The Argentinean fine to intermediate types (Group IV) are unique to that country, with expected similarity to the Sea Island, Georgia (Group II) and Hawaiian (Group III) material (refer to Chapter 4). Two of the AP types clustered in Group II, indicating some introgression from Sea Island to Alden Pines, Florida.

3. The Adalayd-Excalibur (Group V) of Australian origin obviously was the source material for the AP material. One accession from Hawaii clustered with this group, indicating a possible movement of material either from California or Florida into Hawaii. Adalayd and Excalibur are closely related with a similarity coefficient of 0.97. The ecotypes can be split into two subgroups, one closely allied to Adalayd with coefficients near 1, and the second group related to Excalibur with coefficients near 0.85.

5.3. CULTIVARS/ECOTYPES

In the United States, the oldest known fine-textured ecotypes have been found on Sea Island, Georgia. When the Sea Island golf course was built in 1925, the grass was already established in the salt marsh adjacent to the course. Coarse types can be found sporadically from North Carolina to Florida on the eastern U.S. coast, on Gulf of Mexico coastal sites and various Caribbean Islands, on the Hawaiian Islands, and along the Pacific Rim.

'Saltene' is a lawn-type, intermediate texture paspalum grown in Western Australia, while 'Salpas' has been grown in the Adelaide, Australia area (Table 5.3). 'Futurf' and 'Adalayd' were introduced into California during the 1970s and dispersed (see Section 4.3) over the southern and southeastern United States. 'Adalayd,' 'Excalibur,' and 'Fidalayel' were all names used synonymously for **Adalayd** during the late 1970s and through the 1980s, especially in California.

No additional breeding work was conducted on Adalayd after its introduction into the United States. Additionally, no management packages were developed for this grass and it was essentially handled like the hybrid bermudagrasses. The use of too much fertilizer and untimely irrigation scheduling eventually led to disenchantment about its performance and its ultimate demise. Adalayd was not well adapted to the United States, was intermediated in leaf texture resembling common bermudagrass, and its salinity tolerance was only slightly higher than the bermudagrasses. Consequently, its impact on the turf industry in the United States during the 1970s and 1980s was minimal compared to bermudagrass and other warm season grasses.

Attitudes about paspalum usage on golf courses gradually started to shift in the late 1980s when a fine-textured ecotype was carried to Hawaii and established on Honolulu International Country Club on Oahu. The establishment site was next to a salt water lagoon along a fairway and the introduction flourished in that high salinity environment. Paspalum started moving to other salt-affected sites on the islands and several sod companies started growing the grass on Oahu and Maui. Unfortunately, some paspalum ended up in bermudagrass sod/sprig fields because of contamination, and was unintentionally supplied to several new golf courses during bermudagrass planting and establishment. Some superintendents viewed the paspalum as a weed and tried diligently to eradicate it from their bermudagrass courses by using various phytotoxic herbicides. Others elected to manage the paspalum rather than fight it because of their high salt environment, poor quality irrigation water, the fact that paspalum tolerates the low light intensity prevalent in the islands from November through April due to frequent cloudy and rainy weather, and the fact that paspalum tolerates wet soil conditions better than bermudagrass. Tropic Shore, a coarse type and Mauna Kea (Sea Island, Georgia derivative), were selected during the early 1990s in Hawaii.

Table 5.3. Paspalum Cultivars and Their Origin

Year	Name	Origin	Distributor/Company[c]	Leaf Texture
1951	Saltene	Western Australia	The Turf Farm, Wanneroo Turf Farm	intermediate
1972	Salpas	Adelaide	—	intermediate
	Futurf[a]	Toguay, Victoria, Australia	—	intermediate
1975	Adalayd[a] (Excalibur)	Adelaide, Australia	Pacific Sod (CA) Coastal Turf (TX)	intermediate
—	Fidalayel	California	—	intermediate
1991	Tropic Shore	Oahu, Hawaii	Plant Materials Center-Molokai, Hoolehua, HI	coarse
—	Mauna Kea	Sea Island, GA source: Hawaii	—	intermediate
1998	Salam[b]	Hawaii selection out of Sea Island, GA	Southern Turf Hawaii, Alabama, Florida, Egypt	fine (fairway/sports type)
1999	Sea Isle 2000[b]	Old Adalayd mutation from CA; Alden Pines CC, near Ft. Myers, FL	[d]	fine (greens type)
1999	Sea Isle 1[b]	Argentina	[d]	fine (fairway/tee/sports type)
—	Durban Country Club	South Africa	Superlawn, Natal, S. Africa	fine (fairway, tees, roughs)

[a] Patented.
[b] Patent or PVP Pending.
[c] See Table 14.2 for a more extensive list of distributors.
[d] Release pending through the University of Georgia. Distributors to be determined.

Southern Turf® became a major supplier of paspalum for the Hawaiian islands as well as the Pacific Rim. They eventually named their cultivar 'Salam,' which means **peace** in Arabic (Table 5.3). They have sod farms on the north shore of Oahu (grown on plastic), near Elberta, Alabama (between Mobile, Alabama and Pensacola, Florida), near Punta Gorda, Florida, and near Cairo, Egypt.

Golf Courses with Seashore Paspalum

The distribution and use of the seashore paspalum cultivars on golf courses in the world is shown in Table 5.4. The use of specific cultivars reflects a regional pattern of availability for planting material, but the number of courses and their locations signal the potential global impact that this grass will have in the twenty-first century.

Table 5.4. Golf Courses with *Paspalum vaginatum*

Course Name	Location	Cultivar
Sea Island GC	St. Simons Island, GA	SIS[a]
The Little Club	Del Ray Beach, FL	SIS
Gulf Stream CC	Del Ray Beach, FL	SIS
Mauna Lani Bay Resort	Kona side, Big Island, HI	SIS
Ewa Beach Int'l CC	Oahu, HI	SIS
Honolulu Int'l CC	Oahu, HI	SIS
The Challenge @ Manele Bay	Lanai, HI	SIS
Koolau GC	Oahu, HI	SIS
Kapolei GC[b,c]	Oahu, HI	SIS
Luana Hills GC	Oahu, HI	SIS
Kiahuna GC	Kauai, HI	SIS
Wailua GC	Kauai, HI	SIS
Coral Creek GC[c]	Oahu, HI	Salam
Putting course– Hilton Waikoloa	Big Island, Hawaii	Salam
Royal Thai GCC[d]	Bangkok, Thailand	Salam
Club Intramuros	Old Fort, Manila, Philippines	Salam
Punta Fuego GCC	Punte Fuego, Philippines	Salam
Laguna National CC	Singapore	Salam
Ibai Bina GCC	Kaula Tengganu, Malaysia	Salam
Sand River GCC	Shenzhen, China	Salam
El Gouma GC	Hurghada, Egypt	Salam
HH Khalifa Sheikh Mana Bin Khalifa Al Maktoum GC	Dubai, United Arab Emirates	Salam
Kings Crossing GCC	Corpus Christi, TX	Adalayd/ Excalibur
Alden Pines CC[c]	Bookelia, FL	Adalayd/ Excalibur
Fairbanks Ranch GC[c]	Rancho Santa Fe, CA	Excalibur
El Niguel CC	Laguna Niguel, CA	Excalibur
Flumini Di Quartu	Sardinia	Adalayd
LPGA—Legends GC	Daytona Beach, FL	ET
Old Memorial GC	Tampa, FL	ET
Colleton River Plantation	Hilton Head, SC	ET
Hilton Head National	Bluffton, SC	ET
Palm Aire CC	Pompano Beach, FL	ET
Oak Harbor	Vero Beach, FL	ET
Bonita Bay (Cypress/Sabal) GCS	Bonita Springs, FL	ET
Caye Chapel	Belize	ET
Alaqua Lakes	Longwood, FL	ET
Amelia Island Plantation	Amelia Island, FL	ET
Twin Eagles	Naples, FL	ET

Table 5.4. Golf Courses with *Paspalum vaginatum* (Continued)

Course Name	Location	Cultivar
Jolly Harbour GC	Antigua	local
Durratt Al Avus GC	Jeddah, Saudi Arabia	Excalibur
Riffa GC	Bahrain, United Arab Emirates	DCCS
Bahrain Int'l GC	Bahrain, United Arab Emirates	DCCS
—[e]	Mauritius	DCCS
Swakopmund[e]	Namibia	DCCS
Royal Swazi Sun[e]	Swaziland	DCCS
South Coast[e]	Zwa-Zulu Natal coastal	DCCS
Selbourne[e]	belt-South Africa	DCCS
Wild Coast Sun[e]		DCCS
San La Meer[e]		DCCS
Uvongo[e]		DCCS
St. Michaels[e]		DCCS
South Broom[e]		DCCS
Beachwood[e]	North Coast-South Africa	DCCS
Mt. Edgecombe		DCCS
Princess Grant[c]		DCCS
Caesarea GC	Israel	Futurf
Country Club de Villa	Lima, Peru	ARG
San Isidro GC	Argentina	ARG
Mar del Plata	Argentina	ARG
Jockey Club GC[e]	Buenos Aires, Argentina	ARG
Durban CC[e]	Durban, South Africa	DCCS

[a] SIS = Sea Island selection; ET = Ecoturf Alden Pines CC selections; DCCS = Durban CC selection; ARG = Argentina selection.
[b] LPGA Hawaiian Open played on this course.
[c] entire course = paspalum.
[d] Asian Pacific Open played on this course.
[e] greens.

Part II
Environmental Stress Resistance

CHAPTER 6

Breeding for Multiple Environmental Stresses

Seashore paspalum evolved on sand dunes in a coastal environment, with periodic exposure to salt spray, severe prolonged drought, total inundation by salt water during high tides or storm surges, and low light intensity from cloudy days and monsoonal weather patterns. As a result, this grass developed mechanisms to withstand ocean level salt exposure (34,400 ppm salt), a root system capable of adapting to extremely severe drought and waterlogging conditions, an efficient root system capable of extracting nutrients supplied in low volumes from ocean water, a turfgrass with low innate but efficient nutrient requirements, a turfgrass that developed resistances to biotic (insects, diseases) constraints that were prevalent in the salt-affected microclimates, an aggressive turfgrass, and a grass that could function effectively during reduced light situations. The degree of resistance and the diversity among paspalum ecotypes for specific stresses can be found in Chapter 7.

This chapter emphasizes how a traditional breeding program was used to identify the level of stress resistance and diversity among ecotypes, assess stress resistance for different environmental stresses, enhance stress resistance in the breeding program, and incorporate biotechniques into paspalum developmental programs.

6.1. TRADITIONAL BREEDING AND GENETICS

Two foundational principles are essential for maximizing enhancement of multiple stress resistance in *Paspalum vaginatum*. **Multiple stress resistance** is necessary, because seashore paspalum will normally be grown in environments where other warm-season grasses have been challenged and turf quality and long-term performance have been unacceptable or less than desirable with other grasses. Each ecotype must be assessed for its specific level of resistance to individual abiotic and biotic stresses. Those ecotypes with the highest and lowest levels of stress resistance can be used to determine mechanisms of resistance for each stress. Turf quality and performance traits coupled with stress resistance traits are absolutely compatible in the enhancement program.

Genetic tolerance to soil chemical and physical stresses that limit root development (plasticity) and viability/functionality is the *first step* to successfully enhance multiple stress resistance in breeding programs. Without an extensive, flexible (balance between shallow and deep rooting/regeneration capabilities), and stress-tolerant root system, key individual stresses (salinity, drought) and nutrient uptake/utilization efficiency traits cannot be effectively exploited in an enhancement program.

Multiple Stress Resistance

All turfgrasses are exposed to multiple abiotic/edaphic and biotic environmental stresses during their growth and development (Figure 6.1). The sequence and cyclic nature of individual stress exposure, intensity and duration of each stress, and maintenance regimen will dictate the level of turfgrass persistence and ultimately influence their survivability. A high degree of genetic resistance to the various stresses is essential for turfgrasses, since (1) the perennial plant system is intended to persist and perform long term, and (2) inadequate genetic resistance greatly increases maintenance costs since cultural inputs that are needed to alleviate specific stresses are less effective.

Current warm-season turfgrass cultivars within a species are adapted to a general region or climatic zone and exhibit variable performances across their broad region of adaptation. Exposure to site-specific environmental extremes normally diminishes their persistence, and maintenance costs increase in an effort to minimize loss in turf quality traits and overall performance.

Development of cultivars that are genetically buffered against environmental extremes (not only for the climatic zone, but also the microenvironment within the zone) requires breeding programs to focus on site-specific stresses (Carrow and Duncan, 1996; Duncan, 1996; Duncan and Carrow, 1998). The breeding program must be all-inclusive to incorporate **multiple stress resistance** involving pest (biotic) problems, climatic factors, man-made factors, and edaphic (soil) constraints (Figure 6.1) at a site-specific level. Management protocols also need to

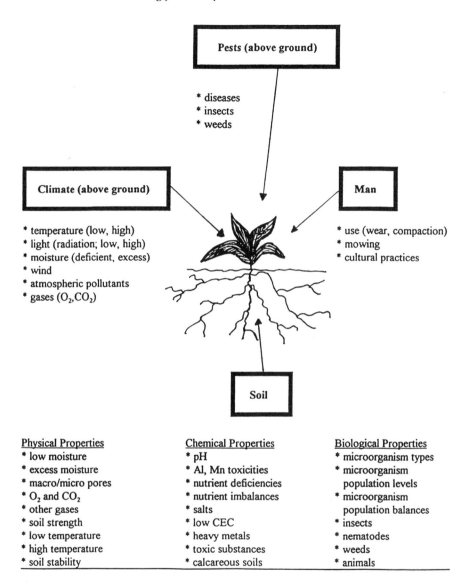

Figure 6.1. The Turfgrass System: plant-soil-atmosphere-man.

be stress-specific, starting with selection of species and cultivars that are resistant to the primary environmental stresses expected at the site.

The most essential component to enhancement of multiple stress resistance is genetic-based root resistance. Genetic root resistance

(1) encompasses the inherent ability of the turf plant to **develop an extensive, deep root system** to extract water from deep in the soil profile during periods of severe drought or water deprivation while at the same time maintaining sufficient shallow root volume to utilize rainfall or irrigation infiltrating the soil surface and percolating through the soil profile (the dynamics of these root characteristics in response to soil and climate stresses are referred to as **root plasticity**); (2) to **maintain the root system (root regeneration)** through growth cycles and stress periods of variable duration; and (3) to **maintain root viability (physiological function)** for water/nutrient uptake; and (4) **genetic control of the carbohydrate load** in the crown region and the subsequent partitioning of carbohydrates during and after severe environmental stress exposure will govern long-term root persistence and viability (i.e., the root cells require a consistent supply of carbohydrates for energy). Breeding programs must address each of these stress resistance components during the screening and evaluation phrases to identify the most resistant cultivars. Exposure to more than one abiotic/edaphic and biotic stress during germ plasm screening and ecotype evaluations will result in multiple stress-resistant turf cultivars.

Root Stresses

Several environmental constraints relative to paspalum will be discussed in the remainder of this chapter. There is no utopian grass, and understanding the specific limitations as well as advantageous traits for specific turfgrass cultivars will help to define the boundaries under which that cultivar should be grown as well as provide initial clues to short- and long-term management strategies.

Certain soil chemical and soil physical factors limit turfgrass root development and persistence in field situations. Genetic resistance to these edophic stresses is essential in developing a healthy, extensive root system under stress conditions. *Soil chemical* constraints include **root toxicities** associated with low pH <5.0 (Al, Mn, H) salt-affected soils (Na, Cl, B, OH), anaerobic conditions (sulfides, methane, cyanide gas), and soil pollutants (heavy metals, organics, herbicides, poor irrigation water quality). **Nutrient deficiencies or imbalances** impact the root system indirectly through their influence on the physiology and metabolism of overall plant growth and development. Soil chemical conditions that favor nutritional deficiencies or imbalances include acid pH (Mg, P, K, Ca, Mo);

calcareous and noncalcareous alkaline pH (P, Fe, Mn, Zn, B); gypsic (Mg, K, Mn, Zn, Ca); salt-affected (Ca, Mg, K); low CEC (N, K, Mg, Ca, Mn); anaerobic (N); and heavy metals (micronutrients). Among the various soil chemical constraints to rooting, the direct toxicities of Al/Mn (soil pH <5.0) and Na (sodic soil situations) are especially important. Nutrient deficiencies or imbalances can be alleviated with proper fertilization, resulting in healthier roots and better turf-grass growth. However, these toxicities (Al/Mn, Na) occur over wide geographical areas and are costly and time-consuming to correct. Genetic-based resistance to these toxicities is critical to successful turfgrass management.

Soil physical factors limiting rooting include: **low soil oxygen** inhibits growth and root viability and is associated with waterlogged sites, compacted sites, sodic soils; **high soil strength** impedes root growth and is enhanced by soil drying, compaction, fine-textured soils, sodic conditions, and layers with minimal macropores; **high soil temperature** is detrimental to summer maintenance of grass roots and is strongly associated with aerial temperatures, humidity, nonirrigated turf, limited air drainage, and low soil oxygen. Direct temperature stress kills the crown tissues and causes root death below the crown region. Indirect temperature stress results from insufficient net carbohydrate balance to supply adequate photosynthate to the roots during stress periods, thereby reducing root viability and functionality with repeated stress cycles; *low soil moisture* primarily limits root growth by its effect on increasing soil strength and is associated with lack of water/water availability in coarse-textured soils, poor water infiltration on fine-textured, compacted, sodic soils, or hydrophobic sands, and physiological (or salt-induced) drought from the low osmotic potential of saline soils. Soil drying can injure or kill turfgrass roots and cultivars differ in their genetic resistance to this stress.

Since there are six major soil chemical and physical constraints to rooting (salinity, drought, low oxygen, extreme high and low temperatures, high soil strength or bulk density, low pH or acidity), each of these can be incorporated into breeding programs. Genetic resistance to two or more of these constraints is an example of multiple stress resistance. The ecotype screening and evaluation procedures for seashore paspalum include assessment to all six major stresses, and subsequent development of management protocols based on level of resistance to specific microclimatic field situations.

Several morphological, anatomical, and physiological types of drought resistance must be addressed in the breeding program. *Drought avoidance* is the ability of the turf plant to avert tissue damage during a drought period by postponement of dehydration. The turfgrass is able to maintain adequate tissue water content and postpone the stress through uptake of more water (deep, extensive root system, high root length density, high root hair density, good root viability and functionality) and/or reducing water loss (low evapotranspiration) through leaf rolling or folding, thick leaf waxy cuticle layers, hairy leaf surfaces, leaf area reduction (smaller leaves or senescence/death of lower leaves), slow leaf extension rates after mowing, leaf densities and orientations that contribute to high canopy resistances, stomatal closure, high stomatal density, stomatal positioning, smaller conducting tissues, and smaller leaf mesophyll cells. *Drought tolerance* is the ability of the turf plant to withstand tissue dehydration during a drought period by escape (dormancy state) or by genetically controlled hardiness traits (functions at low tissue water deficits, osmotic adjustment, maintenance of membrane integrity).

Cultivar Development Principles

In order to make genetic advancements in the breeding program, diversity of response to specific stress resistance traits is needed among paspalum ecotypes. Highly tolerant and highly susceptible types within the turf species must be identified for each stress. Crosses between high and low tolerant types may produce tolerant progeny if the traits are dominant and mostly single gene inheritance is involved. If multiple genes for the tolerance trait are involved or if recessive genes are functioning, trait expression may be variable. Planting the progeny, selfing to produce F_2 (second generation) seed, and then growing the segregating F_2 generation in a stress environment provides one way of selecting tolerant types.

If high and low stress tolerant types are not available, then breeding program options for enhancing stress tolerance include interspecies (crossing with other compatible species of the same genus) hybridization, somaclonal variation from tissue culture, or transformation of alien stress tolerance genes. If the turf species is self-incompatible (as is the case for *Paspalum vaginatum*) and interspecies crosses are difficult to make, variability for stress tolerance improvement can be created using somaclonal variation, by interspecific/intergeneric hybridization, or by the addition of alien genes. Regardless of the breeding option, the stress evaluation program must utilize severe, highly discriminating screening environments and identify the highest level of tolerance that is available in the turf species. Wherever possible, field screening should involve multiple stresses (both abiotic/edaphic *and* biotic) for maximum efficiency, or integrate single laboratory-based screening techniques with hybridization and screening of progeny in severe field stress environments to identify highly tolerant ecotypes.

Most turf species have one stress tolerance trait; i.e., bermudagrass and centipedegrass are noted for drought resistance while zoysiagrass and St. Augustinegrass generally are noted for their tree-shade tolerance. Zoysiagrasses generally are considered to have better cold tolerance than the hybrid bermudagrasses. Regardless of their species reputation or prior performance history, different cultivars must be assessed as to their specific level of tolerance for each of the environmental stresses. The objective is to identify or develop specific cultivars with the highest stress tolerance level and with adaptation to as many stresses as possible. If the turf species has developed a high level of resistance during its evolution, then the breeding program can progress very rapidly. An example of this multiple stress resistance is seashore paspalum that has salt resistance, drought resistance, wear tolerance, waterlogging (low oxygen) tolerance, low light intensity tolerance, wide adaptability across extreme acid and alkaline soil conditions, low mowing tolerance, and resistance to a number of insects and diseases. However, this grass has low tolerance and limited diversity to cold temperatures and tree shade conditions. Each of the stress tolerance attributes and limitations for paspalum will be addressed in Chapter 7.

6.2. BIOTECHNOLOGY

Biotechnology techniques have been used to enhance seashore paspalum diversity (somoclonal variation via tissue culture), to develop transformation protocols, and to analyze the genome. This approach improves traditional breeding method efficiency and accuracy in characterizing the different accessions in the paspalum collection.

Tissue Culture

Several species of *Paspalum* have been cultured *in vitro* (Table 6.1). The protocol for culture of seashore paspalum ecotypes has been documented (Cardona, 1996; Cardona and Duncan, 1997). The basic medium for callus induction from immature inflorescence segments included 1 mg L⁻¹ 2, 4-D plus 5% coconut milk, Murashige and Skoog basals salts, 3% (30 g L⁻¹) sucrose, and 1 mg L⁻¹ 1000X Gamborgs B5 vitamins. The medium is sterilized by autoclaving for 20 minutes at 121°C. The cultures are maintained in the dark at 26–28°C for callus initiation and proliferation. Clumps (2–5 mm) of callus are then replated to half-strength basic medium. For initiation of embryogenesis, the best medium was 1 mg L⁻¹ BAP (6-benzylamino purine) plus 0.5 to 2 mg L⁻¹ NAA (∝-napthaleneacetic acid). The cultures are subjected to a 16 hr light (46–60 μmol sec⁻¹) and 8 hr dark photoperiod. After 4 weeks, ecotype cultures producing shoots are cultured in half-strength, hormone-free medium with 8% sucrose for root proliferation.

Callus induction efficiency (% explants producing viable calli); i.e., [total number of explants ÷ total − contaminated plants × 100] ranged from:

50% (PI 299042)	12% (Mauna Kea)
39% (SIPV-1)	9% (AP-6)
31% (PI 509021)	7% (Adalayd)
25% (K-7)	4% (HI-1)

Ecotypes that were prolific producers of regenerated plants included HI-1, Mauna Kea, K3, and PI 299042; AP-6, S1PV-1, and K7 were intermediate in production, while PI 509021 and Adalayd were poor producers. Variability for genetic color, spread (growth rate over time), density (internode length), and winter hardiness was documented (Cardona and Duncan, 1998). A total of 2,851 tissue-culture-regenerated (TCR) plants were evaluated for somaclonal variation at two Georgia field locations during 1993–1996. Mowing height was 25 mm during the evaluation period.

Somaclonal variation provides an additional method for creating diversity within this species beyond the traditional crossing program or through new ecotype collection. A comparison of mean internode length and ranges for parents and regenerants is presented in Table 6.2. The means of the regenerants were greater than the parents for all five paspalum ecotypes. However, the range for the regenerants was wider than the parents, reflecting somaclonal variation from the culturing process. Selection of shorter internode somaclones was possible since 136 out of

Table 6.1. *In vitro* Propagation of *Paspalum* Species

Species	Year	Explant	Source
15	1985	immature inflorescence	Bovo and Mroginski
dilatatum	1992	immature inflorescence	Akashi and Adachi
	1992	—	Davies and Cohen
	1993	immature inflorescence	Burson and Tischler
notatum	1989	mature/immature inflorescence	Bovo and Mroginski
	1990	mature caryopsis	Marousky and West
	1993	mature/immature inflorescence	Akashi et al.
	1994	leaf blades	Shatters et al.
almum	1993	immature ovaries	Bovo and Quarin
scrobiculatum	1991	—	Nayak and Sen
vaginatum	1996	immature inflorescence	Cardona
	1997	immature inflorescence	Cardona and Duncan
	1998	immature inflorescence	Cardona and Duncan

Table 6.2. Somaclonal Variation for Internode Length (mm) Among 1848 Tissue Culture Regenerated *Paspalum vaginatum* Plants

	Parent			Regenerants		
Ecotype	Mean	Range	N	Mean	Range	N
HI-1	7.4	6–10	20	9.5	2–26	565(43)[a]
PI 509021	7.6	5–11	20	9.0	3–20	421(22)
K-3	9.3	7–12	20	10.6	4–30	400(34)
Mauna Kea	6.9	5–9	20	11.1	3–30	280(12)
Adalayd	11.2	9–16	20	12.6	4–23	182(25)

[a] Number of regenerated plants ( ) with internode lengths less than the shortest internode length of the parents = 136 plants out of 1,848 (Cardona and Duncan, 1998).

1,848 (7%) of the regenerated plants exhibited lengths that were less than their parents. For HI-1, TCR plants exhibited the following turf trait variation:

Trait	Range
spread	2–8 (8 = rapid growth and diameter of spread)
density	2–8 (8 = most dense canopy)
color	5–8 (8 = darkest green)

Assessment of winter survival in field plots was made after short-duration low temperatures of –11.1 (12°F) in 1993, –14.4°C (6.1°F) in 1994, –10.6°C (12.9°F) in 1995, and –13.9°C (7°F) in 1996 (Table 6.3). Mowing height going into the winter was 25 mm each year. A total of 2,851 TCR plants from six paspalum ecotypes were evaluated (Cardona and Duncan, 1998). Finer-textured ecotypes HI-1 and Mauna Kea had 28 and 24%, respectively, of the TCR plants killed by cold temperature, but 63 and 67% survived as healthy plants. Intermediate leaf texture types PI 509021, K-3, and Adalayd had 53, 41, and 44%, respectively, of the TCR plants killed and 34, 52, and 32% healthy survivors.

The coarse-textured PI 299042 lost 95% of the TCR plants to cold winter temperature and only two of the 43 survivors were in good condition. One group of TCR plants from PI 299042 had no coarse-textured survivors, but had mutated to 15 (out of 61 total plants) intermediate (Adalayd-type) texture somaclones with improved cold tolerance compared to the donor parent. Some of the healthy somaclones have shown a tendency to break winter dormancy at 10°C (50°F) soil temperature (100-mm or 4-in. depth) and prior to bermudagrass emergence.

Transformation

A transformation protocol has been developed using *Agrobacterium tumefasciens* (*At*) (Cardona and Duncan, 1998). Highly embryogenic callus of HI-1, Mauna Kea, SIPV-1, and PI 299042 were inoculated separately with two different binary vectors of *At*. Two cultures of *At* strain EHA105 were cotransformed with two vectors:

1. pBI 121 with NPTII (Nos promoter) and GUS (CaMV 35s promoter).
2. pGE203 with NPTII, GUS, and HPH (CaMV 35s promoter)

The inoculated callus was initially cultured for two days at 26°C in a callus induction medium, followed by sequential culturing in a shoot induction medium, followed by sequential culturing in a shoot induction medium with 150 mg L⁻¹ Claforan, and then transfer four days later to a medium containing 100 mg L⁻¹ each of Claforan and Kanamacin. Nonphenolic calli were reselected and transferred to fresh media plus selection agents on 30-day cycles.

Table 6.3. Winter Field Survival[a] of (*Paspalum vaginatum*) Tissue-Culture-Regenerated Plants in Georgia

Ecotype	Total	Dead	Poor Condition[b]	Survivors
HI-1	606	171(28)[c]	52	383(63)[c]
PI 509021	409	216(53)	52	141(34)
K-3	432	177(41)	29	226(52)
Mauna Kea	296	70(24)	28	198(67)
Adalayd	207	92(44)	48	67(32)
PI 299042	901	858(95)	0	43(5)
Total	2851	1584(56)	209(7)	1058(37)

[a] Cold thermal threshold = -7 to $-8°C$.
[b] Plants were small and struggling to recover by July.
c Percentage of total.
Source: Cardona and Duncan, 1998.

After 90 days on selection media, all calli inoculated with *At* strain pBI 121 were discarded with no transformation. Calli transformed with *At* strain pGE 203 showed active growth in the selection media. Only one plant of HI-1 exhibited a fast growth rate on the selection medium. The surviving plant was transferred to fresh media with 50 mg L^{-1} each of Claforan and Kanamacin to stimulate rooting. A preliminary GUS expression test was negative and no additional polymerase chain reaction tests have been performed to identify whether the resistant plant is the product of transformation, an epigenic mutation, or a somaclonal variant resulting from the *in vitro* process.

Genome Analysis

Random Amplified Polymorphic DNA (RAPD)

DNA Isolation (Liu et al., 1994)

Leaf tissue of approximately 20 individuals of each ecotype was bulked for DNA extraction. Young leaf tissue (5 g) was ground to a fine powder with liquid nitrogen and added to an extraction buffer composed of 50 mM Tris-HCl (pH 8.0), 0.7 M NaCl, 100 mM EDTA (pH 8.0), 1% (w/v) hexadecyltrimethylammonium bromide (CTAB), and 0.5% (w/v) polyvinylpyrrolidone (PVP-40). DNA was ethanol-precipitated, resuspended in TE, treated with RNase at a final concentration of 10 μg/mL for 30 minutes at 37°C, extracted 1–2 times with phenol/chloroform/

isoamyl alcohol (25:24:1) and 2–3 times with chloroform/isoamyl alcohol (24:1), ethanol-precipitated and resuspended in TE. DNA concentrations were determined with a Hoefer mini-fluorometer (TKO 100).

Polymerase Chain Reaction (PCR) Amplifications

Decamer random primers (Operon Technologies, Inc., Alameda, California) were used for amplification of seashore paspalum DNA. The PCR reaction mixtures (25 µL) contained 10 mM Tris HCl (pH 8.3), 50 mM KCl, 2 mM $MgCl_2$, 100 µM each of dATP, dTTP, dCTP, and dGTP, 0.75 units of AmpliTaq DNA polymerase (Perkin Elmer Cetus, Norwalk, Connecticut), 0.2 µM of primer and 30 ng of template DNA. The reaction mixture was overlaid with 25 µL of mineral oil. PCR was performed in a DNA thermocycler (Perkin Elmer Cetus) using 45 cycles of the following: 1 minute at 94°C, annealing for 5 minutes at 38°C, a 3-minute ramp time to 72°C, and an extension of 2 minutes at 72°C. PCR products were separated electrophoretically on 1.4% agarose gels in 1 x TAE buffer. The gels were stained with ethidium bromide (0.5 µg/mL) for 25 minutes and then destained in water for 30 minutes. The PCR products were visualized on a transilluminator and photographed under UV light.

RAPD Polymorphisms

Sixty random 10-mer primers (Operon Technology sets E, G, and H) were evaluated for their ability to prime PCR amplification of seashore paspalum genomic DNA. Twenty-six out of 60 printers (43%) either did not amplify all three DNA templates, or resulted in only limited amplifications that were visualized on gels as faint bands or smears. The remaining 34 primers (E-01, E-04, E-06, E-08, E-09, E-10, E-11, E-12, E-14, G-03, G-04, G-05, G-06, G-07, G-08, G-09, G-11, G-12, G-13, G-14, G-16, G-17, G-18, H-01, H-04, H-05, H-08, H-11, H-12, H-16, H-17, H-18, H-19, and H-20) gave reproducible RAPD amplification patterns with individual fragments that stained intensely.

A total of 195 RAPD fragments were unambiguously scored, with a range of 1–9 fragments (average of six fragments) per primer. Twenty-six of the 195 fragments (13%) were invariant across the 46 samples and 169 (87%) were polymorphic between at least two ecotypes. These polymorphic fragments were subjected to further data analyses. Simple matching

(SM) similarity coefficients ranged from 1.0 for the most closely related ecotypes to approximately 0.4 for those most distantly related. Relationships among the seashore paspalum ecotypes were consistent when the number of primers was 14 or higher, corresponding to 65 or more polymorphisms.

Simple Sequence Repeats (SSRs) (or Microsatellites)

DNA Extraction (Brown et al., 1998)

DNA was purified by a modified CTAB procedure (Colosi and Schaal, 1993). Leaf tissue harvested from greenhouse-grown plants was lyophilized, then ground in a mortar and pestle with liquid N_2. Powdered tissue (approximately 100 mg) was mixed with 300 µL CTAB extraction buffer [1.5% CTAB, 75 mM Tris (pH 8.0), 100 mM EDTA, 1.05 M NaCl, 0.75% PVP (40K)], incubated at 65°C for 15 minutes, then extracted twice with chloroform/isoamyl alcohol (24:1). DNA was precipitated by addition of 300 µL CTAB precipitation buffer [1% CTAB, 50 mM Tris (pH 8.0), 10 mM EDTA] and 600 µL isopropanol, incubated at room temperature for 30 minutes, then centrifuged at 12,000 RPM for 10 minutes. DNA pellets were resuspended in TE buffer, incubated with RNase A (1 µg/mL) for 30 minutes at 37°C, and extracted with phenol/chloroform/isoamyl alcohol (25:24:1). DNA was precipitated at −20°C in 70% ethanol, dried, and resuspended in HPLC-grade water at a concentration of 10 ng/µL.

SSR Primer Design and Preparation

Paspalum SSR loci were previously cloned from a genomic library and flanking PCR primers were designed by Liu et al. (1995). Primer sequences, the SSRs that they flank, optimal annealing temperatures, and fluorescent labels are shown in Table 6.4. Fluorescent oligonucleotides were obtained from Perkin-Elmer/Applied Biosystems Division, Foster City, California. Primers were labeled at the 5′ end by incorporation of a phosporamidite tagged with a fluorescent dye, either 6-carboxyfluorescein (6-FAM), tetrachloro-6-carboxyfluorescein (TET), or hexachloro-6-carboxy-fluorescein (HEX), during DNA synthesis. Only one of the oligonucleotides from each primer set (the "forward" primer) was labeled. (CA) and $(GA)_n$ repeats (screened in a Taq I genomic library of paspalum) were chosen because of their frequency in paspalum (Figure 6.1). Esti-

Table 6.4. Characteristics of Dye-Labeled SSR Primers for *Paspalum vaginatum*[a]

SSR Primer	Fluorescent Dye Label[b]	Sequence	Tm[c]	Repeat	Allele Size Range (bp)[d]	Number of Alleles[e] A	Number of Alleles[e] P
Pv-3	Hex	5': TATGGACCGACTGCATGATTCTT 3': GTAGCTAGGTGAGAGGCATTC	48	$(CA)_{14}$	145–235	16	17
Pv-11	Tet	5': AGGTTTGTAGGTTGGGTGCACTGA 3': TTGGCCGGCGGAGGGTAAT	60	$(GA)_{13}$	75–140	14	17
Pv-35	Hex	5': TCGAAATCGAAAAAGAAGATCGTTC 3': GGCGCCAGCTACAAGGTTAG	54	$(GA)_{21}$	95–130	14	14
Pv-51	Tet	5': TCCCATCATCAGTTCTTCCAATC 3': GCCCTGTGTCTATTATTCATCATCTT	55	$(GA)_{13}$	90–130	6	7
Pv-53	Fam	5': CTCGGAAACCGCAGCTCA 3': GCTCCGCCTCCTCTATTCCA	55	$(GA)_{15}$	95–135	16	17
					$\bar{X}$	13	$\frac{17}{14}$

[a] From Liu et al., 1995 and Brown et al., 1998.
[b] HEX = Hexachloro-6-carboxyfluorescein
   FAM = 6 = carboxyfluorescein
   TET = tetrachloro-6-carboxyfluorescein
[c] Annealing temperature (Tm) calculated by the nearest-neighbor method using Right Primer (registered trademark of BioDisk Software Inc., San Francisco, CA).
[d] Size in base pairs (bp) was computed using the "local Southern" algorithm.
[e] A = Agarose gel
   P = Polyacrylamide gel

mated genetic diversity values for the 5 SSRs averaged 0.79 with a range of 0.74 to 0.87 (Brown et al., 1998). The number of alleles resolved averaged 14 (Table 6.4) with a range of 6 to 16.

DNA Amplification

PCR reactions were performed in 25 μL volumes containing 25 ng of template DNA, 1X Perkin-Elmer PCR Buffer II, 0.25 mM dNTPs, 1.5 mM MgCl$_2$, 1.25 U Taq polymerase (AmpliTaq, Perkin-Elmer), and 10 pM of each primer pair. Temperature cycling was done using the GeneAmp 9600 (Perkin-Elmer) with 1 second ramp times. The amplification profile consisted of initial denaturation of the template DNA at 95°C for 4 minutes, 25 cycles of 95°C for 1 minute, 55°C for 2 minutes, and 72°C for 2 minutes. In the final PCR cycle, the extension time at 72°C was increased to 10 minutes.

Electrophoresis and Detection

Samples containing 0.5 μL of the PCR products, 0.5 μL GENESCAN 500 internal lane standard labeled with N, N, N′, N′,-tetramethyl-6-carboxyrhodamine (TAMARA) (Perkin-Elmer/Applied Biosystems) and 50% formamide were heated at 92°C for 2 minutes, placed on ice, then loaded on 6% denaturing acrylamide gels (24 cm well-to-read format). DNA samples were electrophoresed (29 watts) for 7 hours on an ABI model 373A automatic DNA sequencer/fragment analyzer equipped with GENESCAN 672 software v. 1.2 (Perkin-Elmer/Applied Biosystems). DNA fragments were sized automatically using the Alocal Southern@ sizing algorithm.

DNA Library

A genomic enrichment DNA library using PI 509018-1 (Sea Isle 1, a selection from Argentina) has been constructed for SSR screening. Southern blot hybridization was used to screen the restriction enzymes and microsatellite oligonucleotides for the paspalum enrichment library. Southern blot results showed Sau3A1 and Rsa1 were the best enzymes for use among the five enzymes tested. Four SSR trinucleotides [(TTG)$_6$, (TTC)$_6$, (TGG)$_6$, and (TAC)$_6$] were used for library construction.

Enrichment protocols were established and optimized for the paspalum genome. One hundred fourteen positive clones were identified and sequenced. Eight polymorphic SSR primers (out of 40) have been multiplexed and optimized into two sets, based on their ability to produce unique DNA profiles. These primers will be used for cultivar identification, differentiation, and plant variety protection or patenting.

CHAPTER 7

Paspalum Abiotic/Edaphic Stress Resistance

Seashore paspalum ecotypes exhibit varying degrees of resistance to many abiotic stresses (i.e., climatic, soil, and use-related) (Figure 6.1). In this chapter, the focus is on genetic-based resistance and specific responses to individual stresses. Management information to enhance performance of paspalum under such stresses is presented in Chapter 9.

7.1. SALINITY RESISTANCE

Salinity resistance or **salt tolerance** refers to the ability of a turf plant to maintain growth and metabolic function (such as photosynthesis) when exposed to a high concentration of salt in the soil or from irrigation water. At high soil or water salinity levels, two major injuries may occur (Carrow and Duncan, 1998):

- High total salinity can induce drought stress since excessive salt concentrations reduce soil water uptake in turf plants. This **physiological or salt-induced drought** occurs even when soil moisture appears to be adequate, such as shortly after irrigation or after a rainfall event.
- Salt buildup within turfgrass root or shoot tissues can cause **specific ion toxicity**, where the concentration of an individual ion (Na^+) can cause direct toxicity and subsequently injure the tissues. Sodium (Na^+) will replace Ca^{+2} in roots, including outer cell wall exchange sites, interior cell wall structural sites, and in the plasma membrane on the inner cell wall. The net effect is deterioration of root cell wall and membrane structures, reduced root viability, and eventually root death. Excessive salt uptake and accumulation in turfgrass shoots can cause direct toxicity and desiccation of leaf blades and crown re-

gions. The most common salts that cause shoot injuries are Na^+, Cl^-, and B; however, frequent mowing practices in turf removes these toxic ions in clippings and minimizes their effect on turf performance.

When screening turfgrasses and evaluating their salt tolerance levels, physiological drought and specific ion toxicity exposure are both present. Other salt-related problems may or may not be present, such as (1) deterioration of soil structure by excess Na^+, which induces low soil aeration, waterlogging, and high soil strength—all of which hinder turfgrass rooting, and (2) nutrient imbalances caused by excessive additions of particular nutrients (Mg) in the irrigation water.

Grasses and landscape plants are assessed for salinity tolerance based on their shoot and root growth responses to increasing salinity levels using soil salinity measured as **electrical conductivity** (EC_e, dSm^{-1}). The **threshold EC_e** is the soil EC_e where growth starts to decline in response to increasing EC_e. Turf plants classified as "very tolerant" can tolerate a threshold EC_e >10 dSm^{-1} and typically exhibit an EC_e >21dSm^{-1} for 50% growth reduction. For comparison, ocean water has a total salinity equal to 54 dSm^{-1} or 34,400 mg L^{-1} (or ppm), where 1 dSm^{-1}=640 mgL^{-1}.

Paspalum is the most salt tolerant warm-season turfgrass (Carrow and Duncan, 1998), with an average threshold EC_e=8.6 dSm^{-1} and EC_e @ 50% growth reduction = 31 dSm^{-1} for shoot growth (Table 7.1). Alkaligrass (*Puccinella* spp.) is the most salt tolerant cool-season grass species. Based on published literature up to 1998, Adalayd, the least salt tolerant paspalum cultivar, had the following salinity tolerance shoot characteristics: threshold EC_e <1.5 dSm^{-1}, EC_e 50% growth reduction = 18 dSm^{-1} (shoots) and 33 dSm^{-1} (roots). Adalayd has a level of salinity tolerance similar to the hybrid bermudagrasses. The highest salinity tolerance reported for a paspalum ecotype was for FSP-3 (a Sea Island, Georgia selection) with threshold EC_e (shoots) = 14 dSm^{-1}, and EC_e 50% growth reduction = 35 dSm^{-1} (shoots) and >42 dSm^{-1} (roots) (Carrow and Duncan, 1998).

During 1998–1999, Lee (Geungjoo Lee, Comparative Salinity Tolerance and Salt Tolerance Mechanisms of Seashore Paspalum Ecotypes. Ph.D. Dissertation. Crop & Soil Sciences Department, University of Georgia, 2000) assessed 94 paspalum and four bermudagrass ecotypes for salinity tolerance. Several paspalum ecotypes exhibited very high levels of salinity tolerance based on topgrowth and root growth (Table 7.2). Turfgrasses

Table 7.1. Salinity Tolerance Ranking of Selected Turfgrass Species Based on Shoot Growth[a]

Common Name	Scientific Name	Threshold EC_e		50% Growth Reduction EC_e[b]	
		Avg.	Range	Avg.	Range
		dSm^{-1}			
Seashore paspalum	*Paspalum vaginatum*	8.6	0–20	31	18–49
Alkaligrass	*Puccinella* spp.	8.5	6–12	25	20–30
Saltgrass	*Distichlis stricta*	8.0	6–10	—	—
Kikuyugrass	*Pennisetum clandestinum*	8.0	6–10	—	—
St. Augustinegrass	*Stenotaphrum secundatum*	6.5	0–18	29	22–44
Tall fescue	*Festuca arundinacea*	6.5	5–10	11	8–12
Perennial ryegrass	*Lolium perenne*	6.5	3–10	9	8–10
Hybrid bermuda	*Cynodon* spp.	3.7	0–10	22	11–33
Creeping bentgrass	*Agrostis palustris*	3.7	0–10	8	8
Zoysiagrass	*Zoysia* spp.	2.4	0–11	16	4–40
Centipedegrass	*Eremochloa ophiuroides*	1.5	0–3	8	8–9

Very sensitive = ≤1.5 dSm^{-1}
Moderately Sensitive = 1.6–3.0 dSm^{-1}
Very tolerant = >10.1 dSm^{-1}
Tolerant = 6.1–10.0 dSm^{-1}
Moderately tolerant = 3.1–6.0 dSm^{-1}

[a] Adapted from Carrow and Duncan, 1998.
[b] Top growth.

Table 7.2. Salinity Tolerance Characteristics of Seashore Paspalum Ecotypes and Tifway Bermudagrass for Topgrowth (Shoots) and Root Growth

Grass	Threshold EC_e	EC_e 25% Growth Reduction	EC_e 50% Growth Reduction	Growth[a] EC_e O	Growth[a] Threshold EC_e	Growth[a] EC_e 40
	dSm^{-1}			g		
Topgrowth						
HI101 SP	20	31	40	0.43	0.61	0.30
HI36 SP	16	28	38	0.61	0.65	0.30
K3 SP	14	19	40	0.60	0.77	0.36
Sea Isle 2000	9	17	34	0.61	0.74	0.28
Sea Isle 1	8	14	34	0.70	0.77	0.25
HI34 SP	16	21	26	0.41	0.77	0.15
Adalayd SP	2	7	23	0.23	0.23	0.08
Tifway B	20	28	34	0.11	0.23	0.09
Roots						
HI101 SP	24	>40	>40	0.40	0.44	0.38
HI36 SP	24	>40	>40	0.39	0.48	0.45
K3 SP	16	22	>40	0.39	0.47	0.42
Sea Isle 2000[b]	10(32)	20(38)	>40(>40)	0.40	0.47	0.36
Sea Isle 1[b]	10(32)	24(40)	>40(>40)	0.42	0.43	0.32
HI34 SP	16	30	>40	0.32	0.45	0.24
Adalayd SP	2	8	>40	0.20	0.15	0.13
Tifway B	18	34	>40	0.22	0.37	0.23

[a] Growth rate at O, threshold, and 40 dSm^{-1} EC_e values.

[b] These seashore paspalum grasses exhibited two threshold EC_e values for root growth (i.e., root growth increased to the first threshold EC_e, then declined; but a second increase followed to the second threshold value in parentheses).

Source: Geungjoo Lee, Comparative Salinity Tolerance and Salt Tolerance Mechanisms of Seashore Paspalum Ecotypes. Ph.D. Dissertation. Crop & Soil Science Dept., University of Georgia. 2000.

that are adapted to very high salinity conditions (i.e., one-half or greater seawater salinity, >27 dSm^{-1}) must possess certain characteristics:

- A **high inherent growth rate** is essential, since increasing salinity causes growth rate to eventually decrease even in the most salt tolerant turfgrasses. Wear injury is enhanced under high salinity for all turfgrasses. Consequently, growth rate must be sufficiently high under increasing or excessive salinity conditions to recover from wear (see Section 7.4 on wear-traffic tolerance) or other stresses. A comparison of Adalayd versus Sea Isle 1, Sea Isle 2000, K3, HI 101, HI 36, HI 6, and SIPV 35-2 demonstrates the value of a 3.1 to 4.5 fold higher shoot growth rate for these ecotypes compared to Adalayd (or Tifway bermudagrass).
- Grasses with the best salinity tolerance must have high **root and shoot** threshold EC_e, EC_e 25% and EC_e 50% growth reduction values as well as unrestricted overall growth and turf trait performance. Otherwise, the data can be misleading. For example, the most tolerant paspalum ecotypes (Sea Isle 1, Sea Isle 2000, AP-10, HI 101, HI 36, and K3) demonstrate minimal decline in rooting even at 40 dSm^{-1} salt and maintain high absolute growth compared to less tolerant grasses (Adalayd paspalum, Tifway bermudagrass).

7.2. DROUGHT RESISTANCE

Water quality and quantity will be the number one problem facing the turf industry in the twenty-first century. Potable water demands will continue to increase on the human and industrial side, while recreational turf will be relegated to mandatory and widespread utilization of recycled (nonpotable, gray, wastewater, effluent) water. Many recreational turfgrasses typically have water use rates ranging from 3 to 12 mm d^{-1} (Beard, 1989). Adalayd has an evapotranspiration rate of 8.1 mm d^{-1} (Casnoff et al., 1989). One long-term strategy to reduce irrigation requirements is the development and use of drought tolerant cultivars (Carrow et al., 1990).

In assessing the relative drought resistance among grass cultivars, duration of exposure to drought, the presence or absence of edaphic stresses that can limit rooting in a soil profile, and the pattern of soil drying when the data are collected can influence the rankings (Carrow, 1996b). Soil drying from the surface through the subsoil is the typical pattern of drought stress in the field. Soil drying in the upper soil profile can profoundly impact root functionality and turf growth (Smucker et al., 1991). Turfgrasses often concentrate their roots in the upper 30 cm (Beard, 1976). Shoot growth responses to drought stress include leaf firing, wilt, bleached color, increased canopy temperature, reduced shoot density, and reduced verdure (Aronson et al., 1987; Carrow, 1996ab; Minner and Butler, 1985).

Drought resistance among cultivars involves the capability to produce an extensive, deep root system (Hays et al., 1991; Marcum et al., 1995), maintenance of a viable, functional, multilayered root system (referred to as root plasticity) during severe drought (Huang et al., 1997a–D), and root growth recovery from transient drought stress following rainfall or irrigation events (Bassiri Rad and Caldwell, 1992; Brady et al., 1995; Nobel and Huang, 1992). Paspalum has a history of tolerating quite harsh droughty regions in saline soils (Houerou, 1977).

In a study comparing shoot morphological and physiological traits in response to surface soil drought stress and rewatering among seven warm season turfgrasses, the rank in drought resistance for the 0- to 40-cm drying regime was (Huang et al., 1997b):

Sea Isle 1 paspalum = TifBlair centipedegrass > AP-14 paspalum = PI 299042 paspalum > Adalayd paspalum > Common bermudagrass = Emerald zoysiagrass.

Shoot dry matter production after rewatering recovered fully for the TifBlair centipedegrass and all paspalums except Adalayd, but only partially for Common bermudagrass and Emerald zoysiagrass. The superior drought resistance for Sea Isle 1 and TifBlair centipedegrass was associated with enhanced root growth, rapid root water uptake at deeper soil layers, maintenance of root viability at the surface drying soil, and rapid root regeneration after rewatering (Huang et al., 1997c). (Figures 7.1 and 7.2). Reductions in shoot growth for Adalayd paspalum, Common bermudagrass, and Emerald zoysiagrass was attributed more to root viability than to root length ($R^2 = 0.83$), which suggested that following a dry-down period, roots were present but nonfunctional (dead).

Considerable genetic diversity for drought resistance can be found among paspalum ecotypes (Huang et al., 1997 bcd). In a field study (on a nonexpanding, kaolinitic clay) to assess multiple root stress resistance [severe drought/nonirrigated, high soil strength/hard soils, high tem-

Root mortality in top 20 cm of soil

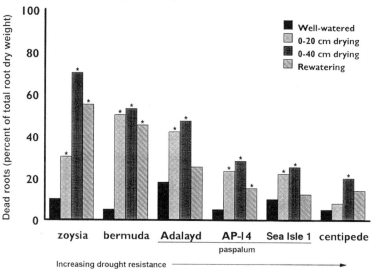

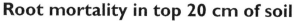

If a species' roots can survive drought conditions, the plant is likely to be more drought-resistant than grasses with greater root mortality. Each asterisk indicates a cultivar response that is significantly different from the cultivar's response in the well-watered treatment (under a statistical analysis where probability equals 0.05)

Figure 7.1. Root mortality in top 20 cm of soil in response to soil drying (Huang, 1997).

peratures and the acid soil complex (see Section 7.6—soil pH adaptability)], a **stress index** was developed to determine paspalum ecotype performance (Table 7.6). Several ecotypes (HI 32, HI 34, HI 37, Hyb 7) ranked in the superior range (**<20**), which was better than Common and Tifway bermudagrasses (very high range 21–39). Adalayd had a Stress Index = 67 (moderate) compared to Meyer zoysiagrass (75, low). Sea Isle 2000 (greens type) and Sea Isle 1 (fairway, tee, sports type) from the Georgia breeding program ranked 38 (very high) and 48 (high), respectively. Drought was the predominant stress in this field study, even though other stresses were involved.

Seashore paspalum has very good adaptation to low soil aeration that often occurs in conjunction with sodic or saline-sodic conditions, where excess Na⁺ causes soil structural deterioration. To determine the **sodium permeability hazard** (i.e., the severity of soil structure breakdown by Na⁺), either the sodium adsorption ratio (SAR, relationship of Na⁺ to Ca^{+2} + Mg^{+2} content) or exchangeable sodium percentage (ESP, rela-

Water uptake from deeper soil

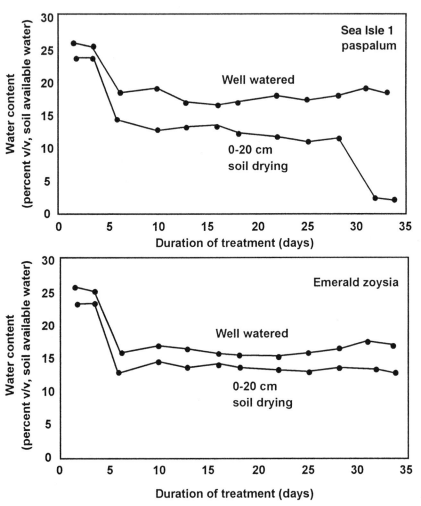

Grasses vary in their ability to take water from deeper soil when the surface has dried out. Paspalum is more able to extract moisture from deep in the soil when the surface 20 cm are allowed to dry compared with zoysiagrass.

Figure 7.2. Water uptake from deeper soil during dry-down and well-watered conditions (Huang, 1997).

tionship of exchangeable Na^+ on CEC sites to total cation exchange capacity) are used. A soil is classified as "sodic" if it has a SAR > 12 meq L^{-1} or ESP > 15%. Paspalum turfgrass tolerates the combined soil stresses of very high Na^+ content, soil structural breakdown by excess Na^+, and the resulting poor soil aeration.

With good management, especially involving an aggressive leaching strategy, ocean water can consistently be used for irrigation of the most salt-tolerant paspalum ecotypes (see Chapter 16). These tolerant ecotypes can withstand SARs > 26 meq L^{-1} and EC_e (electrical conductivities) > 22 dSm^{-1}. The key is to prevent salt buildup in the root zone through high-water-volume leaching and use of gypsum or lime plus sulfur additions where Na^+ is a problem (Carrow and Duncan, 1998).

When managing seashore paspalum for turfgrass, water quality and the level of salinity stress will dictate the level of salt tolerance for the ecotype grown and the management strategy needed to maintain long-term turf performance. If the irrigation water is consistently adding appreciable total salts or high Na^+ levels, the most salt tolerant paspalum ecotype should be chosen. Under these stress conditions, water management must provide excess water for leaching while allowing only moderate to low drought stress. In contrast, rather than using best quality water where salt/Na^+ leaching is not necessary or is needed infrequently, drought resistance would be emphasized in the management strategy. These latter sites could be managed with more flexibility in allowing a higher degree of drought stress before irrigation is applied. Sandy soil profile sites might require more frequent irrigation scheduling than clay sites. However, clay sites will require appropriate scheduling that will allow infiltration, percolation, and salt movement through the profile.

In most situations where paspalum is grown in salt-affected environments, ecotypes with very high salinity tolerance (i.e., tolerance to high total salts and specific ion toxicities) should be the first priority when moderate to high drought resistance will be needed. Those paspalum ecotypes that have multiple stress tolerance to root-limiting soil chemical/physical stresses will also have at least moderately high drought resistance due to the presence of a good, viable root system.

7.3. LOW TEMPERATURE TOLERANCE

Paspalum vaginatum is generally considered to be adapted to 30–35° N–S latitudes and its zone of cold adaptation is similar to most hybrid bermudagrasses and seeded Arizona common bermudagrass. In the continental United States, a line drawn roughly from Raleigh, North Carolina to Chattanooga, Tennessee to Little Rock, Arkansas to Dallas, Texas to south of San Francisco, California would designate the north-ern-most point of survival potential for the currently available fine-tex-tured cultivars and ecotypes in the world collection. On sites where excess total salts or Na^+ inhibit performance of other turfgrass species, seashore paspalum could be used with appropriate management strategies to mini-mize periodic winter injury. Greens and tees can be covered with plastic, hay, or snow prior to the severely cold temperatures. Irrigation can be turned on as the temperatures drop to coat the turf area in an ice blanket.

With or without poor irrigation water quality, sites located about 60 miles south of the northern-most limit would be a conservative and real-istic zone for paspalum adaptation. Similar to other warm season grasses, low temperature sensitivity is greater (1) during the first year of establish-ment, especially if plantings occurred in late summer or early fall, (2) if the paspalum ecotype is subjected to high nitrogen during late summer or early fall and is not allowed to acquire low temperature hardiness, (3) if soils or salt-challenged environments are low in potassium, and (4) on waterlogged, compacted, shady, or close-cut areas.

Cold Hardiness

Among the paspalums, the coarse-textured ecotypes exhibit the least **cold hardiness** and generally, the finer the leaf texture, the greater the cold hardiness. The low temperature tolerance range for acclimated plants of Adalayd and Futurf is –4 to –7°C (24.8 to 19.4°F) (Beard et al., 1991a; Campbell, 1979; Ibitayo et al., 1981) under field conditions.

A study involving electrolyte leakage and freeze shock-recovery of three paspalums of variable leaf texture and Midiron bermudagrass (Cardona et al., 1997) revealed a major cold response difference between paspalums and bermudagrass (Table 7.3). Based on electrolyte leakage, the LT_{50} for the paspalums was –4 to –7.5°C (24.8 to 18.5°F) (acclimated) and –2.5 to –3°C (24.5 to 26.6°F) (nonacclimated) compared to Midiron bermuda (–9.5°C or 14.9°F acclimated and –5.2°C or 22.6°F nonacclimated). Ac-cording to freeze shock-recovery assessment, acclimated paspalums ranged from –8 to –9°C (17.5 to 15.8°F) compared to –12°C (10.4°F) for Midiron bermuda; nonacclimated paspalums ranged from –7 to –8°C (19.4 to 17.5°F) compared to –10°C (14°F) for Midiron. Somaclonal variation

Table 7.3. Comparison of Paspalum Ecotypes Using Electrolyte Leakage (EL) and Freeze Shock-Recovery Methods to Assess Lethal Temperature (LT_{50}) °C at which 50% of the Plants are Killed

| Ecotype | Leaf Texture[a] | Electrolyte Leakage | | | | Shock–Recovery | |
| | | AC^b | | NA^b | | | |
		LT 50	EL (%)	LT 50	EL (%)	$AC\text{-}LT_{50}$	$NA\text{-}LT_{50}$
HI-1	F	−7.5b[c]	NE	−2.5a[d]	NE	−9.2b	−7.0c
Adalayd	I	−5.2c	32	−2.8a	28	−8.5c	−8.0b
PI 299042	C	−4.2c	32	−3.2a	28	−8.0c	−7.2bc
Midiron bermuda	I	−9.5a	58	−5.2b	35	−12.0a[e]	−10.0a

[a] F = fine-leaf texture.
I = Intermediate.
C = Coarse.
[b] AC = Acclimated.
NA = nonacclimated.
[c] °C Mean separations based on Waller – Duncan K ratio = 100
NE = not evaluated.
[d] High value −2.5°C = 27.5°F.
[e] Low value −12.0°C = 10.4°F.
Source: Cardona et al., 1997.

may be one way to improve cold hardiness in paspalum (Cardona and Duncan, 1998). Somaclonal paspalum variants have been selected with a 6°C (11°F) lower cold thermal threshold (survived –14°C or 6.8°F for two winters and –22°C or –7.6°F for one winter) (Cardona and Duncan, 1998; Duncan, 1999). Many paspalum ecotypes develop ample rhizomes that move down in the soil profile if managed properly and these rhizomes provide recovery from severe cold injury. If severe cold temperatures (< –15°C or < 5°F) persist long enough to freeze the moisture in the soil below the rhizome layer, most paspalums will not survive.

Chill Tolerance

Chill tolerance refers to the sensitivity of a grass to lose chlorophyll (color) and go dormant as temperatures become cooler during fall periods (< 55°F or 13°C). Adalayd-type paspalums go dormant at about 55°F (12–13°C) (Harivandi and Gibeault, 1983; Duble, 1989). The coarse-type paspalums go off-color and turn brown at 32°F (0°C), similar to the other warm-season grasses. However, the fine-textured paspalum ecotypes will generally be the last warm-season grass (2–3 weeks later) to go off-color and it normally takes about 26°F (–3.3°C) for them to completely shut down and go into full winter dormancy. The fine-textured types also sometimes take about two weeks longer in the spring to emerge from winter dormancy and start greening up (Beard et al., 1982, 1991c; Harivandi and Gibeault, 1983). If these types never go fully dormant during the winter, they will green up faster than other warm-season grasses. However, as a general rule, compared with the other warm-season grasses, paspalums tend to be less responsive to mild midwinter or early spring temperatures that may break winter dormancy in other warm-season species and thus are less subject to winterkill from premature breakage of winter dormancy.

Winterkill effects can be enhanced by a number of factors: (1) too much shade, especially tree shade, (2) excessive traffic, (3) improper mowing heights (especially heights that are too low, (4) soil physical factors such as compaction in high bulk density soils, (5) improper fertilization, (6) improper irrigation protocols, (7) inadequate drainage, (8) nonadapted grass species and specific cultivars, (9) stress-induced predisposition to insects and diseases, and (10) excessive competition with weeds or other grasses. Proper management can minimize these effects and help in long-term maintenance strategies for maximum turfgrass persistence.

7.4. WEAR-TRAFFIC TOLERANCE

Wear injury may result from physical abrasion or tissue tearing caused by maintenance vehicles, golf cars, or players' shoes. Grasses displaying the highest shoot density and highest shoot growth rate usually show less wear injury and faster recovery rates than less dense and slower growing grasses (Carrow and Petrovic, 1992). Additionally, grasses with high tissue potassium concentrations normally have better wear tolerance and recoverability (Shearman and Beard, 1975).

One study involving seven paspalums and three bermudas (Trenholm et al., 1998, 1999) revealed two fine-textured paspalums (Temple 1, SIPV-2) had substantially less wear injury than the bermudas of similar texture (Table 7.4) seven days after wear treatment. After 14 days, three paspalums (K1, Temple 1, SIPV-2) were equal to Tifway bermuda on recoverability and had the least amount of remaining tissue damage. Potassium tissue concentration in the paspalums was significantly greater than in the bermudas. The mechanisms for wear tolerance are different between paspalums and bermudas. **Paspalum wear tolerance** is governed by low total cell wall content (51% of variation), high leaf moisture content (8%), low leaf strength (3%), high shoot density (11%), and low stem total cell wall content (2%). **Hybrid bermudagrass wear tolerance** is governed by high stem moisture content (41% of variation), low stem cellulose content (32%), high shoot density (9%), high leaf lignin content (3%), high leaf moisture content (9%), high stem lignocellulose content (3%), and high leaf lignocellulose content (1.5%). Paspalums had more lignocellulose and lignin but less hemicellulose in leaves than bermudagrass. Paspalum had more total cell wall contents, less cellulose and lignocellulose, and more hemi-cellulose in stems than bermudagrass.

When nutrient content was evaluated for their influence on paspalum wear tolerance, **high leaf** tissue **K content** accounted for 48% of the variation in wear tolerance. Paspalum wear tolerance was enhanced by factors that (1) imparted canopy cushioning against wear stress—i.e., high shoot density, (2) provided elasticity to cells and tissues, which absorbed wear without injury—i.e., low leaf and stem total cell wall contents and low leaf strength/rigidity, and (3) allowed for high turgor pressure within cells to resist wear pressures—i.e., high leaf moisture content and high tissue K concentrations.

In bermudagrass, high leaf K content was associated with better wear tolerance (61% of the variation). Similar to paspalum, plant characteristics that provided canopy cushioning (high shoot density) and turgor

Table 7.4. Wear Simulation Responses of Turfgrasses on Native Kaolinitic Clay-Soils

		% Leaf Tissue Damage			
		After 7 days		After 14 days	
Ecotype	Species[a]	1st Study	2nd Study	1st Study	2nd Study
AP8	SP	82a[b]	88a	15	23
Adalayd	SP	74a	82ab	12	13
PI 509022	SP	72a	78ab	15	21
Tifgreen[c]	B	38b	63a-d	10	23
TifSport	B	38b	85a	10	32
Tifway	B	30b	68a-c	7	35
HI-1	SP	33b	35de	10	9
K1	SP	30b	28e	8	7
SIPV-2	SP	14c	43c-e	8	9
Temple 1	SP	13c	53b-e	8	9

[a] SP = seashore paspalum.
B = bermudagrass.
[b] Numbers followed by the same letter are statistically equal. Wear supplied by a slip-wear device with rubber-coated rollers. Machine abrades turf tissue while applying minimal compaction. Total wear = five back-to-back soccer games (approximately).
[c] Tifgreen selection from Sea Island, GA golf course.

pressure (high leaf and stem moisture and high K levels) were associated with better wear tolerance. However, factors that enhanced cell or tissue rigidity (stiffness), rather than elasticity, imparted wear tolerance in bermudagrass. Cells and tissues that have higher lignin and lignocellulose, and therefore less cellulose, result in greater rigidity.

The high degree of paspalum wear tolerance exhibited by high shoot density coupled with high salt tolerance is important to ensure adequate growth and wear recovery under saline conditions. Since high salinity reduces growth of even the most tolerant ecotypes (see Section 7.1, salinity tolerance), use of paspalum ecotypes with high inherent growth rates and wear tolerance are essential to long-term performance in these stress environments. Additionally, adequate irrigation and K fertilization will ensure proper cell turgor pressure for turf growth and development. High paspalum wear tolerance would be important on sites where wear is more predominant than soil compaction, such as (1) sandy soils that resist compaction, (2) sports fields not subjected to large studs on (football) shoes, or (3) players that are not large in size/weight. Consequently, wear is normally the dominant stress on high sand sports fields, golf greens, and for soccer or baseball. American football often uses relatively large studs on the shoes, players can be heavy, and considerable localized pressure and tearing actions govern turfgrass wear responses.

Traffic (wear + soil compaction) comparisons of paspalum ecotypes and hybrid bermudagrasses (Table 7.5) attempted to simulate American football on a fine-textured kaolinitic, nonexpanding clay. A differential-slip, double roller with studs (0.40-in. diameter × 0.56-in. length) applied 270 lb per square inch to the top of the stud. The device applied the equivalent of two American football games (center of field) under a near-saturated soil condition (i.e., traffic applied as soon as free water was no longer visible on the surface). This type of treatment applied pressure on grass tissues, provided a tearing action, and imparted soil compaction from the studs penetrating into the soil surface and from the roller weight.

At seven days after treatment (DAT), paspalum ecotypes with high shoot density (Temple 1, SIPV-2, K1) had a similar degree of turf loss compared to the bermudagrasses. All grasses continued to decline in quality traits from 7 to 21 DAT in response to the initial injury and to induced soil compaction. At 21 DAT, dense-canopied paspalums exhibited similar response to the three bermudagrasses in terms of turf coverage and visual quality.

Under saturated field conditions, the softer canopy and more prostrate leaves of paspalum were pushed into the soil by the shoe studs, while the stiffer, more rigid canopy and leaf/stem tissues of bermudagrass did not show this response. However, based on 7 or 21 DAT injury ratings, the visual quality and turf cover responses did not reveal a detrimental overall effect for either grass species. In most instances, American football traffic would be less intense than the traffic stress applied in this study, especially if the soil is not at a near-saturated moisture level.

The high density paspalums and the three bermudagrasses had similar growth and turf performance under compacted soil conditions at 21 DAT. The paspalum ecotypes would be expected to tolerate the low soil oxygen conditions better than the bermudagrasses. For most sports played on finer-textured soils, soil compaction and wear injury would occur, but not at the level caused by the studded tearing action and localized pressure of American football.

In another paspalum wear study involving AP-10 (Sea Isle 2000, a greens type) and SIPV-2 (fairway/tee/sports type), wear tolerance was

Table 7.5. Turfgrass Tolerance to Studded Roller Traffic (Simulated American Football) on a Kaolinitic Clay Soil[a]

Ecotype	Species	% Turf Cover[b]				Visual Quality at 21 DAT	
		No Traffic		Traffic		No Traffic	Traffic
		7 DAT	21 DAT	7 DAT	21 DAT		
AP8	SP	86d[c]	88b	75bc	57cd	5.7c	4.0d
Adalayd	SP	92bc	94ab	70cd	53d	5.4c	3.2e
PI509022	SP	89cd	95a	66d	63c	6.4b	4.6c
Tifgreen	B[d]	97ab	96a	92a	83ab	6.4b	5.4b
TifSport	B	98a	99a	94a	89a	7.0a	6.0a
Tifway	B	98a	98a	95a	87a	6.9ab	5.7ab
HI1	SP	94abc	97a	81b	75b	6.9ab	5.2b
K1	SP	99a	98a	89ab	84a	7.1a	5.8a
SIPV-2	SP	97ab	99a	91a	85a	7.4a	5.8a
Temple1	SP	96ab	98a	89ab	82ab	7.1a	5.5ab

[a] Carrow and Duncan, 1998. Traffic approximates two games on the same day under near soil-saturated conditions.
[b] Data are an average of two separate treatments applied in the fall on 8 and 25 September 1998.
[c] Treatment comparison based on LSD (0.05).
[d] Selection from Sea Island, GA.
DAT = days after treatment. SP = seashore paspalum. B = hybrid bermudagrass.

equal between the two ecotypes on a native clay soil. (Trenholm et al., 2000a). A greens wear study involving Sea Isle 2000 with N and K fertility variables revealed high wear tolerance imposed by 74 passes of the differential-slip rubberized roller device when applied all in one day (Trenholm et al., 2000b).

7.5. SHADE/LOW LIGHT INTENSITY TOLERANCE

Paspalum does not tolerate tree shade very well based on preliminary evaluations of several different ecotypes under oak (*Quercus* spp.) tree canopies in Georgia, with turf performance resembling the bermudagrasses. Tree shade stress includes reduced light intensity, reduced light quality in the photosynthetically important wavelengths, and tree root competition for moisture and nutrients. The grass evolved on sand dunes in full sun or with low light intensity conditions caused by cloudy days and monsoonal climatic conditions. Adaptations to low light is quite complex (Dudeck and Peacock, 1992; Wilson, 1997). *P. vaginatum* has performed exceptionally well in environments that receive over 270 days of rain annually; the grass maintained its dark green color and high turf quality, but did not exhibit elongated, spindly leaves that are typical of bermudagrass responses in the same low light environment. The grass is gaining popularity in the Hawaiian islands because of this trait plus the fact that it can tolerate nonpotable water for irrigation. Additionally, the grass may have utility in reduced light venues such as enclosed dome sports facilities. Additional research is needed to assess the exact level of low light intensity tolerance in *Paspalum vaginatum* as well as the wavelengths absorbed to maintain growth and development. Two shade-tolerant *Paspalum* species (*P. wettsteinii* and *P. malacophyllum*) have been identified (Wong and Stur, 1996), but neither have been evaluated for turfgrass use.

7.6. SOIL pH ADAPTATION

Paspalum will tolerate a pH range from a highly acidic pH 3.5 to a highly alkaline 10.2 (Duncan, 1994, 1997). It can root equally well in sands, heavy clays, silts, or mucks (Duncan and Carrow, 1998). The performance of seashore paspalum under extreme acid and alkaline conditions is discussed in the following sections.

Acid Soils

A wide diversity exists within the paspalum collection for response to the **acid soil complex** (Table 7.6). Soil acidity stress involves a complex of elemental toxicities (Al, Mn), potential nutrient deficiencies/imbalances (K, Mg, P, Ca), and high soil strength (from hard, nonexpanding kaolinitic soils such as those found in the Piedmont region in the southeastern United States). The acid soil complex is a major soil stress problem in humid tropical and subtropical areas that limits turfgrass growth. High soil temperatures and severe drought (no supplemental irrigation) can enhance the level of stress from the acid soil complex. Grasses that develop and maintain a vigorous and functional root system under these multiple stress conditions are adapted to and perform well across many turf sites. In a field study, superior tolerance to multiple root limiting stresses (acid soil complex, high soil strength, drought, high soil temperatures) included three selections from Hawaii (32 and 34 that came from Kauai and 37 from the Kona side of the Big Island–Hawaii), and Hyb 7, a cross of unknown heritage. (Table 7.4). A low/high ratio near 1.00 indicates similar growth at pH 4.2 and at 6.5. All four ecotypes are in the top four statistical groups when grown on low pH. HI 37 is unique in acid soil response, since it grew very little at the higher (6.5) pH, but grew extremely well at the low (4.2) pH. This ecotype would be a potential candidate for an acid sulfate soil.

The cluster of ecotypes in the very high tolerance range includes Common bermuda, Tifway bermuda, and an excellent greens type Sea Isle 2000. Native common bermudagrass (not AZ Common) is extremely aggressive at both pHs and had the greatest spread among all entries evaluated. The closest paspalum in aggressive growth at both pHs was PI 509023, a selection from Argentina. Two Hawaii selections (10 and 106 from Oahu) and three selections from Alden Pines country club on Pine Island in north Ft. Myers, Florida (AP 4, AP 10 (Sea Isle 2000), AP 15) have very high acid soil tolerance.

The high tolerance group includes: Q36313, a selection from an oasis in the Negev Desert in Israel; Cloister, a selection from a lawn bowling green at the Cloisters Hotel, Sea Island, Georgia; Sea Isle 1, an excellent fairway/tee/sports ecotype from Argentina; and Salam, a selection from Hawaii tracing back to Sea Island, Georgia origin. Adalayd is in the moderate tolerance range; Meyer zoysiagrass is in the low tolerance group; and, Excalibur and Mauna Kea paspalums are in the very low tolerance (susceptible) group.

Table 7.6. Acid Soil Field Tolerance Response of Selected Paspalum Ecotypes[a]

Cultivar/Ecotype	Grass	Low pH (ft²)	High pH (ft²)	Low/High Ratio	Stress Index[b]	Category
HI 32	SP	1.35d (10)[c]	1.23 (42)[c]	1.10 (5)[c]	15 (1)[c]	
Hyb 7	SP	1.58cd (7)	1.65 (31)	0.96 (9)	16 (2)	
HI 34	SP	1.95cd (4)	2.35 (14)	0.83 (13)	17 (3)	
HI 37	SP	1.14d (16)	0.14 (69)	814.00 (1)	17 (3)	SUP
AP 4	SP	1.33d (11)	1.84 (27)	0.72 (16)	27 (4)	
Common	B	6.88a (1)	12.55a (1)	0.55 (28)	29 (5)	
PI 28960	SP	0.93 (27)	0.56 (63)	1.66 (2)	29 (5)	
TCR6	SP	1.70cd (5)	2.83d (5)	0.60 (25)	30 (6)	VH
HI 10	SP	1.28d (12)	1.85 (26)	0.69 (18)	30 (6)	
HI 106	SP	1.68cd (6)	2.79d (7)	0.60 (25)	31 (7)	
Tifway	B	2.18c (3)	4.40c (3)	0.50 (31)	34 (8)	
AP 15	SP	0.96 (24)	1.01 (48)	0.95 (10)	34 (8)	
PI 509023	SP	4.05b (2)	8.65b (2)	0.47 (34)	36 (9)	
Taliaferro	SP	1.40cd (9)	2.40d (11)	0.58 (27)	36 (9)	
TCR3 (K3 der.)	SP	0.85 (33)	0.75 (58)	1.13 (4)	37 (10)	
Sea Isle 2000	SP	1.00 (21)	1.40 (37)	0.71 (17)	38 (11)	
Q36313	SP	0.98 (23)	1.44 (36)	0.68 (19)	42 (15)	
Cloister	SP	1.25d (14)	2.40d (11)	0.52 (30)	44 (17)	H
SIPV 1	SP	0.80 (36)	0.85 (53)	0.94 (11)	47 (19)	
Sea Isle 1	SP	1.05 (19)	1.93 (25)	0.54 (29)	48 (20)	
Salam	SP	0.99 (22)	1.69 (30)	0.59 (26)	48 (20)	

Table 7.6. Acid Soil Field Tolerance Response of Selected Paspalum Ecotypes[a] (Continued)

Cultivar/Ecotype	Grass	Low pH (ft²)	High pH (ft²)	Low/High Ratio	Stress Index[b]	Category
FSP-1	SP	0.63 (44)	0.89 (52)	0.71 (17)	61 (28)	
Adalayd	SP	0.85 (33)	1.80 (28)	0.47 (34)	67 (32)	Mod
Meyer	Z	0.34 (58)	0.48 (66)	0.71 (17)	75 (38)	L
Excalibur	SP	0.21 (64)	0.44 (67)	0.48 (33)	97 (48)	
Mauna Kea	SP	0.18 (65)	0.64 (61)	0.28 (48)	113 (54)	VL
Lsd (0.05)		0.82[d]	1.13[d]			

[a] Low pH = 4.2, kaolinitic nonexpanding clay (25%); high pH = 6.5. (Carrow, 1999. USGA Annual Research Report).

[b] SI = Low pH rank (absolute growth on acid soils), i.e., rapid establishment and good growth under stress) + pH ratio rank (growth pattern similarity between low and high pH, i.e., low value indicates multiple root stress tolerance = acid soil complex + high soil strength + soil drought + high soil temperatures).
Superior range = 15 (best)–17   Very High range = 27–39
High range = 40–48   Moderate range = 49–67
Low range = 68–75   Very Low range = 76–113(worst)

[c] Rank among 84 entries. Top four statistical groups are designated by a → d notation. Ecotypes not listed performed at the moderate to very low category.

[d] Significance of F-test is denoted in supra-notation on LSD value.

SP = seashore paspalum; B = bermuda, Z = zoysia.

When soil pH < 5.5, paspalum response to applied NH_4-N is often limited. In studies involving various N carriers, paspalum rapidly responded to NO_3^- forms, especially $Ca (NO_3)_2$ (Duncan and Carrow, personal observations). Seashore paspalum apparently has developed a strong preference to NO_3^--N versus NH_4-N for uptake, probably because the grass was only exposed to dissolved nitrates in ocean water during its evolution. Under soil acid pHs < 5.5, nitrification ($NH_4^+ \rightarrow NO_3^-$ by *Nitrosomonas* and *Nitrobacter* microorganisms) is inhibited and little NO_3^- is actually available for uptake by the grass (see Chapter 9). The low pH N availability problems can be resolved by using NO_3^--N carriers, by light applications of lime or other Ca sources that can stimulate microbial activity, or by direct application of highly soluble N sources such as Ca $(NO_3)_2$. The nitrification organisms will respond to applied Ca even if soil pH is not increased.

Alkaline Soils

Paspalum has been observed consistently surviving sodic soil conditions where soil pH > 8.5 (Carrow and Duncan, 1998; Miles and Tainton, 1979). In extremely sodic conditions where pH fluctuated between 9.5 to 10.2 due to poor quality effluent on a Caribbean island, it was the only turf-type grass species that was surviving. In these extremely challenging salt-affected environments, paspalum is the preferred grass of choice because of its excellent turf quality traits and its performance when the salts are properly managed. If the salts are not consistently flushed from the root zone, paspalum might survive, but quality and performance will be compromised, and the grass could struggle to maintain adequate density because of reduced growth rate caused by increasingly high salt concentrations. If salts are allowed to accumulate at EC_e values that are substantially higher than seawater (>34,400 ppm TDS or EC_w >54 dSm^{-1}), the potential for severe turf deterioration, even with the most salt-tolerant paspalum ecotypes, significantly increases.

7.7. LOW OXYGEN/ANOXIA/HYPOXIA TOLERANCE

Paspalum has a history of tolerating complete inundation (Colman and Wilson, 1960) by ocean water and the low oxygen problems caused by waterlogged or wet, boggy ecosystems (Ferguson, 1951; Straatmans, 1954; Glenhill, 1963; Chaudhri et al., 1969; Malcolm 1977). The grass is ideally suited to low drainage areas that tend to stay wet for long periods and other sites that do not drain properly. Paspalum may actually firm up those areas through water extraction and allow sports or other recreational activities to occur on those sites. Many recreational fields are constructed on inadequately drained sites.

7.8. MOWING TOLERANCE

Paspalum is highly responsive to variable cutting heights, with greens types preferring 0.125 to 0.156 in., fairway/tee types at 0.188 to 0.300 in., and coarse types at 1.5 to 3.0 in. This grass reportedly develops higher shoot densities, is more competitive against weeds, and maintains higher quality turf at lower (≤13 mm or 0.50 in.) mowing heights (Beard et al., 1991bc; Duble, 1988ab) than at higher mowing heights. Paspalum greens ecotypes mowed at 3–4 mm (about $^1/8$-in.) maintains a denser canopy, darker green color, and higher turf quality than Tifgreen bermudagrass mowed at the same height (Duncan, 1999).

Height of cut had more influence on Adalayd paspalum turf quality than N fertility level (Beard et al., 1991abc; Sifers et al., 1990). Paspalum mowed above 13 mm (0.5 in.) was more subject to broadleaf and annual grassy weed invasion than plots mowed less than 13 mm (Beard et al., 1991bc). Cutting height (≤13 mm) was more important than N fertility level in terms of fall low temperature color retention (Beard et al., 1991abc; Henry and Gibeault, 1985; Sifers et al., 1990).

Mowing heights should be reduced gradually in order to avoid scalping the fine-textured ecotypes (Gibeault et al., 1988). With gradual reduction in height, internodes become shorter and leaf cluster density increases, providing a uniform surface with a soft, cushiony feel to it. On golf courses such as Kapolei on Oahu, Hawaii (where the LPGA Hawaiian Open is played), regular verticutting, light topdressing, and periodic rolling can provide a fast ball rolling surface with stimp readings consistently in the 9–10 foot range. Management is the key.

Two approaches are used in the paspalum breeding program in Georgia to identify potential greens type paspalums: (1) collect ecotypes from the greens of old Adalayd/Excalibur golf courses with a history for mowing at heights close to $^1/8$-in. (0.125 in. or 3 mm), or (2) establish all new ecotypes on 10 × 10 ft blocks on a green and gradually reduce mowing height down to $^1/8$ in. This approach allows for the identification of potential greens types with a moderate growth rate (that will adequately recover from ball marks) and fairway/tee/sports field types with an aggressive growth rate (that will adequately recover from high traffic/injury situations). The potential greens types are reestablished on larger greens for long-term performance evaluations at a 3–4 mm mowing height. The potential fairway/tee/sports types are reestablished on larger tees, fairways, or sports fields with mowing heights between 7–13 mm (0.25 to 0.50 in.) for long-term performance evaluations involving judicious inputs. Fairway reel mowers are used to identify types that cut cleanly and mow consistently throughout the growing season. Old Adalayd types have a reputation of being tough to mow during late summer, leaving serrated leaf tips that are cosmetically unappealing. These types also cause mower blades to become dull.

CHAPTER 8

Paspalum Biotic Stress Resistance

This chapter deals with **biotic stresses** (pests) that influence seashore paspalum (Figure 6.1). The emphasis is on (1) potential pest problems, and (2) the degree of genetic resistance or susceptibility observed in *P. vaginatum*. Management options for these pests can be found in Chapter 10.

8.1. DISEASE RESISTANCE

Seashore paspalum does not have a wide variety of pathogen problems that tend to plague other warm season grasses, probably because the grass evolved in a wet, humid ecosystem with widespread and multiple disease exposure where ecotypes that survived could develop resistance. When salt water (brackish, straight ocean water) is used for irrigation, disease problems are almost negligible since most of the pathogens do not function well at high salt levels. While a number of pathogens have been reported on various *Paspalum* species, especially *P. notatum*, relatively few have been associated directly with *P. vaginatum* (Table 8.1).

Nematodes

Little information is available on paspalum sensitivity to nematodes. In nonsaline conditions, nematodes can build up over time to cause problems (Morton, 1973). During 1997, a nematode assay was conducted on 18-year-old paspalum greens at the Alden Pines Country Club, Bokeelia, Florida. The greens had not been treated for nematodes during the previous four years. The following nematodes were found:

Minimal Problem		Serious Problem	
sting	*Belonolaimus*	lance	*Hoplolaimus*
spiral	*Peltamigratus*	sheathoid	*Hemicycliophora*
ring	*Criconemella*	spiral	*Helicotylenchus*
dagger	*Xiphinema*		

Table 8.1. Pathogens That Attack Various *Paspalum* Species

Organism	Species	Disease/Location
Alternaria sp.	notatum	seed rot
Angiopsora compressa Mains	other	rust
Ascochyta paspali (Syd.) Punithalingam	other	leaves, sheaths
Balansia clavula (Berk & M.A. Curtis) C.G. Lloyd	other	black choke
Balansia epichloe (Weese) Diehl	notatum	black choke
Balansiopsis pilulaeformis (Berk, & M.A. Cirtis) Diehl	other	black crust
Bipolaris cynodontis (Marignoni) Shoemaker	dilatatum	eye spot
Bipolaris micropus (Drechs.) Shoemaker	notatum, others	leaf spot
Bipolaris sorokiniana (Sacc.) Shoemaker	urvillei	leaf spot
Chaetospermum chaetosporum (PAT.) A.L. Sm. & Ramsb.	other	dead culms
Chaetospermum tubercularioides Sacc.	other	dead culms
Claviceps paspali F. Stevens & J. G. Hall	dilatatum, notatum, urvillei, **vaginatum**, others	ergot
Colletotrichum sp.	notatum	leaf spot
Colletotrichum (Ces.) G.W. Wils.	dilatatum	anthracnose
Curvularia sp.	notatum, **vaginatum**, others	leaf mold
Curvularia eragrostidis (Henn.) J.A. Meyer	notatum	leaf necrosis
Curvularia lunata (Wakk.) Boedijn	notatum	seedling blight
Drechslera sp.	notatum	leaf spot
Exserohilum sp.	notatum	leaf spot
Fusarium sp.	notatum, **vaginatum**	root rot
Fusarium heterosporum Nees:Fr.	dilatatum, notatum, others	head mold
Fusarium lateritium Nees:Fr.	notatum	stem/seed
		head rot

Fusarium solani (Mart.) Sacc.	notatum	root rot
Gaeumannomyces sp.	notatum	decline
Helminthosporium sp.	dilatatum, notatum, urvillei, **vaginatum**, others	leaf spot
Lepiota sp.	notatum	fairy ring
Leptosphaeria sp.	other	crown rot
Marasmius sp.	notatum	fairy ring
Melanconium sp.	notatum	culms
Myriogenospora atramentosa (Berk. & M.A. Curtis) Diehl	notatum, other	black streak
Myriogenospora paspali Atk.	notatum, other	black streak
Neottiosporina paspali (Atk.)	notatum, others	leaf spot
Phyllachora sp.	other	tar spot
Phyllachora cornispora Atk.	notatum, others	tar spot
Phyllachora guianensis F. Stevens	others	tar spot
Phyllachora minutissima (Welw. & Curr.) G.W. Sm.	notatum, others	tar spot
Phyllachora paspalicola Henn.	other	tar spot
Phyllachora punchtum (Schwein.) Orton & F. Stevens	other	tar spot
Phyllachora wilsonii (Orton)	other	tar spot
Physarum cinereum (Batsch) Pers.	notatum	slime mold
Physopella compressa (Mains) Cummins & Ramachar	elongatum	rust
Puccinia sp.	urvillei	rust
Puccinia araguata Kern	microstachyum	rust
Puccinia chaetochloae Arth.	other	rust
Puccinia coronata Corda var. *coronata*	other	rust
Puccinia dolosa Arth. & Fromme	other	rust
Puccinia dolosoides Cummins	commersonii	rust

Table 8.1. Pathogens That Attack Various *Paspalum* Species (Continued)

Organism	Species	Disease/Location
Puccinia emaculata Schw.	stramineum	rust
Puccinia esclavensis Diet. & Holw.	laxum	rust
Puccinia levis (Sacc. & Bizz.) Magnus	urvillei, others	rust
Puccinia levis Sacc. & Bizz. var. *panici-sanguinalis* (Rangel) Ramachar & Cummins	other	rust
Puccinia macra Arth. & Holw.	candidum, prostratum	rust
Puccinia pseudoatra Cummins	pallidum, prostratum, penicillatum	rust
Puccinia paspalina Cummins	other	rust
Puccinia substriata Ellis & Barth.	notatum, others	rust
Puccinia thiensis Huguenin	orbiculare	rust
Pyricularia grisea (Cooke) Sacc.	other	leaf spot
Pythium sp.	notatum	root rot
Rhizoctonia sp.	dilatatum notatum, others	brown patch
Rhizoctonia solani Kuehn	notatum, others	brown patch
Sclerotinia homoeocarpa F.T. Bennett	notatum, **vaginatum**	dollar spot
Sorosporium sp.	other	smut
Sphacelotheca cordobensis (Speg.) H. Jacks.	other	head smut
Sphacelotheca paspali-notati (Henn.) G.P. Clinton	other	head smut
Stagonospora sp.	other	leaf spot

Tilletia sp.	other	smut
Tolyposporium sp.	other	smut
Uredo sp.	notatum	rust
Uromyces paspalicola Arth. & Holw.	candidum, commersonii, elongatum, laxum, microstachyum, orbiculare, pallidum, penicillatum, prostratum, racemosum, setaceum, stramineum, tenellum	rust
Ustilago schroeteriana Henn.	other	seed smut
Sugarcane mosaic virus (SMV)	other	mosaic
Paspalum striate mosaic virus (PSMV)	conjugatum, dilatatum, longiflorum, plicatulum, urvillei	mosaic
Chloris striate mosaic virus (CSMV)	dilatatum	mosaic
Cocks foot streak potyvirus	other	streaks

Sources: Alfieri et al., 1994; Cummins, 1971; Greber, 1989; Smiley et al., 1992; Watson and Dallwitz, 1992.

As more paspalum is grown as recreational turf with alternative water resources, more data will be accumulated on response of specific cultivars. No systematic screening of paspalum ecotypes from the world collection has been conducted for response to these obligate parasites. Other potential problem nematode species include: stubby-root (*Paratrichodorus*), root knot (*Meloidogyne*), cyst (*Heterodera*), lesion (*Pratylenchus*), pin (*Paratylenchus*), awl (*Dolichodorus*), and stunt (*Tylenchorhynchus*).

Bahiagrass (*P. notatum*) is apparently resistant to the root-knot nematode. Nematode symptoms in turfgrasses include stunted, off-color, or necrotic roots and shoot stress symptoms associated with slow growth and development, thinning of turf density and stands, and no response to fertilizer or water applications. Nematode population dynamics parallel the environmental conditions. Turf symptoms are seasonally expressed when nematode populations are high (Overstreet, 1999).

Pathogens

Dollar spot (*Sclerotinia homoeocarpa* F.T. Bennett) can be a problem on fine-textured paspalums mowed less than 6 mm. Increasing irrigation intervals or adding nitrogen fertilizer are methods to reduce the damage. Using ocean water is also a good biocontrol. Diversity exists within the ecotype collection of paspalums, with Hawaiian and Australian (Adalayd or Excalibur) sources being quite susceptible and types from Argentina having a good level of resistance (Duncan, 1999) (Table 8.2).

Since paspalum can be maintained under lower N regimes than bermudagrass, these conditions could favor dollar spot development on susceptible ecotypes. Selection for dollar spot resistance has been a priority in the Georgia breeding program (Table 8.2). Sea Isle 1, a fairway/tee type, has demonstrated excellent resistance while Sea Isle 2000 has a high level of resistance.

Fusarium has been suspected on paspalum in Central America and observed in the greenhouse in Georgia on specific fairway type paspalums. This systemic disease is fairly cosmopolitan in availability, but should rarely cause problems in paspalum turf. Sea Isle 1 and Sea Isle 2000 were not affected by the organism in the greenhouse, even though the open flats were positioned next to the diseased turf. Using ocean water or delaying irrigation with no additional nitrogen fertilizer applications are methods for control.

Table 8.2. Dollar Spot Resistance for *Paspalum vaginatum* Ecotypes

Ecotype	Origin	5/18/95	6/6/95	8/15/95	Mean
Sea Isle 2000	GA	6[a]	6	6	6.0
Sea Isle 1	Argentina	9	8	9	8.7
Salam	GA/HI	9	6	5	6.7
Excalibur	Australia	6	5	5	5.3
Mauna Kea	GA/HI	5	5	2	4.0

[a] 1 = poor resistance, 9 = best resistance.

Curvularia was observed (with no damage or injury) on paspalum on Kauai, Hawaii at about 200 m altitude above sea level and away from the sea (Duncan, 1999). Similar to all other warm-season grasses, viruses have been observed on a few of the introduced paspalum accessions from foreign countries while in quarantine, and those accessions were immediately destroyed. No viruses have been observed on *P. vaginatum* in turf plots. Paspalum striate mosaic virus (PSMV) is one virus documented in the genus *Paspalum* (Greber, 1989), but not on *P. vaginatum*.

Rhizoctonia has been observed on other *Paspalum* species (Wong and Stur, 1996), but not on *P. vaginatum*. Several species of *Paspalum* serve as hosts for rust (*Puccinia* spp.) fungi that attack cereals, other grasses, and bamboo (Cummins, 1971), but this disease has not been reported on *P. vaginatum*. Ergot (*Claviceps paspali* Stev. et Hall) has been found in several species of *Paspalum* including *P. distichum* (Botha et al., 1996; Brown and Rank, 1915; Cole et al., 1977; Langdon, 1963; Lefebvre, 1939; Raynal, 1992/1996) and *P. vaginatum* in Georgia (C. Cardona, personal observation). *Fusarium heterosporum* Nees: Fr. has been found on dallisgrass (*P. dilatatum* Poir.) inflorescences infested with ergot in Australia (Ali et al., 1996), on *Spartina* (Preece et al., 1994) and on *Lolium perenne* (Gay and Shattock, 1980).

8.2. INSECT RESISTANCE

Eighty-one species of *Paspalum* were evaluated for fall armyworm (*Spodoptera frugiperda* Smith) resistance (Wiseman and Duncan, 1996). *Paspalum vaginatum* cv. Tropic Shore had a good level of resistance, but the highest level of antibiosis (high insect mortality, slowed insect growth, or reduced insect feeding) occurred in *P. modestum* and *P. scrobiculatum* accessions.

Hunting billbugs (*Sphenophorus venatus vestitus* Chittenden) are sporadic problems on paspalum turf, with outbreaks recorded in Pine Island, Florida and Bangkok, Thailand golf courses. Very little research has been conducted on this insect in warm-season grasses, but has been documented in cool-season species (Johnson-Cicalese et al., 1989).

Seashore paspalum has an excellent level of resistance to yellow sugarcane aphid (*Sipha flava* Forbes) in Hawaii (G.K. Fukumoto and T.N. Sugi, University of Hawaii at Manoa). Tropical sod webworms (*Herpetogramma phaeopteralis* Guerne) will attack paspalum turf in nonsaline micro environments and under drought stressed conditions. Outbreaks have been reported in Hawaii, Thailand, Curacao, and Florida (Morton, 1973).

Two-lined spittlebug (*Prosapia bicincta* [Say]) studies have revealed the following general ranking of warm season grasses: centipedegrass (most susceptible) < bermudagrass < seashore paspalum < zoysiagrass. Among 28 paspalum ecotypes, the most resistant ones included Sea Isle 1, AP-14, Sea Isle 2000, Mauna Kea, PI 509023, and PI 299042. Laboratory bioassays have been developed to identify resistant plants (Braman and Ruter, 1997).

Tawny mole cricket (*Scapteriscus vicinus* Scudder) and southern mole cricket (S. borellii Giglio-Tos) evaluations have included 21 paspalums in the greenhouse and 35 paspalums plus seven bermudas in a field study on sandy soil in Tifton, Georgia. A no-choice (paspalum was only available food source) laboratory test (Table 8.3) conducted on 21 paspalum ecotypes showed that tawny mole crickets (TMC) caused a significantly greater reduction in quality than southern mole crickets (SMC). Both caused a significant loss in quality compared to uninfested controls (8.00). Cricket-induced injury was quite variable among the ecotypes when comparing response between the two mole crickets. Overall, the most tolerant paspalum ecotypes to TMC injury were 561-79, HI-1, HI-2, and Excalibur. Sea Isle 1 retained 82% of its normal growth on uninfested plots. PI 509023 and PI 509022 were the most susceptible, losing 76 and 75% of their normal growth, respectively.

Armyworm [*Pseudaletia unipunctata* (Haworth)] evaluations have been conducted on 31 paspalums and 7 zoysia/centipede/bermuda/tall fescue cultivars. Armyworms can be a sporadic problem under field conditions on paspalum turf (Morton, 1973). A laboratory free-choice (multiple ecotypes available) test indicated ovipositional preference or differential larval survival among 21 paspalum ecotypes (Table 8.4). Ad-

Table 8.3. No-Choice Test Response of Paspalum Ecotypes to Southern Mole Cricket (SMC) and Tawny Mole Cricket (TMC) Infestation

Ecotypes	SMC Quality[a]	TMC Ecotype	Quality
Tropic Shore	8.00a	Excalibur	6.25a
Mauna Kea	7.75ab	SIPV-1	6.25a
HI-1	7.75ab	SIPV-2	5.50a
PI 377709	7.75ab	HI-1	5.50a
PI 509023	7.50abc	Temple 2	5.25ab
HI-2	7.50abc	PI 509023	5.00ab
PI 509022	7.50abc	Temple 1	5.00ab
Fidalayel	7.25abc	HI-2	4.50abc
Temple 2	7.25abc	561-79	4.00abc
Sea Isle 1	7.25abc	Sea Isle 1	4.00abc
SIPV 2	6.75a-d	PI 299042	4.00abc
Excalibur	6.50a-e	Mauna Kea	3.75abc
PI 509020	6.50a-e	PI 509020	3.75abc
PI 299042	6.25a-e	Fidalayel	3.75abc
PI 509022	6.25a-e	Tropic Shore	3.50abc
PI 364985	6.00a-e	PI 509022	3.25abc
Temple 1	6.00a-e	PI 377709	3.25abc
310-79	5.75b-e	310-79	3.00abc
561-79	5.50cde	PI 364985	2.75abc
SIPV-1	5.25de	PI 509022	1.75bc
G.O. Adalayd	4.50e	G.O. Adalayd	1.25c
	$\bar{x}$ = 6.702		$\bar{x}$ = 4.06

[a] 1=dead plant, 10=maximum quality. Uninfested controls = 8.00. Data courtesy of S.K. Braman, University of Georgia–Griffin.

ditional fall armyworm evaluations have revealed the following ecotypes are the most susceptible; Sea Isle 2000, Sea Isle 1, AP-14, K-6, K-7, K-8, HI-2, Salam, HI-39, Temple 1, PI 377709, and PI 299042. Ecotype 561-79 from Argentina demonstrated lower larval weights and a lengthening of larval development time.

Leafhoppers have been reported to prefer young, tender seedlings of seashore paspalum during establishment (Morton, 1973). The degree of insect activity when seashore paspalum is grown using straight seawater, seawater blends, or poor quality effluent should be minimal, since these stress environments do not normally favor high insect populations.

Table 8.4. Free-Choice Laboratory Test Preference of True Army-worms on Selected Seashore Paspalum Ecotypes

Ecotype	Leaf Texture[a]	Larvae/Pot (n=12)[b]	Origin[c]
PI 364985	C	1.417a	AF
S1PV-2	F	1.167ab	SI
PI 509021	F	1.083ab	AR
Excalibur	I	1.083abc	AU
HI-1	F	1.000a-d	SI
Temple-1	F	0.750a-e	AR
PI 509022	F	0.750a-e	AR
Mauna Kea	F	0.583a-e	SI
HI-2	F	0.583a-e	SI
310-79	F	0.583a-e	AR
Tropic Shore	C	0.333b-e	HI
S1PV-1	F	0.250b-e	SI
PI 377709	C	0.250b-e	AF
PI 509020	F	0.167cde	AR
PI 299042	C	0.167cde	AF
Temple 2	F	0.083de	AR
G.O. Adalayd	I	0.083de	AU
PI 509018	F	0.083de	AR
PI 509023	F	0.083de	AR
Fidalayel	I	0 e	AU
561-79	F	0 e	AR

[a] C = coarse, I = intermediate, F = fine.
[b] O = nonpreference resistance (best rating or no surviving army-worms). Data courtesy of S.K. Braman, University of Georgia.
[c] AF = Africa; AU = Australia; AR = Argentina; SI = Sea Island, GA; HI = Hawaii.

8.3. WEEDS

In salt-affected environments, many weeds lack the necessary level of tolerance to be competitive with seashore paspalum in turf situations. Close paspalum mowing heights (<13 mm or 0.50 in.) provides a tight, dense canopy that deters aggressive growth in most weeds. The exceptions include those grassy weeds like kikuyugrass (*Pennisetum clandestinum* Hochst ex Chiov.), which is extremely aggressive, inhabits warm coastal venues, and tolerates wet soil conditions, and torpedograss (*Panicum repens* L.), that also inhabits equatic biotopes and waste places. A problem perennial weed is kyllinga [*Cyperus brevifolius* (Rottb.) Hassk.]. Weed control management options are presented in Chapter 10.

Part III
Management Practices

CHAPTER 9

Management of Abiotic/Edaphic Stresses

9.1. INTRODUCTION

Proper management of paspalum is essential for achieving high quality performance, regardless of whether this grass is grown for recreational turf, for landscaping, for bioremediation, or for transitioning into environmentally sensitive areas. In this chapter, the focus is on management:

- of abiotic/edaphic factors, including soil stresses, climatic stresses, and use-related (often man-made) stresses such as traffic and mowing.
- during establishment and on mature turf.

When Futurf and Adalayd were introduced into California during the 1970s, no additional breeding work was allowed on the grass and no management packages were developed for short- or long-term maintenance. These older cultivars were essentially maintained similar to bermudagrasses and coupled with the fact that Futurf and Adalayd were not that well-adapted to U.S. conditions nor were they high quality fine-textured types, the cultivars failed to gain widespread popularity or use. Part of that apathy could be attributed to relatively economical amendments (water, fertilizer, and pesticides) at that time and the broad adaptation traits of the bermudas. Environmental concerns were less of a priority during the 1970s and 1980s, compared to the late 1990s. With an increased emphasis on environmental regulations, escalating demands for nonpotable water use on recreational turf sites in order to meet the potable water needs of a growing population and for industrial uses, an enhanced sensitivity to the pollution-contamination-pesticide-fertilizer paradox, and rising overhead costs to maintain high quality turf, the entire turf industry is changing in response to these issues (Duncan, 1998a).

The release of a whole new regimen of warm-season grasses; for example, the new superdwarf (or ultradwarf) bermudagrasses—TifEagle, Floradwarf, Champion, Miniverde, MS Supreme—have changed the thinking concerning management strategies for each of these new grasses. The new superdwarf bermudagrasses are different grasses than the older 328 (Tifgreen), 419 (Tifway), and Tifdwarf cultivars. These new bermudagrasses are niche-specific in terms of environmental adaptation and culture, and as such, often require different management tactics (closer mowing, more verticutting to prevent thatch buildup) than other bermudagrasses.

In the same context, **paspalums are different from other warm-season grasses** in two major areas. First, they have tolerance to multiple stresses (drought, salt, waterlogging, low light intensity, extremely high and extremely low pH). They require less fertilizer than bermudagrasses. They need only minimal pesticide applications. They tolerate most types of alternative water resources (wastewater, effluent, brackish, gray, ocean water) for irrigation. Since paspalum cultivars will often be grown in stress-challenged environments, management strategies must be adjusted on a site-specific basis—i.e., salt-affected sites, wastewater- or seawater-use sites, acid-soil-complex sites, alkaline sandy soils. This turfgrass is the first species targeted for its initial use where severe stress problems predominate and where other turfgrasses have failed. Consequently, its management must be tailored to the unique microenvironments under which the grass is being grown. Secondly, the old bermudagrass management book must be discarded. Seashore paspalum evolved in unique, extremely harsh environments, and consequently requires different management protocols than other warm-season turf species. Even the original methods used to grow the Adalayd types during the 1970s to the early 1990s are not applicable when trying to grow the new finer-leaf-textured paspalum cultivars. This chapter will outline the basic management principles for paspalum and will emphasize the flexibility needed for adjusting management decisions to site-specific, environmentally-stressed areas. Proper management will allow the paspalum cultivar to express its proper level of stress tolerance, and to maintain an acceptable level of turf quality and performance, while encompassing the most stringent environmental regulations.

9.2. UNIQUE MANAGEMENT SITUATIONS

Seashore paspalum can be established in four microenvironmental situations, each of which requires specific management considerations.

More detail is provided on each situation in later chapters, but management considerations, grass requirements, and specific site concerns involving stresses will be addressed in this section.

Ocean-Influenced Ecosystems (refer to Chapter 16)

Coastal sites offer a multitude of challenges to managing high quality turf. Most warm-season grasses can be grown at these sites if management strategies and resources are available to proactively meet and stay ahead of the challenges for this environment unless salt problems arise. Then, few of the warm-season grasses have sufficient multiple stress tolerance levels needed for the environment. The result is often a 50% or more increase in management costs and man-hours needed to maintain an acceptable quality of turf using nonadapted cultivars than if these cultivars were grown in a less stressful environment. The margin of flexibility in response to cyclic stresses tend to be less for grasses that are not well adapted to these environments compared to growing the same grass in a less challenging environment. Choosing the right species and the best specific cultivar for the area will lead to more cost-effective and environmentally friendly management protocols.

Multiple stresses challenge the performance and persistence of grasses in ocean-influenced ecosystems. These stresses include:

1. Soil profiles with poor water and nutrient holding capacity (sands), heavy clays, mucks or silts that maintain a constant level of water ("wet feet" or waterlogged syndrome), usually accompanied by reduced soil oxygen levels that can impede or diminish active root growth and high salt levels.
2. Salt-water inudation, either in the form of storm surges, flooding at high tides, or intrusion into the root zone. A common scenario found on golf courses or sports fields in coastal areas includes high water tables, especially during rainy seasons, or extensive pumping from wells drilled in the area. As long as fresh water is replenished at the same volume as that being pumped, the irrigation scheduling is not a major problem. But if too much fresh water is pumped (such as during prolonged drought periods) and is not replenished at the same volume, salt water intrusion can change the situation to a salt-affected environment almost overnight. If this happens, management

protocols will change also. Less salt tolerant grasses can get into trouble very quickly unless management is adjusted to meet the salt stress challenges.

3. A combination of high *humidity* that increases pathogen problems and *wind* that depletes soil moisture (especially sands), increases evapotranspiration, and challenges the specific level of drought tolerance for the grass cultivar provides a dual challenge to management. Pathogens, however, may be suppressed by high salt levels from seawater or poor quality effluent. Again, choosing the right species and cultivar can make management much easier.

Management challenges in this environment include: irrigation (volume, quality, and timing), nutrient management (micronutrient imbalances, macronutrient availability, leaching losses, prescription fertilization), pesticide applications (which are often less effective and less durable), and drainage of excess water that is often salt-laden.

Effluent Water (refer to Chapter 15)

With an escalating demand on fresh water for human and industrial use coupled with a continually rising discharge of recycled water from that segment of the population, use of wastewater on recreational turf will continue to increase in the twenty-first century. The quality of this water will depend on the number and type of industrial discharge in the sewage system for the area. Water quality monitoring will be crucial to proper adjustment of management practices to meet the limitations imposed by the water. Water quality will vary in levels of heavy metals, carbonates and bicarbonates, salts, and other micronutrients. Whether the recycled water can be blended with ocean water or with potable water sources will change the level of management for the specific turf. Water pH changes can rapidly alter management tactics, particularly >8.5.

Most warm-season grasses can tolerate "good" recycled water, but as quality decreases, the need for turfgrass cultivars that can tolerate poor quality effluent increases. Management must also adjust to these changes, through water treatment prior to or during irrigation and through soil amendments.

Management considerations include (a) constant water monitoring and adjustment of rates/scheduling of macro- and micronutrient fertilizer amendments, (b) pH adjustments using lime amendments if irrigation water contains high sulfates, acids or sulfur amendments if the pH >8.5, (c) nutritional monitoring with high leaching volumes, (d) avoiding salt-based amendments in salinity-affected sites, (e) drainage, and (f) using highly soluble NO_3-N fertilizer sources; e.g., $Ca(NO_3)_2$.

Acid Soil Sites (refer to Chapter 17)

Excessive acidity (pH < 5.0) in surface and subsoil horizons is usually found in humid cool temperate as well as subtropical/tropical regions where high rainfall leaches base cations. The B horizon of many soils usually contains a zone of clay accumulation, especially nonexpanding (kaolinitic or Al/Fe hydrous oxides) clay forms. Turfgrass management must deal with (1) Al/Mn root toxicities in the rhizosphere, (2) nutrient imbalances (usually deficiencies) of Mg, Ca, K, P, Mo S, and B, (3) diminished bacterial and actinomycete populations needed for thatch/organic matter decomposition, and $NH_4 \rightarrow NO_3$ conversions, (4) reduced earthworm activity, (5) high soil strength that impedes rooting, (6) very low basic soil cation (Ca^{+2}, Mg^{+2}, K^{+1}) content (loss of pH dependent CEC), (7) indirect problems associated with root pruning (from toxic Al or Mn), leading to increased drought susceptibility (reduced water uptake) or predisposition to insect and disease attack, (8) low organic matter content (usually less than 3%), and (9) acid rain or acidic irrigation water.

Management strategies include (a) lime or gypsum applications on the surface (relatively easy) and in the subsoil (more difficult, unless renovating the soil or using specialized equipment without major renovation), (b) nutrient applications to correct deficiencies or imbalances, (c) organic matter incorporation, (d) utilizing basic N-carriers instead of acid N-carriers (sulfate or nitrate fertilizers) and avoiding sulfur-containing amendments (unless lime is also applied), (e) surface lime applications to enhance microbial activity or NH_4 to NO_3 conversions, and (f) using acid soil tolerant species/cultivars with high genetic root tolerance to the acid soil complex.

Acid sulfate soils (pH 1.5 to 3.5) are normally found in tropical coastal plain or tidal swamps where pyrite (FeS_2) accumulates under waterlogged conditions. Sulfates are reduced to sulfides and Fe is reduced to Fe^{+2}, forming FeS_2. Bacteria decomposes the organic matter. Drainage causes pyrite oxidation and generates sulfur acid, creating the extremely acid problem (Al toxicity, P-Ca-Mg-K deficiencies, salinity, high bulk density soil layers). Management options during reclamation include (a) soil mixing and landscape contouring to move pyrite, (b) drainage to control the water table, (c) leaching of Al^{+3} from the profile, d) organic matter additions, and (e) a good budget and plenty of patience.

Moderate acidity (decreasing from pH 6.0 down to pH 5.0) is found in subtropical, temperate-humid, and cool-humid soils. Subsoil pHs are normally >5.0 and acid surface problems cause nutrient deficiencies (Mg, Ca, K, P, especially in acidic sand soils), cause slow conversion of ammonia-base fertilizers to nitrates (inefficient microbial conversions), and reduce bacterial/actinomycete populations that are instrumental in thatch/ organic matter decomposition in the surface. Management options include (a) scheduled lime additions, (b) applying base N sources, (c) limiting S applications, (d) nutrient applications to reduce deficiencies/ imbalances, and (e) thatch/organic matter management: reduce accumulation, light lime applications to enhance microbial decomposition, avoid excessive leaching of bases from the thatch layer.

Environmentally Sensitive Areas (Wetlands)
(refer to Chapter 18)

As environmental concerns continue to increase, recreational turf occupies a very visible place in the total ecosystem. Contamination of potable water supplies, loss/destruction of wildlife habitats for recreational turf purposes, and the utilization of potable water for recreational turf irrigation are all at the forefront of these concerns. Environmental impact statements are primary documentation prior to any construction projects. Turf management considerations include (a) use of alternative water resources for irrigation, (b) establishment of buffer strips to minimize the movement of pesticides or fertilizer into groundwater or wetland sites, (c) prescription fertilization techniques, (d) judicious and carefully timed pesticide applications to minimize the impact on the user community, (e) efficient water use/improved irrigation technology, (f) water-use-efficient and multiple-stress-tolerant turfgrass cultivars, (g) wildlife and habitat management (Audubon Cooperative Sanctuary Program, Wildlife Links Program), (h) water quality management, (i) integrated pest management, (j) environmental planning, and (k) impact of management practices on the user community.

9.3. ESTABLISHMENT AND GROW-IN

Paspalum must be vegetatively propagated since seed are not available, similar to the hybrid bermudas. Stolons, rhizomes, verticut material, and sod can be used for establishment. The species is amenable to hydrosprigging. Coral Greek Golf Course on Oahu, Hawaii was established in Salam paspalum using this latter technique in 1997.

Preestablishment

Seed bed preparation should be similar to that used with other warm season grasses. The soil surface should be soft and pliable. If the soil pH is < 5.5, apply lime topically at 2–5 lb/1000 ft^2 and incorporate into the top 1–2 in. surface layer. If sufficient lime is added to raise the pH to 6.5, till as deeply as possible. If the pH is > 8.5 and/or salt-laden water is used for irrigation, apply gypsum (20–80 lb/1000 ft^2) or the equivalent amount of granulated sulfur and lime and work into the surface 4 in. Other options include treatment of irrigation water with gypsum and agitation prior to application, or lime plus sulfur additions to the soil. If the irrigation water is high in sulfates, add lime to the soil surface to form gypsum.

In salt-affected environments, avoid using soil deposits dredged from surrounding bays or inlets for the top soil, if possible. Collect water quality and soil analysis data prior to deciding on the grass species and specific cultivars for the site. If the soil surface has a white appearance (from excess salts), collect soil samples from 0–2 in., 2–6 in., and 6–12 in. for analyses. If saline, sodic, or saline-sodic conditions are present, always start managing (pretreatment) the salt problems prior to sprig or sod establishment. Both soil and water amendments may be needed, depending on the degree of salinity (Carrow and Duncan, 1998b). Young seedling roots are quite sensitive to salt-affected soil conditions, especially high total salts in the soil surface. High sodium can also cause establishment problems if a sodic condition (soil structural deterioration) reduces water infiltration and causes poor aeration in the rhizosphere and at the surface.

For saline soils, pretreatment includes high irrigation water volumes to provide leaching and flushing of salts from the top few inches of soil at least one week prior to planting. Treating the soil with deep tillage and gypsum or lime plus sulfur incorporation will diminish the impact that excess Na would have on causing deterioration of soil structure (sodic) (Carrow and Duncan, 1998b). The addition of 40–80 lb gypsum/1000 ft^2 to the soil surface followed by 1–2 high volume irrigations at least 2–3 weeks prior to planting will dislodge excess Na^+ from the soil surface exchange sites and enhance establishment in sodic soils. However, treating the soil is only the first step. The long-term problems will come from salt-laden, poor quality water. Since irrigation will be essential for establishment, grow-in, and long-term maintenance, the water may need treatment prior to planting and continuously thereafter to minimize adverse effects. One frequent problem that is often encountered during grass establishment (when irrigation water has a high salt level) is salt accumulation from light frequent irrigation. Grass establishment will be successful if periodic leaching is used to reduce the salinity hazard to young turf plants. If water conservation programs are used, irrigation scheduling and duration must be sufficient to keep salts from rising through the soil profile due to evaporation. Rising salts will kill the root systems of young turfgrass seedlings.

Establishment Techniques

Tillage, sprig dispersal, and rolling to maximize node-soil contact are essential for successful establishment. Maximum rooting will be accomplished when the vegetative material is covered by a thin layer of soil, organic matter, or synthetic polymers to minimize light exposure (Ferreira and Valio, 1992) and dessication. Sprigging rates can vary from 5 bu (1.26 ft^3 = 1 bu)/1000 ft^2 or 200 bu/ac up to 600 bu/ac. The lower volume will take at least 3 months for grow-in. High sprig volume will take less time for grow-in, depending on fertility and irrigation scheduling, and water quality. Salt-laden irrigation water will slow down turfgrass growth rates and extend the grow-in period for even the most salt-tolerant turf cultivars.

Paspalum can be planted into wet, boggy areas or low drainage ways. To avoid compaction problems, a light topdressing might be preferable to rolling in order to provide the grass node-soil contact.

Mowing height should be maintained at 13–25 mm during establishment and early grow-in to avoid vertical growth and to promote horizontal growth. Lower cutting heights (< 7 mm) shortens internodes and creates a dense canopy faster than higher (> 20 mm) cutting heights.

Fertilizer

Paspalum absorbs limited amounts of nitrogen during the first month of establishment. Instead, the grass prioritizes root development during this period and medium to high levels of P and K are essential for rhizo-sphere development, especially in salt-affected environments. Beginning at establishment, basic fertilizers with ratios of 1:2:3 or 1:3:4 N:P:K are adequate when applied at 0.33 to 0.50 lb N/1000 ft² biweekly for the first month. When stolon growth is observed, the emphasis should be shifted to high N sources in a starter formulation or highly soluble NO_3-N sources for grow in.

Herbicides

Granular Ronstar can be used at planting for crabgrass, goosegrass, bluegrass, and broadleaf weed control (see Tables 10.1 and 10.3 for chemical names and a summary of herbicide responses during initial establishment, grow-in, and on mature turf). Kerb, Dimension, Drive, Prograss, Vanquish, Manage, Trimec Southern, Mecomec, and Basagran are non-injurous to paspalum turf applied postemergence. *Do Not Use* Surflan, Asulox, Aatrex, Sencor, Daconate, Vantage, Princep, Image, Bueno, Trimec Plus, Trimec Classic, Turflon, Confront, or Acclaim, since these herbicides are phytotoxic to paspalum.

Irrigation

For the first two weeks after sprigging, irrigation applications should be scheduled to minimize any drying of the soil surface. With high evaporative demand conditions on sandy profiles, short duration (every 10–15 minutes during daylight hours for 5 minutes) applications may be needed if full sun exposure and winds are constant. If native soil conditions (with some water-holding capacity) are being used, irrigation 2–3 times daily for 15 minutes per application may be adequate to prevent the surface from drying out. If poor quality water is being used, the strategy is to use sufficient volumes to keep the salts moving through the profile.

Once rooting has been initiated (usually 3–4 weeks after planting with sprigs), the irrigation scheduling (duration, intervals) should be *gradually* lengthened to force the roots deeper into the soil profile. Paspalum responds to short duration and frequent irrigation applications by maintaining a shallow root system. Adjustment to a less frequent, longer duration irrigation schedule is essential to transitioning paspalum roots deeper into the soil profile and is critical on salt-affected sites where salts must be leached deeper into the profile. If the pump breaks down or scheduling is suddenly altered, the young shallow-rooted seedlings might not survive long enough to adjust their root systems deeper into the profile if drought conditions are severe. The management strategy is to gradually increase the intervals between irrigation and the duration for each application; e.g., 2-hour intervals for 5 minutes increased to once daily applications for 30–45 minutes. The transition time will vary on a site-specific basis and be dictated by use (greens, tees, fairways, roughs on golf courses, sports fields, landscapes), soil conditions, water quality and availability, and climate.

Kapolei Renovation/Conversion Technique

Steve Swanhart, superintendent at the Kapolei golf course on Oahu, Hawaii and his assistant devised a renovation technique on a golf course that was planted in bermuda contaminated with paspalum. He decided to reestablish paspalum uniformly on the golf course, and through trial and error developed an effective technique to transition the course into one species with no "down" time. He modified an aerator by replacing the spikes/corers with a blunt "shovel" that would push the sprigs into the established grass surface.

His stepwise technique included:

Greens:
1. Roping off one-half of each green as "out of bounds."
2. Deep verticutting of sprigs from his paspalum nursery.
3. Hand application of sprigs over the roped-off greens area.
4. Using the modified aerator, pushing the sprigs into the surface at last 3 passes over the area from different directions.
5. Rolling 3–4 times from different directions.
6. Hand watering initially, then regular frequent irrigation during the establishment phase.

He systematically renovated greens, tees, and fairways during early 1996. Even though the bermuda became more aggressive during the May to October period, the paspalum was sufficiently established to be competitive and survive. When the rainy period began in November and the bermuda slowed down its growth rate, he began a systematic application of Prograss® (1.5 ai/ac) + Cutlass® (0.75 ai/ac) to transition out the bermuda and finish growing in the paspalum. He was able to accomplish complete grow-in by February 1997 in time for the LPGA Hawaiian

Open. Using straight ocean water would have accomplished the same thing as the reduced light intensity or the Cutlass concerning its growth regulation effect to slow down the growth rate of bermuda. With this water source, only Prograss® would be needed to effectively control the bermuda.

Grow-In After Establishment

Fertility

Normal grow-in time from sprig planting until full coverage is between 2 and 3 months, depending on volume of sprigs planted and water quality/quantity. Paspalum response to urea or ammonium -N fertilizers can be minimal (Beard et al., 1991c), either because of slow microbial conversion of NH_4 to NO_3, the inability of paspalum to rapidly absorb NH_4^+-N, or an inherently low N requirement. Since this grass evolved on sand dunes that were subjected to ocean storm surges and periodic inundation, it has developed the capability to absorb NO_3^--N (dissolved in ocean, groundwater, or rainwater) and to thrive on lower amounts than most other warm-season grasses.

A dual-phase tactic to enhance stolon-rhizome-shoot growth is to lightly verticut (cut rooted stolons) on a regular schedule (weekly or biweekly, depending on how fast the grass needs to grow) beginning at week 5–6 after sprig planting, followed by 1 lb/1000 ft²/application of a highly soluble N source, such as $Ca(NO_3)_2$. Irrigate immediately after fertilizer application. Paspalum should respond in 24–36 hours. Repeat as necessary to escalate grow-in.

About 4 weeks after planting, apply about 1 lb/1000 ft² of a complete fertilizer (i.e., 16-8-24, 12-12-24, 9-18-18, or something comparable). Repeat every 2–3 weeks until grow-in is >90% complete. Beginning at week 5 or 6, verticut one time, apply 1/2–1 lb/1000 ft² (2.4 to 4.8 g/ m²) $Ca(NO_3)_2$, and irrigate. Repeat on 7–14 day cycles, verticutting in different directions each time. If verticutting is not performed, grow-in time will be lengthened. Once established, N-carriers containing urea or NH_4^+-N can be used as long as soil conditions (temperatures > 55°F; pH > 5.5 at least in the surface one or two inches) allow for conversion of NH_4^+ to NO_3^- in a timely manner. If the site is sodded, fertilization would be the same as the initial establishment of stolons and for the second treatment. Thereafter, a mature turf program would be used. Whether established by sod or by stolons, N fertilization rates should be reduced to that of a mature turf program as quickly as possible (see Section 9.6).

Irrigation

Water should be applied each time fertilizer treatments are made. The strategy is to gradually transition the schedule to longer intervals between applications and a longer duration during each application in order to force the roots deeper into the soil profile. This scheduling must be balanced with keeping the soil profile wet enough after verticutting to foster rapid root development from new nodes while moving moisture deeper into the profile to enhance deeper rooting.

Mowing

Cutting heights should be no higher than 25 mm (1 in.), and preferably closer to 13–20 mm (0.50 to 0.75 in.) to promote shorter internodes and a denser canopy during grow-in after establishment.

9.4. MOWING PRACTICES

After initial grow-in, cutting height should be gradually reduced to that of the eventual use for the grass. Rotary or reel mowers can be used, depending on the eventual desired height, but for mowing under 25 mm (1 in.), a reel mower is required. Paspalum will scalp if too much leaf blade is removed during a single cutting, and the practice of removing no more than 35–40% of the existing blade area is appropriate for paspalums as well as other grasses.

Scalping of seashore paspalum turf has been associated with:

1. use of ecotypes that are not adapted to the mowing height; i.e., intermediate-leaf-texture types such as Adalayd or Excalibur.
2. overapplication of N fertilizer either during grow-in or on a routine basis. While paspalum does not require as much N as bermudagrass, it will efficiently take up N (except during the early weeks of establishment), which can lead to excessive uptake if too much is applied. The net result is excessive growth and thatch accumulation, and succulent leaf blades.

3. waterlogged sites, or
4. combinations of these.

The soft leaf blades and the cushion-type canopy of paspalum will enhance scalping if these conditions exist, especially if excessive N is applied.

Bermudagrass produces leaf blades on the end of stems and rarely has leaves below the stem tip. Stem elongation during the growing season elevates the leaves above the mowing height, which can promote scalping, unless plant growth regulators are applied prior to mowing or the mowing height is raised. In contrast, paspalum produces more horizontal growth, with a layering of leaves and very few stems growing upright. With multiple leaf layers and the lack of stem elongation, scalping is not a problem in seashore paspalum if the proper ecotype, N fertility program, and topdressing practices are used. If scalping occurs due to excessive leaf growth and succulence or inappropriate mowing schedules, Ca $(NO_3)_2$ can be used to rapidly mend scalped areas.

Greens

Using ecotypes developed for greens, the normal mowing heights can range from 3–5 mm. Sea Isle 2000 can perform well at 3 mm ($1/8$ in.) mowing height. Color and density will normally be darker green and more dense than the bermudas cut at the same height. Precision reel mowers with sharpened blades will be necessary for uniform cuts and smooth ball roll. Stimp readings of 9–10 feet are possible with proper management (regular light verticutting, light topdressing, and periodic rolling).

Tees

Heights ranging from 13–20 mm (0.5 to 0.8 in.) will provide a nice firm surface. To mend scalping problems or to escalate divot recovery, use highly soluble N sources, such as Ca $(NO_3)_2$ after verticutting the damaged area.

Fairways

Optimum mowing heights should range from 13–20 mm, depending on the ecotype or cultivar. Sea Isle 1 grows well between 13–16 mm

(0.5 to 0.64 in.) height and can maintain good density even at 7 mm (0.28 in.). Repair of ball landing zone areas can be enhanced by verticutting and spot application of highly soluble N fertilizers. Consideration should be given to raising the mowing height between 20–25 mm (0.8 to 1.0 in.) going into the winter to improve the carbohydrate load in the crown region and in the rhizomes and to enhance winter hardiness in the northern U.S. transition zone.

Roughs

Short roughs can be maintained between 25 and 50 mm (1–2 in.). Density will be less than areas mowed at shorter heights. The higher the cutting height, the more difficulty in hitting balls out of the rough. Paspalum roughs left unmowed or with heights >50 mm will be true penalty roughs.

Sports Fields

Optimum heights should be 13–25 mm (0.5 to 1.0 in.), with the shorter heights for soccer and baseball and the taller heights for football. Paspalum is much softer and more "cushiony" than bermudagrass (which tends to be more upright and stemy). The cushiony effect of paspalum comes from the horizontal layering of multiple leaves and the lack of tendency for upright growth. The result is a denser canopy than bermudagrass at these mowing heights.

9.5. PLANT GROWTH REGULATORS (PGR)

Minimal data on PGR effects on seashore paspalum are available. A few golf course superintendents and Southern Turf® have used Primo® (trinexapac-ethyl) with success on paspalum for growth regulation. Primo rates and timing for use on *Paspalum vaginatum* have yet to be determined, but rates generally should be no more than $1/2$ x (label rate). At rates normally applied to bermudagrass, paspalum will turn brown. A nitrogen fertilizer application after Primo® application apparently minimizes the "browning" effect.

Cutlass® has been used in conjunction with Progress to control bermudagrass in paspalum, with minimal effect on paspalum during the fall and spring seasons. But Cutlass (flurprimidol) will slow down paspalum growth rates when temperatures exceed 90°F during the summer months or with temperatures <70°F during the fall and spring. What effect Proxy® (ethephon), Limit® (amidochlor), Shortstop® (EPTC), TGR® or Parlay® (paclobutrazol), Maintain® (chlorflurenol), fluoridimide, ancymidol, fluorinol, DMSO (dimethyl sulphoxide), Alar® (B-995), CCC (chlormequat), or Phosphon® (phosphonium chloride) might have on this paspalum species is unknown (Diesburg, 1999).

As discussed in Section 9.4 (Mowing Practices), the use of PGRs to reduce stem elongation and minimize scalping problems is not necessary on paspalum due to its horizontal growth habit as compared to bermudagrass. PGR application to maintain a prostrate, dense turf under low light intensity, such as during monsoon seasons in tropical environments, apparently is not required for paspalum. PGR use to reduce growth during rainy seasons and as a harvest aid in sod production may be beneficial. As more data and grower experience become available, the role of PGRs in the overall management of seashore paspalum will become more evident.

PGR response on bahiagrass (*P. notatum*) has been documented (Table 9.1). In general, Oust G (sulfometuron-methyl), Image SL (imazaquin), Royal MH-30SL or Slo-Gro (maleic hydrozide), Pursuit SL (imazethapyr), and Cadre (imidazolinone) SL have provided seed head or vegetative growth suppression. Embark SL (mefluidide) and Glean WG (chlorsulfuron) were ineffective or inconsistent. Whether *P. vaginatum* will respond to these specific PGRs in the same manner as *P. notatum* has yet to be determined.

9.6. FERTILIZATION ON MATURE PASPALUM TURF

Seashore paspalum evolved on infertile, sandy sites where certain nutrients would be adequate to abundant from seawater, such as Mg, SO_4, Ca, K, Cl, and Na (see Section 16.3). In seawater, Na (10, 560 ppm), Mg (1272 ppm), and Ca (400 ppm) account for most of the total cations, while K (380 ppm) constitutes less than 1% of the cations. The anions in the highest quantities include Cl (18,980 ppm) and SO_4 (2649 ppm). Other nutrients such as N and P are present in very low concentrations (Table 15.1).

In this ocean-exposed ecosystem, paspalum developed mechanisms for sufficient uptake of nutrients in the presence of (1) very high Na^+ concentrations that could limit K^+ and Ca^{2+} availability and because of

Table 9.1. Plant Growth Regulators Used on *Paspalum notatum* (Bahiagrass).

Chemical Family	Names/Formulations (U.S.)	Source
Sulfonylurea	Sulfometuron 75% ai (Oust wg)	Nelson et al., 1993
Imidazolinone	Imazapyr 240 g ai/L (Pursuit SL)	Nelson et al., 1993
—	Maleic hydrozide 180 g ai/L (Royal MH-30 SL)	Nelson et al., 1993
Mefluidide	Mefluidide 240 g ai/L (Embark SL)	Nelson et al., 1993
Sulfonylurea	Chlorsulfuron 75% ai (Glean WG)	Nelson et al., 1993
Imidazolinone	Imazaquin 180 g ai/L	Goatly et al., 1996
Imidazolinone	AC 263,222 240 g ai/L (Cadre SL)	Goatly et al., 1996

EC = emulsifiable concentrate   SL = soluble liquid
WG = water dispersible granules   AS = aqueous suspension.

toxic levels could potentially cause replacement of Ca^{2+} in root cell walls and membranes, (2) a high Mg^{2+} content that could inhibit Ca^{2+} and K^+ uptake, and (3) very high Cl^- levels that could inhibit NO_3^- uptake. Since paspalum thrived in this environment, it evolved nutrient uptake and utilization mechanisms that provide functional growth and development under very low nutrient availability and severe nutrient imbalance situations. Consequently, paspalum fertilization requirements differ substantially from bermudagrass requirements.

Nitrogen

Most warm-season grasses respond to and utilize both NO_3^- and NH_4^+ forms of N. Paspalum will use the N in NH_4^+-N if it is transformed to NO_3^--N form by the nitrification process. *Nitrosomonas* and *Nitrobacter* require soil temperatures >55°F (12.8°C) and a soil pH >5.5 or readily available soluble Ca. If these conditions are present, nitrification can transform NH_4^+-N to NO_3^--N in a few days, but under less favorable conditions, seashore paspalum will not utilize NH_4^+-N directly. Paspalum demonstrates the same response to urea $[CO(NH_2)_2]$ as it does to NH_4^+-N. It apparently will not take up the urea-N form efficiently, and nitrification to NO_3^- must occur before the grass will take up the N. Paspalum rapidly responds to highly soluble NO_3^--N, such as Ca $(NO_3)_2$.

Seashore paspalum apparently has a low N requirement compared to bermudagrasses. Additionally, paspalum has very efficient mechanisms for NO_3^- uptake and N utilization, since less applied N is needed for comparable plant responses. Several factors may account for these N requirements (Dubey and Passarakli, 1995):

1. Nitrogen levels would be low in the ocean ecosystem under which seashore paspalum evolved and NO_3^- would be more abundant than NH_4^- in this system. The NO_3^--N preference is probably an enhanced energy-dependent process with a carrier protein for transport of NO_3^- across the root cell membrane in an active manner.

2. Many halophytes (salt-adapted plants) are adapted to NO_3^- uptake because increasing salinity induces uptake and accumulation in these plants. Salinity often increases the activity of nitrate reductase, an enzyme necessary for reduction of NO_3^- to NH_3 in halophytic plants. These attributes would favor development of a preference for NO_3^--N.

3. Salinity adversely affects the glutamine synthetase/glutamine-oxoglutorate aminotransferase (GS/GOGAT) pathway where NH_4^+ becomes assimilated into various N-compounds in plants.

4. The presence of Ca^{2+} in saline environments enhances NO_3^- uptake, probably due to maintenance of root cell membrane integrity and enhancement of NO_3^- transporter protein activity.

5. In acid environments, NH_4^+ becomes a much more dominant N- form than NO_3^- and transformation of NH_4^+ to NO_3^- by nitrification requires an appropriate environment for *Nitrosomonas* and *Nitrobacter* activities (soil temperature > 55°F, pH > 5.5 or presence of a soluble Ca source). Since paspalum does not use NH_4^+, management must apply NO_3^- sources or must allow sufficient time for nitrification and the subsequent paspalum response under acidic conditions.

The following nitrogen fertilization guidelines are based on the integration of published literature for paspalum (limited to and primarily involving Adalayd types), ongoing research, field observations, and field practices by turf managers. Fertilizer application **schedules** for paspalum are similar to a cool-season grass protocol: high rate applications during the fall and spring (0.50 to 1.0 lb $N/1000$ ft^2 or 0.25 to 0.49 kg $N/$ 100 m^2) and minimal (0.33 to 0.66 lb $N/1000$ ft^2 or 0.16 to 0.32 kg/ 100 m^2) applications during the summer months (Gibeault et al., 1988;

Harivandi and Gibeault, 1983; Duble, 1988ab). Paspalum needs little fertilization once established (Beard et al., 1982, 1991c). Optimum N fertilizer rates for fairways, tees, and sports fields are 2–4 lb/1000 ft^2 (0.98 to 1.96 kg/100 m^2) annually (Duble, 1989) within the region of adaptation in the United States. On greens, annual N applications of 3–6 lb/1000 ft^2 (1.47 to 2.94 kg/100 m^2) would be adequate for this region. In more humid tropical regions with year-round growing seasons, annual N rates of 5–8 lb/1000 ft^2 (2.45 to 3.92 kg/100 m^2) (greens) and 3–6 lb/1000 ft^2 (1.47 to 2.94 kg/100 m^2) (fairways/tees/sports fields) would be sufficient. Sandy soils or salt-affected sites that require extra irrigation for leaching salts would require N rates at the higher end of the range. When salinity is not a problem, the soil is not a sand or in tropical arid or semiarid regions, the low to middle N rates within each range would be adequate. Consequently, seashore paspalum normally uses only 40–50% of the annual N used by hybrid bermudagrasses under the same conditions once the grass is established. Nitrogen fertilizer rates exceeding 4 lb/1000 ft^2 (1.96 kg/100 m^2) per year may cause puffiness, thatch buildup, and scalping problems in some environments (Duble, 1988ab, 1989). These potential problems increase during the hottest temperatures when growth rates are high; therefore, fertilizer rates should be minimized during these periods. Prescription fertilization (or spoon-feeding) with low rates (0.33 to 0.66 lb N/1000 ft^2 or 0.16 to 0.32 kg N/100 m^2) per growing month should be the standard fertilization protocol (Duncan, 1999). Both quick release and slow release N carriers should be used in the spoon-feeding program. During the spring period, high N rates (0.50 to 1.0 lb/1000 ft^2 or 0.25 to 0.49 kg/100 m^2) can be applied monthly.

Prior to fall cool temperatures (<55°F) and a slow down in growth rate, applications of K fertilizers (0-20-20, 0-0-39, 0-0-60 or something comparable) should be made at 1–2 lb K$_2$O/1000 ft^2 (0.41 to 0.82 kg/100 m^2) rates to enhance winter hardiness. If the paspalum is to be overseeded, the late summer and early fall N applications should be decreased or omitted prior to the overseeding operation in order to reduce the growth rate and vigor of paspalum. On sites not receiving overseeded cool-season grasses, early to mid-fall N applications can range from 0.50 to 0.75 lb/1000 ft^2 per month. Avoid excess N rates (>0.50 lb N/1000 ft^2) during the late fall until dormant, even when overseeded with cool-season grasses. Paspalum responds to Fe amendments and rates of $1/2$–1 lb/1000 ft^2/application may be beneficial on a monthly basis during the growing season.

If the paspalum is slow to respond to urea or other ammonium-based N fertilizers, applications of lime may enhance microbial activity and the conversion of ammonium to nitrate in acid soils. Sufficient lime should be applied to adjust the surface 4 in. to pH >6.0. However, this may not be possible in some turfgrass sites. Alternative applications could include (1) adding low quantities (2–5 lb/1000 ft^2 or 0.98 to 2.45 kg/100 m^2) of lime (CaCO$_3$) two or three times per year or whenever fertilizer N responses are limited. Low volume Ca applications will cause a rapid paspalum response to NH$_4$$^+$-N, indicating that *Nitrosomonas* and *Nitrobacter* apparently do not require a pH >5.5 as long as Ca is available and present in sufficient quantities; (2) adding gypsum at 2–5 lb/1000 ft^2 two or three times yearly; or (3) adding highly soluble N sources such as Ca(NO$_3$)$_2$ in $^1/_2$–1 lb/1000 ft^2 increments on a weekly or biweekly basis will result in a rapid paspalum response. These highly soluble N sources can be used as spot applications to escalate recovery/repair of scalping problems, divots, or ball landing zones/high traffic areas and to trigger faster grow-in after establishment or renovation. This N source can also be used during spring greenup when soil temperatures are less than 55°F (which is necessary for microbial conversion from ammonium to nitrate) when nitrification is slow and regardless of whether the soil is acid or alkaline.

As noted in the section on Grow-In After Establishment, N needs during the first month are relatively low at 0.33 to 0.50 lb N/1000 ft^2 of a starter fertilizer at establishment and again at two or three weeks, whether the area is established by stolons (sprigs) or by sodding. After the one-month period, areas that were stolonized can be fertilized at 1–2 lb N/1000 ft^2/month (0.49 to 0.98 kg N/100 m^2) until 90% or greater coverage is achieved. At that time, N fertilization should be adjusted to a mature turf schedule to prevent thatch buildup, puffiness, or scalping. For sodded sites, a mature turf program can be used after the first month.

Consistently high rates of fertilizer coupled with frequent, short duration irrigation scheduling should be avoided, since these practices foster shallow root zone development and decrease the overall drought tolerance capability of paspalum (Duncan, 1999). If paspalum is not responding to a judicious fertilization program, especially on sandy profiles or USGA-specification greens and in high rainfall climates, the fertility rates may need to be increased or the duration between applications may need to be shortened. In most U.S. areas, balanced N-P-K fertilizers (i.e., 10-10-10 to 19-19-19) can be used in 0.25 to 1.0/1000 ft^2 increments on a monthly basis from March to June and September to November for normal fertility maintenance.

The fertility practices of using relatively low annual N rates, reducing N rates per application in the most vigorous growing months (summer), and adopting a spoon-feeding approach are necessary because of the high efficiency of N-uptake (particularly NO_3^-) and the vigorous, deep rooting capability of the grass. At higher N rates, paspalum will continue to efficiently take up applied N, but the result is excessive growth (especially during high temperature months) and greater succulence. Paspalum responds by becoming puffy (spongy), with increased thatch buildup, and by increased susceptibility to scalping (Beard et al., 1982, 1991c; Duble, 1988ab, 1989; Gibeault et al., 1988; Harivandi and Gibeault, 1983). Vigorous verticutting, dethatching, and topdressing can moderate these paspalum responses, but the easiest control measure is to adjust the N fertility program to lower rates.

Potassium

Potassium fertilization is very important for seashore paspalum since (1) it is often grown for turf in sites where additional increments of Na, Ca, or Mg are added in irrigation water, soil, or chemical amendments that are needed to alleviate toxic Na problems. Each of these elements can enhance K losses through leaching or through suppression of K uptake, and (2) high tissue K content enhances greater wear tolerance and greater salinity tolerance in paspalum, and is an important component in these stress tolerance mechanisms.

Fine-textured paspalums have 85–95% higher leaf K content than intermediate (Adalayd) or coarse-textured paspalums and hybrid bermudagrasses (Trenholm et al., 1999). Under low K fertilization regimes, Sea Isle 2000 (a greens type paspalum) maintained a higher tissue K content. Paspalum also maintains a higher tissue K content under salt stress than bermudagrasses (Marcum and Murdoch, 1990, 1994).

Seashore paspalum has developed very efficient K uptake and utilization mechanisms, even when soil K levels are low or high levels of other salts (especially Na) are present. Although paspalum has the capability to extract and accumulate appreciable K in leaf tissues in adverse environments, K additions must be included in the management program. Sufficient K must be applied on a regular schedule to prevent "mining" of soil

K to very low levels and to provide adequate K for uptake and use in stress tolerance mechanisms.

On fine-textured soils, extractable K levels and percent K on the CEC sites are the two best guidelines for supplying annual K needs. Moderately high to high extractable K levels are needed for most recreational turf sites and 3–8% K on the CEC sites is recommended. On salt-affected (saline, sodic, or saline-sodic sites) fine-textured soils, several 1–2 lb $K_2O/$ 1000 ft^2 (0.41 to 0.82 kg K/100 m^2) K applications should be made over the growing season to maintain adequate soil K content.

Since seashore paspalum is often grown on salt-affected sandy soils, leaching losses will be greater for K if extra irrigation water is needed to remove salts. High Na, Ca, or Mg amendments will displace K from CEC sites and could suppress K uptake (this is probably less of a problem for paspalum). Even without salinity problems, K is likely to leach on sands in high rainfall humid climates or under heavy irrigation. To address these problems, K should be applied at 1.5 to 2.0 times the N rate (i.e., N:K$_2$O ratios of 1:1.5 to 1:2.0 or N:K ratios of 1:1.25 to 1:1.66). Both K and N can be spoon-fed onto these sites to maximize availability for uptake. While N rates should be reduced during the summer months on paspalum, K needs remain high all year, especially if poor quality effluent is used for irrigation. To compensate for these needs, fertilizers with 1:2.0 (N:K$_2$O) ratios should be applied during summer months or during high leaching months, while 1:1.5 (N:K$_2$O) ratios are acceptable during other periods. During mid-fall in regions where paspalum may be subjected to low temperatures, high K fertilization rates (1–2 lb $K_2O/$ 1000 ft^2 or 0.41 to 0.82 kg K/100 m^2) should be applied to enhance winter hardiness.

Since high total salinity is often present where paspalum is grown on salt-affected sites, turf managers should be aware of the salt index of various fertilizers that contribute to salinity (Table 9.2). The salt index is a measure of the salt concentration that a fertilizer induces in a soil solution. A high salt index implies (1) greater potential to cause total salinity stress on germinating seeds or rooting vegetative plant material during establishment, (2) greater contribution to soil salinity for the same weight of material versus a fertilizer with a lower salt index, and (3) greater potential for fertilizer burn of shoot tissues that are in contact with the fertilizer. The salt index is based on sodium nitrate, which is assigned a relative value of 100. The osmotic pressure increase in soil solution caused by the same weight of a fertilizer is compared to sodium nitrate, where

Table 9.2. Salt Index and Acidification Potential of Selected Fertilizers

Source	Salt Index[a]	Calcium Carbonate Equivalent (Acidity)[b]	
Sodium chloride	153	0	
Potassium chloride	116	0	
Ammonium nitrate	105	62	acid
Sodium nitrate	100	29	base
Calcium chloride	82	68	base
Urea	75	71	acid
Potassium nitrate	74	23	base
Ammonium sulfate	69	110	acid
Calcium nitrate	65	20	base
Potassium sulfate	46	0	
Epsom salts (Mg sulfate)	44	0	
Sulfate of potash-magnesia	43	0	
Diammonium phosphate	34	75	acid
Monoammonium phosphate	30	58	acid
Triple superphosphate	10	0	
Slow release carriers	<10	<2	
Gypsum (CaSO$_4$)	8	0	
Normal superphosphate	8	0	
Potassium monophosphate	8	0	
Limestone (CaCO$_3$)	5	100	base
Dolomite lime	1	110	base

[a] After Roder et al., 1943. *Soil Science* 55:201. Expressed as ratio of change in osmotic pressure of soil solution based on an equal weight of sodium nitrate (100 base). The higher values indicate greater potentials for salt problems.

[b] Calcium carbonate equivalent = measurement of acidity potential expressed as acid (or pounds of calcium carbonate required to neutralize acidity from 100 pounds of fertilizer) and base (or basicity of 100 pounds of fertilizer that is equal to this amount of calcium carbonate). An acid fertilizer lowers pH while a basic fertilizer increases pH.

>100 indicates a high potential for salinity problems compared to sodium nitrate. However, if a fertilizer with a higher salt index than sodium nitrate is applied at a lower weight-per-unit-area of turf than the 100 lb equivalent, its total effect on soil salinity would also decrease.

Phosphorus and Other Nutrients

Seashore paspalum evolved on sites where P and the micronutrients (except Cl⁻) would be limited in availability. Paspalum probably developed a mycorrhizal association for more efficient P uptake over time, but during establishment, this association would be present. During establishment and grow-in (Section 9.3), moderate to high P levels are initially required to enhance rooting. After grow-in, P needs are similar to bermudagrass.

When growing paspalum on salt-affected sites where constant leaching is used, the following guidelines should be followed when applying all nutrients except N and K:

1. Increase annual rates by 25–50% to adjust for leaching losses
2. Use a spoon-feeding approach where light, frequent (3–6 applications annually) applications are made, and
3. Adjust the fertilization of individual nutrients based on additions or nutrient imbalances arising from irrigation water or from soil/water chemical treatments (Section 9.7).

Other Fertilization Observations

In South Africa, paspalum is considered an energetic user of N, and responds quickly to nitrate-N. If leaf N exceeds 3%, paspalum becomes soft; fungus diseases become more prevalent; and wear characteristics are negatively affected. Only judicious amounts of N should be applied to maintain a light brilliant green color with South African ecotypes, rather than a dark blue-green color. South African paspalum ecotypes respond readily to phosphate and as long as plenty of P is available, the grass will grow rapidly. A desirable leaf P content of 0.75% is sufficient for maintenance. Potassium leaf analysis of 3.5% is considered sufficient for maintenance. Once grow-in has been achieved, South African paspalums will grow at the most efficient rate when the nutritional N-P-K ratio is 3:1:5 (Mike Kruger, Cramond, Natal, South Africa—personal communication).

Typical leaf tissue concentrations in fine-textured paspalums grown in the United States (Georgia) ranged from 3.0 to 4.0% N, 0.30 to 0.43% P, and 2.1 to 3.4% K (Trenholm et al., 2000). In the same study, Tifway and TifSport bermudagrasses had similar leaf N and P contents, but K levels were 1.2 to 2.0%. When foliar and drench applications of Si were used to investigate their effect on wear tolerance of seashore paspalum, increased leaf Si content resulted in both decreased K content and wear tolerance (Trenholm et al., 2000). Wear tolerance was enhanced by high leaf K concentration.

9.7. SITE INFLUENCES ON FERTILIZATION

High Leaching and Salt

In salt-affected environments where high irrigation volumes are used to leach excess Na through the soil profile, nutrients such as Ca, Mg, Mn, P, and K may be leached with the excess water. Additionally, if ocean water is used for irrigation, excess Mg found naturally in the water might cause an imbalance problem with other nutrients; i.e., Ca. Fertilization programs must remain flexible in these salinity-stressed environments and through careful soil, water, and plant monitoring (analyses), adjustments made in the program. The problems will be site-specific (Carrow and Duncan, 1998b), and specific amendments may be needed to maintain nutritional balance in the turf plants. The more sensitive the turf cultivar is to salt stress, the greater the problem for toxicities and deficiencies to detrimentally affect quality traits and performance.

Effluent Water and Nutritional Problems (see Chapter 15)

Recycled water varies by location and may vary by season in quality and the content of nutrients. Constant monitoring will provide sufficient data to help in adjusting the type and amounts of fertilizers applied on a scheduled basis. If high volumes of water are applied, particular attention must be paid to Ca, Mg, Mn, P, and K levels since they may be leached out before the turf roots can absorb them. The prescription approach (small volumes of highly soluble sources applied frequently or higher volumes of slow release fertilizers applied less frequently) to fertilization should maintain a level of nutrient availability to sustain high quality turf.

Soil pH Interactions (see Chapter 17)

Soil acidity problems (<5.0 pH) add another dimension to stress environment fertility management. Excess Al or Mn can cause toxicities, which can result in Ca, Mg, K, P, Mo, S, and B deficiencies. Micronutrient fertilizers coupled with regular lime applications may be needed to balance nutrition within the turf plant and to raise the pH >5.5. Low pH and Al/Mn toxicities will also prune turf roots and enhance susceptibility to winter kill. The first management strategy should be to raise the pH with lime additions and amendments of 10–20 lb/1000 ft^2 in conjunction with incorporation (aeration or tillage) may be warranted if the pH in the turf root zone is <5.0. With a pH that low, acid soil tolerant culti-vars should be used since uniform exposure of lime to the subsoil can be difficult unless the area can be completely deep-tilled and renovated. In perennial turf stands where the pH is between 5.0 and 6.0, lime addi-tions of 2–5 lb/1000 ft^2/application may enhance microbial activity, enhance conversion of NH_4 to NO_3, and result in increased utilization of nitrogen fertilizers.

Soil alkalinity problems (pH>8.5) can impact fertility management decisions. These problems are usually associated with sodic conditions (Carrow and Duncan, 1998b) and excess levels of Na, Cl, CO_3, and HCO_3 can create nutritional imbalances (Ca, Mg, K). Only the most salt tolerant turf cultivars should be grown in these stressful environments. Management decisions must be focused initially on Na destruction of soil structure and a combination of gypsum or lime plus sulfur additions coupled with either complete soil profile renovation or at the very least, deep tine (12–14 in. or 300 to 350 mm) aerivation plus high water vol-umes to leach the excess Na out of the turf root zone. Ten to 20 lb/1000 ft^2 of gypsum may be needed initially, followed by 2–5 lb/1000 ft^2 additional amendments on a monthly basis for 1–2 years in order to re-gain control of soil structure. Poor quality water may need additional lime, sulfuric acid, or gypsum treatment prior to applications to mini-mize excess Na, CO_3, or HCO_3 additions. Micronutrient fertilizers may be needed on a prescription basis to minimize imbalances in the turf plant. Regular soil and water analyses will be needed to maintain high quality turf performance in this stress environment.

9.8. IRRIGATION

Paspalum can be irrigated with a wide range of variable quality water, from potable to recycled to straight ocean water. Paspalum water needs will vary with climate, soil type, maintenance level, and cultivar used. But in general, overall needs after establishment will be less than most other warm season grasses (the exception is centipedegrass).

Ocean Water (see Chapter 16)

If ocean water is used for irrigation in a high salinity environment, the principal management strategy is to use high and consistent volumes of water, coupled with frequent applications of sulfur + lime or gypsum, to keep the salts moving through the soil profile. High leaching volumes can cause nutrient imbalances (Carrow and Duncan, 1998b), especially excess Mg and a 3 Ca:1 Mg imbalance plus deficiencies in P, K, and Fe. Using this water source, N fertility amounts can be reduced by one-half because of the dissolved nitrates in the water. Rates can vary from $^1/2$ in. (13 mm) daily with good percolation to 7 in. (175 mm) per week, depending on severity of salt-stress, soil structure, and climate. Irrigation scheduling and volume must be developed on a site-specific basis.

Recycled Water (see Chapter 15)

Water quality monitoring must be performed daily (very poor quality) to every 6 months, depending on the uniformity of the water source on an annual basis, the levels of carbonates/bicarbonates, heavy metals, or other ingredients, and the quantity available on a seasonal basis. Irrigation rates might vary from $^1/2$–1 in. daily (very poor quality, high in salts/carbonates/bicarbonates) to 1 in. per week (good quality water). Again, scheduling and volume must be adjusted on a site-specific basis (USGA, 1994).

Potable Water

Paspalum will produce high quality turf with good quality water. For established turf, rates can vary from 1 inch weekly to 1 inch biweekly, depending on soil conditions and climate. Excess water applied frequently on a daily basis with short duration will promote shallow rooting patterns and actually diminish the drought tolerance capability of paspalum. The irrigation management strategy should be one of looking for drought stress symptoms (bluish-gray color) before application; then applying $^1/2$–1 in. volumes in one application at night and waiting until visual stress symptoms show up again.

Combinations

Management options for using various ocean or recycled water sources are presented in Table 9.3. When these two resources are used for irrigation, either individually or blended, an aggressive management strategy must be implemented to maintain high quality turf. With different blending options, the management of both water and fertility must be adjusted, based on what components are being applied with each application.

In general, irrigation scheduling during establishment (first two weeks after sprig planting) should be frequent enough to maintain moist conditions, not allow the young seedlings to dry out, and to prevent salts from rising with evaporation. The duration between applications can be gradually lengthened during grow-in to force the root system deeper into the soil profile. The irrigation philosophy for long-term maintenance should be one of judicious applications, except in highly saline environments where excess salts must be moved through the soil profile. Paspalum has excellent drought resistance if managed properly, with genetic root tolerance traits that include root growth into deep soil layers, high root viability in the surface zone during moisture stress, and rapid root regeneration after rewetting (Huang et al., 1997ab). Scaling back on irrigation frequency during the fall months will force paspalum roots (rhizomes) deeper and improve its winter hardiness; but in arid regions, maintaining field capacity (−3 bars) during the winter months will minimize cold temperature injury.

9.9. RENOVATION/THATCH/ VERTICUTTING/TOPDRESSING

Excess fertility and water will cause puffiness, thatch buildup, and increased potential for scalping. Both management practices must be reduced to get the grass and its root system back under control and to maintain high quality. In sodic or saline-sodic sites, some low drainage areas may have soil structural deterioration problems caused by excess sodium. Compaction from mowers, golf carts, or other man-made or vehicular traffic sources can enhance the problem. Paspalum can be enticed to grow in these areas, but soil structural problems must be addressed first. Management options include deep aeration/tillage, gypsum or sulfur plus lime application, followed by high water volumes to flush the dislodged excess Na deeper into the soil profile and away from the root zone. In a calcareous soil, the lime can be delayed initially until the sulfur has reacted with the carbonates at the soil surface, but, over time, the extra calcium from the lime will be needed to dislodge the excess NA and to combine with SO_4^- to form gypsum. Approximately 4–5 weeks after planting paspalum sprigs, the area can be verticut and fertilized with $Ca(NO_3)_2$ for faster grow-in.

Table 9.3. Ocean Water or Recycled Water Components, Their Impact, and Turf Management Options

Water Component	Impact	Management
High Mg	Imbalance with Ca	Apply lime or gypsum
Total-N, organic-N, NH_4^+-N, NO_3^--N	Excess nitrogen	Reduce N amendments
	Rapid growth, succulence, increase in diseases	Buffer zones (filter strips)
P, K	Cascading into ponds/rivers/lakes, wetland sites; contamination	Buffer zones, Control runoff, P and K fertility reduction
High Na	Increase sodium absorption rates; physiological drought (saline); destroys soil structure (sodic); toxicity to roots	Apply lime or gypsum; cultivation (aeration, tillage); leach with high water volumes
Soil pH	Increase >8.5 Decrease <5.0	Acid amendments. Lime application
Water pH	>8.5 <5.0 high sulfates	Sulfuric acid plus lime Lime application Lime application
High carbonates/bicarbonates	Increases soil pH	Sulfur plus lime or gypsum
Biological/chemical oxygen demand	Organic loading depletes soil oxygen	Aeration; drainage
Increased conductivity (total soluble salts)	Salt accumulation	Leaching
High B, Cl^{-1}	Cultivar-specific ion toxicity	Plant selection, remove clippings
Heavy metals (Cu, Ni, Zn, Pb, chromium, arsenic mercury)	Complexes P	Increase P applications, micronutrients
Suspended solids	Seals the soil	Aeration, coarse sand topdressing

Sources: USGA, 1994, p. 212; Carrow and Duncan, 1998.

Heavily trafficked greens (>90,000 rounds per year) or high-use sports fields may require verticutting once per month. Less-traveled greens should be verticut 2 to 4 times per year. Fairways should be aerated and verticut at least 2–4 times annually. Landing zone and tees will need to be verticut on a biweekly schedule to stimulate recovery and repair. Verticutting stimulates each node to root and initiate new stolons. The result is shorter internodes and a tighter canopy. Low mowing heights (but not scalping) after verticutting will foster horizontal growth and foster stolon growth into damaged areas. Verticutting or slicing depths should range from 13–25 mm (0.5 to 1.0 in.) deep. Single cuts should be sufficient during grow-in and for damage repair. Direction of verticut should be altered with each application.

In heavily thatched areas, a double verticut may be needed to tighten up (increase density) the canopy. A regular verticutting and aeration program should avoid excessive thatch buildup in most cases, if N fertility is kept below 5 lb/1000 ft^2/year. Seashore paspalum will respond to a topdressing regime that is similar to the one used on bermudagrasses. Light, relatively frequent topdressing applications are better than heavy, infrequent operations for maintaining a firm, uniform surface and for limiting thatch accumulation.

9.10. OVERSEEDING

Paspalum can be overseeded with most cool-season grass species (Table 9.4). Verticutting may be needed to establish proper seed-soil contact during the early fall planting time. Planting should be scheduled when air temperatures near 55°F slow down the growth of paspalum, or about 20 days prior to the first frost date. Since paspalum has a cool-season grass fertility schedule, the fertility program for the overseeded grasses should be highly compatible for both species. The caution on the paspalum is to avoid excess N fertilization in the fall until the paspalum has gone completely dormant (usually after two or three exposures to 26°F or −3°C). Excess N will cause succulence and may predispose the paspalum to cold temperature damage. Periodic slow-release N rates of a $1/3$–$1/2$ lb/1000 ft^2 should be adequate to maintain the cool-season grass prior to paspalum dormancy. Fertilizers high in P and K will benefit both grass species going into the winter months by enhancing winter hardiness in the paspalum and wear tolerance in the cool season grass.

Table 9.4. Cool-Season Grasses That Can Be Used for Overseeding into Seashore Paspalum

Common Name	# Seed/lb	Seeding rate[+] #/1000 ft²	Days to Germinate	Optimum Germination Temperature °F
Creeping bentgrass	6–7,000,000	0.5–1	4–12	59–86
Kentucky bluegrass	950,000–2,000,000	1.5–20	6–30	59–86
Rough stalk bluegrass (*Poa trivalis*)	2,100,000	1–2	10–21	68–86
Annual ryegrass	200,000	7–8	3–7	68–86
Perennial ryegrass	210,000–300,000	7–8	3–7	68–86
Tall fescue	220,000	7–8	6–12	68–86
Alkaligrass	2,000,000	12–15 (greens), 6–10 (tees, fairways) 2–4 (roughs)	7–21	70–75
Fine fescues	550,000–700,000	4–5	10–20	59–77

[a] Note that these are normal rates for establishment, and the overseeding rates into established seashore paspalum mature turf might need to be increased by 25–50% to achieve adequate cool-season grass density.

9.11. TRAFFIC/COMPACTION/WEAR

High traffic areas that cause compaction or excessive wear on paspalum turf will require regularly scheduled maintenance. Regular aeration [deep—12 to 14 in. (300–350 mm) at least twice each year, and shallow—4 to 6 in. (100–150 mm) monthly during high traffic use] with proper fertilization and irrigation scheduling will pay dividends on long-term performance of the grass. On golf courses, restricting cart traffic, roping off highly traveled areas, or application of crumb rubber (Hartwiger, 1995; Shiels, 1998; Leslie, 1995; and McDonald, 1995) are management options. On sports fields (such as the center of football fields and goal mouths on soccer fields), applying crumb rubber to the highest use areas will provide a cushion, will allow grass to grow while healing, and could improve water use efficiency in that area by 50% (Rogers and Vanini, 1994, 1995; Rogers et al., 1998ab). Aeration, verticutting, and application of $Ca(NO^3)_2$ are appropriate management tactics for paspalum repair and regrowth of high use areas. During the winter months, overseeding with cool season grasses, such as perennial ryegrass, can provide good wear tolerance in the high traffic areas and help protect the crown regions of the paspalum while it is dormant. On salt-affected soils (especially sodic soils), a very aggressive surface and subsurface cultivation strategy is necessary to ensure adequate infiltration/percolation/drainage of water and to effectively remove high total salts and toxic levels of Na^+ (Carrow and Duncan, 1998b).

CHAPTER 10

Management of Biotic Stresses

Seashore paspalum generally has fewer pest problems than other warm-season turfgrasses. On salt-affected sites, the lower pest activity is partly due to high salinity suppression of those pests. However, even in non-salt-affected environments, paspalum seems to have few pest problems, especially diseases.

10.1. WEED CONTROL

Weeds are the most *persistent problems* in management of any turfgrass, and when stress environmental conditions are included (drought, salinity, humid climates), effective control becomes a challenge. Herbicide activity or effectiveness may be reduced on some of the stress-challenged sites where seashore paspalum can be grown. On salt-affected sites where paspalum often becomes the grass of choice, most weeds are greatly suppressed by high salinity. Since seashore paspalum is a relatively new grass in the turf arena, less is known about herbicide efficacy than most other warm season grasses. Herbicide response research out of California, Hawaii, Texas, and Georgia is summarized in Table 10.1. Additional herbicide studies from other *Paspalum* species is summarized in Table 10.2., where most of the allied research has been conducted on bahiagrass (*Paspalum notatum*). Herbicides listed in Table 10.2 are safe for other *Paspalum* species, but may not necessarily be safe for *P. vaginatum*. Problem weeds in established seashore paspalum turf such as torpedograss and kikuyugrass can be controlled with Drive® (quinchorac) or Dimension® (dithiopyr). Both kikuyugrass and kyllinga can be controlled with Manage® (halosulfuron).

Safe Herbicides

The only herbicide labeled specifically for use on seashore paspalum turf is granular Ronstar®. *Paspalum vaginatum* exhibits a high degree of

Table 10.1. Summary of Herbicide Responses on Seashore Paspalum

Herbicide	Preemergence or at Planting	Postemergence During Grow-In	Postemergence Established Sod
Goal (oxyfluorfen)$_{EC}$	I		
Ronstar (oxadiazon)$_{WP}$	— —	I	
Ronstar (oxadiazon)$_G$	++++	++	+
Asulox (asulam)$_F$		—	—
Astrex (atrazine)$_W$		—	—
Balan (benefin)$_G$		+	
Betasan (bensulide)$_{EC}$		+	+
Confront (triclopyr+cloryralid)$_{SL}$		—	
Daconate (MSMA)$_{SL}$		—	
Dimension (dithiopyr)$_L$	I,+		+
Drive (quinclorac)$_{DF}$	+	+	++
Gallery (isoxaben)$_{DF}$		+	
Acclaim (fenoxaprop)$_L$			—
Image (imazaquin)$_{EC}$		—	I, — —[a]
Kerb (pronamide)$_W$		+	+
Mecomec (MCPP)			+
Bueno, Daconate (MSMA)			— —
Poast (sethoxydim)$_{EC}$		—	
Princep (simazine)$_{EC}$			—
Sencor (metribuzin)$_W$		—	—
Surflan (DNA)$_{SC}$	— —	+	++
Team (DNA)$_G$	I		
Turflon ester (triclopyr)$_{EC}$		—	—
Trimec Southern L(2,4-D, dicamba, MCPP)		+	++I
Trimec Classic L	— —		
Vanquish (dicamba)$_{SL}$	+		+++
XL 2G (benefin + oryzalin)	—, I	+	
2,4-D			I+
Trimec Plus (2,4-D + 2,4-DP+dicamba+msma)			— — —
Trimec ester (2,4-D+2,4-DP+dicamba)			—
Barricade (prodiamine)	++		
Pre-M (pendimethalin)	++I		+
Prograss (ethofumesate)$_{EC}$		+	+
Manage (halosulfuron)	+	+	
Illoxan (diclofop)	—		I
Ally (metsulfuron)			—
Vantage (sethoxydim)			—

[a] Prolific seed head development.
"—" = phytotoxic; "+" = safe; "I" = intermediate
Sources: Cudney et al., 1995; Davis et al., 1997; De Frank, 1992; Duble, 1989; Duncan, 1999; Harivandi et al., 1987; Johnson and Duncan, 1997, 1998ab; Menn and Baird, 1984, 1995; Tavara and De Frank, 1992.

Table 10.2. Herbicide Responses on Other Paspalum Species

	P. notatum		*P. atratum*		*P. distichum*	*P. hieronymi*
	Post	Pre	Seedlings	Established	Post	Post
imazapyr	—					
acifluorfen	+					
clopyralid	+					
dicamba (Banvel)	++		+	+		
fluroxypyr	+					
picloram	+					
triclopyr (Remedy)	+			+		
asulam (Asulox)	—					
clopyralid	—					
2, 4-D + triclopyr	—					
DSMA, MSMA	—					
imazaquin (Image)	—					
metsulfuron (Ally)	—			+		
metribuzin (Sencor)	—			—		
pronamide (Kerb)	—					
quinclorac	—					
sethoxydim	—					
simazine	—					
fenoxaprop	—					
Atrazine	—					
bentazon (Basagran)	++					
bromoxynil (Buctril)	++					
chlorflurenol	+					
chlorsufuron	+			—		
2, 4-D	++					

Table 10.2. Herbicide Responses on Other Paspalum Species (Continued)

	P. notatum Post	P. notatum Pre	P. atratum Seedlings	P. atratum Established	P. distichum Post	P. hieronymi Post
2, 4-D + dicamba	+					
2, 4-DP	++					
MCPP (Mecomec)	++					
2, 4-D + MCPP + dicamba	++					
benefin (Balan)		+				
bensulide (Betasan)		+				
oryzalin (Surflan)		+				
DCPA (Dacthal)		+				
napropamide (Devrinol)		+				
pentimethalin (Pre-M)		+				
benefin + oryzalin (XL 2G)		+				
benefin + trifluralin (Team)		+				
nicosulfuron (Accent)				+	-(2X rate/surfactant)	
hexazinone (Velpar)				+		+
glyphosate (Roundup)				—		
clomozone (Command)				—		
diuron (Karmex)				—		
fluometuron (Cotoran)				—		
imazethapyr (Pursuit)				—		
norflurazon (Zorial)				—		
trifluralin (Treflan)				—		
fluazifop-P-butyl (Fusilade)				—		
sulfometuron-metyl (Oust)				—		

"—" = phytotoxic; "+" = safe; "I" = intermediate; pre-preemergence application; post = postemergence application

Sources: Akanda et al., 1997; James and Rahmen, 1997; Kalmbacher et al., 1996; McCarty and Colvin, 1988; McCarty and Murphy, 1994.

tolerance to the herbicides listed in Table 10.3. All new cultivars should be tested for their specific tolerance. Check the label of each herbicide to determine whether it has a general use or specific use requirement.

Noninjurious herbicides for preemergence annual grass control use on paspalum turf include bensulide, pronamide, benefin, DCPA, granular Ronstar, and pendimethalin. For postemergent applications, benefin, ethofumesate, quinclorac, Trimec Southern, dithiopyr, dicamba, pendimethalin, MCPP, Pronamide, isoxaben, halosulfuron, mecoprop, and bensulide can safely be used (Table 10.3).

Glyphosate or diquat can be used on dormant paspalum, for renovation, or for border control and maintenance. For control of bermudagrass in paspalum, herbicide options include Prograss + Cutlass at 1.5 and 0.75 ai/ac, respectively, or ocean water plus Prograss. Specific weed control options are presented in Table 10.4.

Marginally Safe Herbicides

Goal and XL G are marginal for use as a preemergence application (Table 10.5). Marginal herbicides for postemergence use include Amine, Team, and Illoxan. These herbicides should only be used at the lowest recommended rate and when other alternative chemicals are not available.

Phytotoxic Herbicides

Preemergent herbicides that cause injury include Ronstar WP, Surflan, and Illoxan (Table 10.6). Postemergent herbicides that cause injury include the triazines (Aatrex, Sencor, Princep); the phenoxys with MSMA, 2,4-DP, or mecoprop in them; the aryloxyphenoxy propionates (Acclaim, Fusilade, Illoxan); the pyridinecarboxylic acids (Turflon ester, Confront), the organic arsenicals (Bueno, Daconate, MSMA); Asulox, Vantage, and Image. These herbicides can be used to control paspalum encroachment into bermudagrass: MSMA, Asulox, Image, Sencor, Illoxan. Multiple applications may be needed to significantly reduce paspalum density, and changing herbicide classes (Table 10.7) may escalate the eventual removal of the paspalum. Confront® plus MSMA (in combination) is proving to be quite effective in preventing paspalum encroachment into bermudagrass greens.

Table 10.3. Herbicides That Are Noninjurous to Seashore Paspalum Turf[a]

| Common | Herbicide | | Broadcast Rate/Acre | |
	Trade	Family	Formulation	lb ai
Preemergence				
bensulide	Betasan EC[b]	—	1.9–3.1 gal	7.5–12.5
pronamide	Kerb WSP	Amide	1–2 lb	0.5–1.0
benefin	Balan G[b]	DNA	80–120 lb	2.0–3.0
DCPA	Dacthal WP	phenoxy	2–3 gal/10 lb/1000 s.f.	see label
—	Ronstar G[c]	oxadiazon	100–200 lb	2.0–4.0
Pendimethalin	Pre-M WDG[b]	DNA	2.9–5.5 lb	1.7–3.3
Postemergence				
ethofumesate	Prograss EC	—	0.67–1.0 gal	1.0–1.5
quinclorac	Drive DF/WD	—	1.9 lb	1.4
MCPP+2, 4-D+dicamba	Trimec Southern SL[b]	phenoxy	see label	0.7+0.4+0.08
dithiopyr	Dimension EC	pyridazine	2 qt	0.5
2, 4-D+dicamba+dicloprop	Super Trimec SL[b]	phenoxy	see label	see label
dicamba	Vanquish SL[b]	benzoic	0.5–1.0 pt	0.25–0.5
halosulfuron	Manage WG	sulfonylurea	0.67–1.33 oz	0.031–0.062
mecoprop	Mecomec 4SL[b]	phenoxy	2.0–2.7 pt	1.0–1.35
bentazon	Basagran T/O[b]	benzothiadiazole	2.0–4.0 pt	1.0–2.0
Dormant Paspalum/Renovation/Border Maintenance				
glyphosate	Roundup	—	0.75 pt	0.375
diquat	Reward	—	1.0–2.0 pt	0.25–0.5

[a] Since only granular Ronstar® is labeled for specific use on *Paspalum vaginatum* turf, check the label as to whether the herbicide is for general or specific turf use.

[b] These herbicides have more than one trade name or similar/slightly different chemical formulations.

[c] Only use the granular formulation on seashore paspalum. Do not use the wettable powder.

Table 10.4. Specific Weed Control Options for Noninjurous Herbicide Use on Seashore Paspalum[a]

Herbicide	Chemical Family	For Control of
Granular Ronstar	oxadiazol	PRE Crabgrass, Goosegrass, Poa, winter broad leaves
Kerb WP	amide	PRE/Post Poa
Balan G	dinitroaniline	PRE Poa, winter weeds PRE crabgrass, short season control
Dimension EC	pyridine	PRE/early POST crabgrass PRE goosegrass/Poa POST kikuyugrass
Pre M WDG	dinitroaniline	PRE crabgrass/ goosegrass/POA
Barricade WDG	dinitroaniline	PRE crabgrass/ goosegrass/Poa
Drive DF	quinclorac	POST crabgrass (juvenile) POST torpedograss, kikuyugrass
Prograss EC	ethofumesate	PRE Poa with Cutlass, POST Bermuda
Vanquish SL	benzoic	POST broadleaf
Team G	dinitroaniline	PRE crabgrass/Poa
Manage WG	sulfonylurea	POST purple/yellow nutsedge POST kyllinga, kikuyugrass
Gallery WG	benzamide	PRE broadleaf weeds
Basagran	benzothiadiazole	POST yellow nutsedge
Trimec Southern	phenoxy	POST spurge, broad leaves

[a] Since only granular Ronstar® is labeled for specific use on *Paspalum vaginatum* turf, check the label as to whether the herbicide is for general or specific turf use.

Using Ocean Water or Rock Salt for Weed Control

Ocean water (34,400 mg/L salt) can be utilized on paspalum turf in weed control management either as a single application, multiple applications, or in combination with reduced-rate herbicides (Couillard and Wiecko, 1998). On Guam, turf sites with access to seawater are being subjected to rate and time-of-application studies to control problem weeds (Wiecko, personal communication). Sites being continuously irrigated

Table 10.5. Marginally Safe Herbicides When Used on Seashore Paspalum Turf[a]

| Herbicide | | | Broadcast Rate/Acre | |
Common	Trade	Family	Formulation	lb ai
Preemergence				
oxyfluorfen	Goal EC	diphenylether	see label	see label
benefin + oryzalin	XL 2G	DNA	100–150 lb	1.0–1.5
Postemergence				
2,4-D	Amine 4SL	phenoxy	see label	0.5–2.0
benefin	Team	DNA	see label	see label
diclofop	Illoxan	aryloxyphenoxy propionate	see label	see label

[a] Since none of these herbicides is specifically labeled for *Paspalum vaginatum* use, check the label as to whether the herbicide is for general or specific turf use. Use only the lowest rates for application.

Table 10.6. Herbicides Phytotoxic to Seashore Paspalum Turf[a]

Common	Herbicides Trade	Family
Preemergence		
oryzalin	Ronstar WP	oxadiazon
diclofop	Surflan As	DNA
	Illoxan EC	aryloxyphenoxy propionate
Postemergence		
asulam	Asulox SL	carbamate
atrazine	Aatrex WP[b]	triazine
metribuzin	Sencor DF[b]	triazine
MSMA, DSMA	Daconate 6SL/Bueno 6SL[b]	organic arsenical
sethoxydim	Vantage EC	cyclohexenone
simazine	Princep WP/Wynstar DF[b]	triazine
imazaquin	Image SL/Scepter[b]	imidazolinone
2, 4-D+2, 4-DP+dicamba	Trimec ester	phenoxy
2, 4-D+MCPP+dicamba+MSMA	Trimec Plus SL[b]	phenoxy
2, 4-D+mecoprop+dicamba	Trimec Classic SL[b]	phenoxy
2, 4-D+triclopyr	Turflon ester EC	pyridinecarboxylic acid
triclopyr+clopyralid	Confront SL	pyridinecarboxylic acid
fenoxaprop	Acclaim EC	aryloxyphenoxy propionate
diclofop-methyl	Illoxan EC	aryloxyphenoxy propionate

[a] Check the label as to whether the herbicide can be used for general or specific turfgrass applications.
[b] These herbicides have more than one trade name or similar/slightly different chemical formulations.

Table 10.7. Herbicide Classes

Class/Chemical Family	Product Trade Name
Amides	Kerb, Enide, Devrinol, Gallery
Sulfonamides	Betasan
Benzoics/benzamide/benzothiadiazole	Banvel, Basagran, Vanquish, Lescosan, Bensumec
Cyclohexanedione/cyclohexenone	Vantage, Prism
Dinitroanilines (DNAs)	Balan, Barricade, Pendulum, Surflan, Team, Treflan, Pre-M, XL G
Diphenylether/Nitrodiphenylether	Goal
Oxadiazoles	Ronstar
Imidazolinone	Image
Pyridazines/pyridine/pyridinecarboxylic acid	Dimension, Confront, Turflon, Chaser
Carbamate/phenylcarbamate	Asulox
Phenoxys	2, 4-D, MCP, MCPA, MCPP, dicloprop, Trimec, Meconec, Amine, Dymec, Weedone
Organic arsenical	Daconate, Bueno, MSMA, Phytar, Cleary's Methar 30
Sulfonylureas	Manage, TFC (Lesco)
Triazines	Aatrex, Atrazine, Princep, Sencor, Simazine, Turfco
Aryloxyphenoxy propionate	Illoxan, Acclaim, Fusilade, Poast
Phythalic acids	Dacthal
Phenylureas	Tupersan
Phosophono amino acids	Roundup, Ortho Kleenup
Benzofuran	Prograss
Benzonitrile	Buctril
Acetamide	Pennant, Ornamental herbicide 5G
Unclassified	Basamid, Betasan, Finale, Drive, Endothal

with seawater or seawater blends (wastewater) will have few annual grass and broadleaf weed problems. An additional weed control strategy could include spot applications of rock salt on problem weeds, followed by light irrigation (too much water will dilute the salt-enhanced stress and diminish its weed control effectiveness). Sodium chlorate was a salt-based herbicide used in the 1960s for control of rhizomatous grasses. Management considerations on non-salt-affected sites include (1) number of seawater applications per week, (2) clay versus sandy soil profiles, (3) probability for percolation through the soil profile or runoff into fresh water resources, and (4) transport distance and method of application (i.e., tanker truck).

10.2. DISEASES

Seashore paspalum has few disease problems. General statements concerning the Adalayd intermediate-leaf-texture types indicated susceptibility to Rhizoctonia brown patch and to leaf spot diseases (Duble, 1989). No brown patch or Pythium blight symptoms have been observed in breeding nurseries or on turf plots at Griffin, Georgia during the development/evaluation program or during collection of ecotypes in native habitats. Specific differences in fungicide tolerance between seashore paspalum and other warm-season grasses have not been documented. Dollar spot is the only disease that has consistently been observed on some ecotypes of paspalum. Other diseases are discussed only from their potential to cause problems.

Dollar Spot

Dollar spot (*Sclerotinia homoeocarpa* F.T. Bennett) can be a problem on paspalum mowed less than 6 mm ($1/4$ in.) on greens (Duncan, 1999). Ecotypes from Hawaii and Australia are particularly susceptible. Ecotypes from Argentina have a good level of resistance. Dollar spot resistance has been an important selection criteria in the Georgia paspalum breeding program, especially since improved ecotypes are also selected for low N use.

Symptoms include straw-colored, light tan, or yellowish diseased lesions near the top of the leaf blade and whitish, cobweb-like, mycelial growth when dew is present during the early morning. Circular patches may be 2–3 in. in diameter (Duble, 1996). The fungus disease is most active during warm (70°–85°F or 21°–29°C) days and cool (60°F or 16°C) nights during the spring, early summer, and fall periods. Cultural control practices to promote healthy paspalum turf include:

1. Aeration to enhance oxygen, nutrient, and water movement through compacted soils.
2. Verticutting to remove excess thatch.

3. Avoiding light, frequent irrigation applications, especially during the late afternoon or early evenings prior to midnight.
4. Adopting a prescription nitrogen fertility program involving a spoon-feeding approach (combination of slow-release N fertilizers and fast release, highly soluble sources on an alternating weekly basis using $1/4$–$1/2$ lb/1000 ft^2/application increments).
5. Decreasing shade stress through tree removal or pruning.
6. Increasing air circulation.
7. Using ocean water for irrigation.
8. Maintain adequate soil moisture (neither too dry not too wet).

Preventive chemical control may be warranted on problem greens or tees when highly susceptible ecotypes are used, especially in cool weather when paspalum recovery might be slowed or less than optimum. Fungicides used to control dollar spot are listed in Table 10.8. Heritage, Prostar, Fore, and pythium fungicides (Alliette, Banol, Termec, Lesan, Koban, Subdue) do not provide effective control of dollar spot.

Fusarium Blight

This systemic fungal disease is caused by *Fusarium roseum* and *F. tricinctum* and can be a serious problem during hot, humid conditions when the paspalum turf is under severe drought stress, or on sandy profiles with low water-holding capacity and high evaporative demand conditions. When temperatures rise above 70°F (75°–90°F) in conjunction with high humidity, spore production can cause systemic death of crown, rhizomes, stolons, and root tissues in 4–7 days. The entire turf plant can be infected and the color change will progress rapidly from dark green to reddish brown to dark brown or black. High nitrogen levels that promote thatch accumulation and excessive, frequent irrigation favor fusarium spore production.

Preventive cultural and chemical control strategies should be used in the maintenance program. Cultural control practices could include:

1. Use ocean water for irrigation.
2. Reduce fall and winter (overseeded cool-season grasses) nitrogen applications. Avoid NH_4-N. Use NO_3-N fertilizers.
3. Maintain high P and K levels.

Table 10.8. Fungicides That Can Be Used to Control Dollar Spot on Seashore Paspalum[a]

Product Name	Chemical Name	Rate of Application oz/1000 ft²	Application Interval (days)
Banner 14.3L	Propiconazole	1–2 fl. oz/2–5 gal water	14–28
Bayleton 25WP	Triadimefon	1–2 oz/2–4 gal water	15–30
Chipco 26019 50WP	Iprodione	1.5–2.0 oz/2–10 gal water	14–21
Daconil, Evade, Prograde 500, Echo DF, Count Down	Chlorothalonil	3–11 oz	7–14
Eagle 40 WSP	Myclobutanil	3 oz pkt/5000 ft²	4
Engage, Penstar Revere	Terraclor, PCNB	7–10 oz/5–10 gal water	21–28
Cleary's 3336, Topsin, Fungo, Systec 1998	Thiophanate methyl	1–2 oz/5 gal water	10–28
Sentinel 40 WG	Cyproconazole	0.16 oz	21–28
Tersan LSR, Protect T/O	Maneb, Maneb + zinc sulfate, mancozeb	3–8 oz/3–5 gal water	7–10
Rubigan A.S.11.6	Fenarimol	0.75–1.5 fl. oz	10–28
Thiram 75WP, Tersan 75	Cycloheximide, Benomyl	3–4.5 oz/5 gal water	3–10
Vorlan, Curalan, Touche	Vinclozolin (dicarboximides)	2 oz/5 gal water	7–21

[a] Since none of these fungicides is specifically labelled for *Paspalum vaginatum* use, check the label as to whether the fungicide is for general or specific turf use.
Adapted from Landry et al., 1998. Other potential new fungicides include Defiant®, Zerotol®, and Junction®.

4. Avoid liming if the pH>5.5.
5. Decrease shade stress.
6. Increase air circulation.
7. Avoid late afternoon or early evening irrigation.
8. Remove thatch.
9. Raise the mowing height.

Chemical control includes several fungicides (Table 10.9), with the thiophanate methyls (Cleary's 3336, Topsin, Fungo 50, Systec 1998) being quite effective. Prostar and the pythium control fungicides (Heritage, Alliette, Banol, Termec, Lesan, Koban, Subdue) are ineffective.

Other Leaf Spot Diseases

Curvularia has been observed on paspalum turf as a weak pathogen (Duncan, 1999). The organism occurs primarily at temperatures near 30°C or 86°F (Smiley et al., 1992) and is capable of saprophytic growth due to its association with necrotic plant tissues. An effective cultural control strategy is to lower soil surface pH to 5.0 using sulfur amendments or acidifying fertilizers such as ammonium sulfate or ammonium chloride (Umemoto et al., 1997). The low pH tolerance (some ecotypes tolerate pH 4.0) of paspalum cultivars makes this species a good choice for this stress environment, as long as NO_3^--N is available.

Helminthosporium leaf, crown, and root diseases may be a sporadic problem on paspalum turf, especially in association with highly compacted soils. Disease severity increases with temperatures 60°–85°F (16°–29°C) and extremely high humidity. Small purplish leaf spots may first appear on stolons, crowns, or leaves. Symptoms include spots with brown centers and a light tan halo with purplish border (Duble, 1996). *Bipolaris micropa* has been documented on paspalum (Smiley et al., 1992).

Cultural control methods for Helminthosporium include:

1. Avoid low N and K levels. Avoid excessive N.
2. Avoid severe drought stress, herbicide injury, or heavy traffic.
3. Maintain good drainage during wet conditions.
4. Use ocean water for irrigation.
5. Avoid late afternoon or early evening irrigation.
6. Maintain a regular aeration schedule.

Plate 1. Kapolei Golf Course, Oahu, Hawaii

Plate 2. Saline Soil Problem—Only
Surviving Grass is Paspalum.

Plate 3. Variability Among Potential Greens-Type Paspalums.

Plate 4. Grand Hyatt Wailea Hotel, Maui, Hawaii. Paspalum Landscaping.

Plate 5. Mary Lou Fraser YMCA Soccer Field, Hinesville, Georgia.

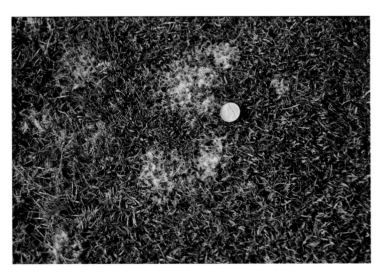

Plate 6. Dollar Spot on Seashore Paspalum.

Plate 7. Root Development–Paspalum Grown on Plastic.
Rapid Turf, Rincon, Georgia.

Plate 8. Stolons and Rhizomes–
Seashore Paspalum.

Plate 9. Fusarium damage on paspalum.

Plate 10. MSMA herbicide damage on paspalum.

Plate 11. Paspalum (brown) vs. bermudagrass (white)–
MSMA damage.

Plate 12. Paspalum inflorescence–developmental stages.

Plate 13. Callus of Paspalum–Plantlet Regeneration from Immature Spike.

Plate 14. Callus Growing in Petri Dish.

Plate 15. Variability in Leaf Texture: Coarse (left), Fine (right).

Plate 16. Paspalum Beach Erosion Control.

Table 10.9. Fungicides That Can Be Used to Control Fusarium Blight[a] on Seashore Paspalum[b]

Product Name	Chemical Name	Application Rates oz/1000 ft^2	Application Intervals (days)
Cleary's 3336 Topsin, Fungo 50, Systec 1998	Thiophanate methyl	2–8 oz	5–14
Engage, Penstar, Revere	PCNB, Terraclor	8 oz/10–15 gal water	21–28
Chipco 26019	Iprodione	4 oz	28
Banner 14.3L	Propiconazole	4 fl. oz	14–28
Bayleton 25WP	Triadimefon	2–4 oz	15–30
Rubigan AS 11.6	Fenarimol	2–8 fl. oz	30
Sentinel 40WG	Cyproconazole	0.33 oz	21–28
Curalan, Touche, Vorlan	Vinclozolin	2–4 oz	7–21

[a] *Fusarium roseum* or *F. tricinctum*
[b] Since none of these fungicides is specifically labeled for *Paspalum vaginatum* use, check the label as to whether the fungicide is for general or specific turf use.
Adapted from Landry et al., 1998.

Preventative fungicide applications on a regular basis are more effective than treating a severe outbreak (Smiley et al., 1992). Fungicides for effective control are listed in Table 10.10.

10.3. NEMATODES

Nematodes can be a problem on paspalum turf in microenvironments that are not salt-affected (Morton, 1973). Although long-term exposure in salinity ecosystems might lead to an increase in this problem, Alden Pines Country Club near Ft. Myers, Florida has been the only report of nematode problems on a paspalum golf course that uses brackish water for irrigation. Nematode-affected turf symptoms have not been observed on various test sites for experimental ecotypes, but as this grass becomes more widely used, nematode populations will be monitored to assess their effect on seashore paspalum.

Chemical control strategies include *Nemacur 10G (systemic)* or *Chipco Mocap (non-systemic) 10G* at 2.3 lb/1000 ft^2 (100 lb/ac) followed by an application of at least 0.5 in. irrigation water. *Nemacur 3* can be applied at 9.7 fl. oz/1000 ft^2. *Ditera G* is a biological nematicide that can be applied at a rate of 100 lb/ac.

Turf symptoms include:

1. Thinned out, damaged areas with weed invasion.
2. Yellow, stunted leaves (looks like nutrient deficiency).
3. No recovery from drought stress after rains or irrigation.
4. Irregularly shaped, damaged areas.
5. Brown or red isolated lesions on very short roots.
6. Discolored or swollen root tips.
7. Excessive root branching with few main feeder roots.

Cultural practices that enhance healthy turf and minimize stress to combat nematode injury include:

1. Long duration, infrequent irrigation scheduling to promote deep root systems.
2. Avoid excessive N fertilization. Keep a balanced nutrition.
3. Avoid scalping. Raise mowing height.
4. Aerate and dethatch regularly.
5. Carefully apply pesticides.

Table 10.10. Fungicides for Controlling Leaf Spot Diseases Such as *Helminthosporium*, *Curvularia*, Rusts, and Anthracnose on Seashore Paspalum Turf[a]

Product Name	Chemical Name	Application Rates oz/1000 ft²	Application Interval (days)
Heritage 50WG (beta-methoxy-acrylate)	Azoxystrobin	0.2–0.4 oz	14–28
Banner 1.1E	Propiconazole	2–4 fl. oz	14–28
Bayleton 25WP	Triadimefon	2 oz	15–30
Cleary's 3336, Topsin, Fungo, Systec 1998	Thiophanate methyl	2 oz/5 gal water	10–14
Chipco 26019	Iprodione	2 oz/2–10 gal water	14–21
Daconil 2787, Evade, Prograde 500, Echo DF, Count Down	Chlorothalonil	3–11 fl. oz	7–10
Eagle WSP 40	Myclobutanil	0.6 oz	14
Fore, Protect T/O	Maneb, Maneb + zinc sulfate, mancozeb	3–8 oz/3–5 gal water	7–10
Engage, Penstar, Revere	PCNB, Terraclor	7–10 oz/5–10 gal water	3–4
Pro Star 50WP	Flutolanyl	1 qt/100 gal water	14–21
Sentinel 40WG	Cyproconazole	0.16–0.33 oz	21–28
Curalan, Touche, Vorlan	Vinclozolin	1–2 oz	14–28
Medallion, Fountain	Fludioxonil (pyrollnitrin analog)	see label	Residual activity enhanced when mixed with Banner MAXX® and Primo®

[a] Since none of these fungicides is specifically labeled for *Paspalum vaginatum* use, check the label as to whether the fungicide is for general or specific turf use.
Adapted from Landry et al., 1998; Dernoeden, 1998; Anonymous, 1999.

6. Control insects and disease before they become a problem.

7. In warmer climates, nematodes are active in the spring, while in northern, temperate climates, they are a problem in the summer.

10.4. ALGAE AND BLACK LAYER ON GREENS

Seashore paspalum is no more susceptible to algae or black layer formation than any other warm-season grass. But, this grass will, at times, be grown under environmental conditions (wet ecosystems) that may be conducive to these problems. For example, on salt-affected sites requiring extra irrigation to enhance leaching of salts, the duration of exposure to wet conditions and the high volumes of water may encourage algae growth if the paspalum has low shoot density. In salinity-challenged environments, several factors can promote the algae/black layer problems: (1) excess Na^+ will cause a deterioration in soil physical conditions, with reduced water infiltration/percolation and aeration. A sodic soil often exhibits a black, slick-like appearance on the surface in low areas. These black areas resemble black layer symptoms or algae scum, but are actually caused by excess Na^+ precipitation of organic matter, which rises to the surface (Carrow and Duncan, 1998), (2) high S amendments in irrigation water or to the soil can enhance black layer formation if anaerobic conditions occur, and (3) prolonged water use on salt-affected sites to remove excess Na^+.

Blue-green algae species (*Lyngbya, Nostoc, Oscillatoria, Phormidium*) of *Cyanobacteria* and green algae species (*Chlamydomonas, Cosmarium, Cylindrocystis*) can develop a black scum on the surface of overly wet soils. Black layer can be a biofilm product of the interaction between cyanobacteria species (i.e., *Nostoc and Oscillatoria*), which produce organic by-products that coat and plug sand micropores, thereby creating an anoxic environment for development of gaseous hydrocarbons like methane, ethane, ethylene, and propylene, and sulfate-reducing bacteria (*Desulfuvibrio desulfuricans*) (Hodges and Campbell, 1998). This can be a problem on sites where water resources have a pH>7.0 (blue-green algae) and come from ponds and/or sewage effluent water containing significant amounts of magnesium, manganese, iron, or sulfur. Fertilizers or pesticides and amendments high in organic matter containing these elements can contribute to the problem (Smiley et al., 1992).

Green algae prefer acidic pH conditions <6.0. Turf grown on sandy profiles may be subjected to black layer formation, which is a soil physical condition characterized by reduced exchange of gases (anaerobic conditions), poor internal drainage, a high water table, a perched water table, and is identified by a rotten-egg odor (hydrogen sulfide gas).

Cultural control strategies are predicated on reducing light that the algae need for growth and gaining control of the soil physical problems. Control options (Elliott, 1997, 1998; Nelson, 1997) include:

1. Improve soil drainage, air drainage/movement with scheduled core aeration, spiking, slicing, or verticutting.
2. Adjust irrigation schedules.
3. Maintain soil and water pH between 6.0 and 7.0.
4. Increase mowing height.
5. Improve air circulation around greens.
6. Reduce tree shade.
7. Maintain a balanced nutrition.
8. Use light, frequent topdressing with sand particle sizes similar to that used in greens construction.
9. Apply wetting agents (Primer®, Cascade®, Aquifer®, Yuccah®, Infiltrix®, Aqueduct®).
10. Use nitrate forms of fertilizer (frequent applications, prescription rates).
11. Avoid elemental sulfur application or S-containing fertilizers.
12. Apply the following fungicides: **chlorothalonil** (Chlorostar, Daconil 2787, Echo, Lite, Manicure, Monterey Bravo, Thalonil); **mancozeb** (Dithane, Fore, Formec, Mancozeb, Protect); quartenary ammonium salts (Physan, Algaen-x); **others** (Junction, Zerotol)

In salt-affected areas or sites with poor water quality, additional cultural control measures are applicable:

1. Aggressively manage sodic soil problems with appropriate cultivation (aeration), amendments, and leaching (Carrow and Duncan, 1998), and
2. When high rates of S are applied as a treatment to irrigation water or as a soil amendment, lime should be applied periodically at rates of 2–10 lb $CaCO_3/1000$ ft^2 (0.98 to 4.90 kg

$CaCO_3/100$ m^2) to react with the excess S to form gypsum ($CaSO_4$). This reactive process effectively "scrubs" the excess S from the system and converts it to a form that is much less affected by anaerobic conditions. Black layer formation is enhanced by reduced forms of S, but while in the gypsum form, it is protected from contributing to the reduced S pool.

10.5. INSECTS

Insecticides and application rates for control of mole crickets, sod webworm, spittlebugs, white grubs and billbugs, cutworms and fall armyworms, and imported fire ants in paspalum turf are listed in Table 10.11. Two novel soil insecticides—Merit® and Mach 2®—can be used at low rates, have very low toxicity to noninsect groups, and pose relatively little hazard to the environment (Potter, 1998). Merit® (imidacloprid) belongs to a new synthetic insecticide class called chloronicotinyls, with selective activity solely on the insect nervous system. This product is translocated systemically within plants, kills by contact and ingestion, and is effective in controlling newly-hatched grubs, billbug larvae, and annual bluegrass weevil. It is not effective against sod webworms, armyworms, or cutworms. It is registered for all turfgrass sites except sod farms and should be applied as a preventative 4–6 weeks prior to egg hatch. Half-life in the soil is about five months (Potter, 1998).

Mach 2® (halofenozide) is a unique insect growth regulator (IGR) that targets the hormonal systems controlling insect growth and molting. This synthetic MAC (molt accelerating compound) mimics the action of ecdysone, a hormone that regulates insect molting, by signaling a premature, lethal molt within 1–3 weeks. The product is registered for sod farms, commercial turf, and golf courses, but not for sports fields, residential lawns/landscapes, or housing complexes. It can be used as a preventative and as a curative, with control on late-instar grubs as well as caterpillars for up to 2–3 months (Potter, 1998).

10.6. ENVIRONMENTAL STEWARDSHIP/ LONG-TERM MAINTENANCE

Few pesticides and herbicides are specifically labeled for use on paspalum turf. Refer to the product labels for proper use (whether general category use or restricted use) under golf course, sports turf, or lawn/

Table 10.11. Insect Control on Seashore Paspalum Turf[a]

Pest	Product Name	Chemical Name	Application Rate per 1000 ft²
Mole crickets	Chipco Choice	fipronil	4.5 oz
	Orthene TTO, Pro 75	acephate	1.5 oz
	Scimitar 10WP	lambdacyhalothrin	0.1–0.2 oz
	Talstar T & O,	bifenthrin	0.23–0.46 oz
	Talstar 0.2G		2.3–4.6 lb
	Crusade 5G	fonofos	1.5–2.0 oz
	Mocap 10G	ethoprop	2.5 lb
	Turcam 2.5G	bendiocarb	2.8 lb
	Dursban 0.5% B, 1.0% B	chlorpyrifos	1–2 lb
	Sevin 20% B	carbaryl	0.5–1.0 lb
Sod webworm	Scimitar 10WP	lambdacyhalothrin	0.1–0.2 oz
	Scimitar 0.8CS		0.12–0.25 fl. oz
	Proxol 80SP	trichlorfon	3 oz
	Conserve SC	spinosyn	0.25–1.25 fl. oz
	Dursban Pro	chlorpyrifos	1.5 oz
	Diazinon 4E		3 oz
	Turcam 76W	bendiocarb	3.2–6.4 oz
	Sevin 50W or 80W,	carbaryl	6.4 oz or 4 oz
	Sevin SL		6 oz
	Mach 2 1.5G 2 SC	halofenozide	Follow label directions

Table 10.11. Insect Control on Seashore Paspalum Turf[a] (Continued)

Pest	Product Name	Chemical Name	Application Rate per 1000 ft²
Spittlebugs	Dursban 2E	chlorpyrifos	1.5 oz
	Dursban 0.5%B	—	1 lb
	Diazinon 4E	—	3 oz
White grubs (Japanese beetle, Chafers, Green June Beetle), Billbugs	Merit 75WP	imidacloprid	Follow label directions
	Merit 75WSP		
	Merit 0.5G		
	Talstar T & O,	bifenthrin	0.23–0.46 oz
	Talstar 0.2G		2.3–4.6 lb
	Diazinon 4E	—	3 oz
	Proxol 80SP	trichlorfon	3.75 oz
	Turcam 76W	bendiocarb	1–2 oz
	Dursban Pro	chlorpyrifos	3–6 oz
	Sevin SL	carbaryl	4–6 oz
	Mocap 5G	ethoprop	1.5 lb
	Mach 2	halofenozide	Follow label directions
	1.5G		
	2 SC		
Cutworms, Fall armyworms	Scimitar 10WP	lambdacyhalothrin	0.1–0.2 oz
	Scimitar 0.8CS	—	0.12–0.25 fl. oz
	Tempo 2E	cyfluthrin	1 tsp
	Proxol 80SP	trichlorfon	3 oz
	Orthene TTO, Pro 75	acephate	0.5–1.0 oz
	Conserve SC	spinosyn	0.25–1.25 oz
	Dursban Pro	chlorpyrifos	1.5 oz

	Product	Active ingredient	Rate
	Sevin 80W	carbaryl	1–2 oz
	Sevin SL		1.5–3.0 oz
	Mach 2	halofenozide	Follow label directions
	1.5G		
	2 SC		
Imported fire ants	Amdro	Baits	1–1.5 lb/ac broadcast
	Award	—	
	Ascend	—	
	Dursban Pro	chlorpyrifos	1 fl. oz/4 gal water
	Oftanol 2	isophenfos	1 mL/3 gal water
	Talstar 7.9%F	bifenthrin	0.5–1.0 oz
	Talstar 0.2%G		2.3–4.6 lb
	Dursban 2E	chlorpyrifos	mound
	Dursban 4E, 50W	—	treatments
	Pageant DF	—	
	Turcam 76W	bendiocarb	2–3 tsp/2 gal
	Sevin SL	carbaryl	3 Tbs/2 gal
	Orthene	acephate	2 tsp/mound
	Pro 75	—	
	Affirm	avermectin/B1	5–7 Tbs/mound
	Triumph	isazofos	0.75 fl. oz
	Award	fenoxycarb	1–3 Tbs/1–1.5 lb/ac
	Diazinon	—	1 Tbs/gal

[a] Since no insecticide is specifically labeled for *Paspalum vaginatum* use, check the label as to general or specific turf use.
Adapted from Landry et al., 1998; Brandenburg and Cooke, 1998/1999; Anonymous, 1999.

landscape situations. Be sure to note any restrictions, mowing intervals before and after application, whether irrigation will be needed for activation, and temperature requirements. Avoid applications, if possible, before high rain events that could cause the products to cascade from the soil or turf surface into wetland sites or other environmentally sensitive areas. If overseeding, certain restrictions might apply.

CHAPTER 11

Golf Course Case Studies

Actual golf course management regimes are presented. One course is located on Oahu, Hawaii and the other is found north of San Diego, California. The two superintendents have several years of practical experience in managing seashore paspalum and were willing to share their insights concerning this grass.

CASE STUDY NO. 1

Kapolei Golf Course   Phone: 808/674-0884
Kapolei, Oahu, Hawaii   Fax: 808/674-0593
Steve Swanhart, Superintendent   (s.swanhart@aol.com)

Course was opened in 1992. Paspalum (Sea Island, Georgia selection) is on greens, tees, and low areas in fairways. Sandy soil profile.

Management

Fertilizer

Starter = $1/2$–1 lb/1000 ft^2/application on 3–4 week cycle.

Maintenance = $1/4$–$1/2$ lb/1000 ft^2/application on 4–6 week cycle. Total 6 applications/year.

Fe = 2% granular applied every 4–6 weeks in a fertilizer blend.

Mn = 0.14% applied occasionally.

Irrigation

Combination brackish/effluent/potable applied nightly.

Mowing

> Greens   = $^1/_8$ in. daily
> Tees   = $^1/_4$ in. MWF
> Fairways = $^1/_2$ in. MWF
> Roughs = $1^1/_2$ in. weekly
> Primo® is being used on greens.

Major disease problem

> Dollar spot (from November through February).
> Control: 1 qt/ac Scotts Fungicide #2 as needed.

Major insect problem

> Sod webworm (early spring).
> Control: 1 oz/1000 ft² Dursban as needed.

Herbicides

> Manage @ 1.3 oz/ac as needed for nutsedge.
> Banvel @ 0.25 oz/1000 ft² as needed for broadleaf weeds.
> Herbicides that should not be used: MSMA, Sencor, Lexon.

Greens speed

> Daily stimp readings = 9–10 ft. Verticut and light topdress every 7–10 days. Can maintain constant speed year-round.

For LPGA Hawaiian Open

> Stimp 10–11 ft. Single cut and roll. Have not experienced any thinning or loss of turf in preparation for the tournament (highest stimp achieved 12 ft 6 in.).

Comments

> Have had to use very little herbicide after establishment. Paspalum holds up much better than bermudagreen to wear and traffic.

CASE STUDY NO. 2

Fairbanks Ranch Country Club   Phone: (619) 259-8811
Rancho Santa Fe, California   Fax: (619) 259-8593
Brian Darrock, Superintendent   "Brian K Darrock"
                                      <frccmain@adnc.com>

Course opened in 1985. Excalibur paspalum on tees, roughs, and fairways.
Greens: Poa, bentgrass SR 1020/1019
Tees, fairways, roughs overseeded in the winter with Seaside bentgrass using a slit seeder going in two directions

Management

Fertilizer

Starter	=	6-20-20 @ 1 lb/1000 ft² for P and K
Total N/yr	=	4 lb/1000 ft² (all applied early spring and late summer)
		2 lb nitrate or organic sources
P/yr	=	0.5 lb/1000 ft²
K/yr	=	4 lb/1000 ft² sulfate of potash

Aerification

2 times/yr—April, June using a G.A.60 and Vertidrain® @ 8 in. depth

Disease

Very light dollar spot

Mowing heights

5/8 in. winter
7/16 in. summer

CHAPTER *12*

Sports Fields

High traffic with the accompanying wear and soil compaction and an escalating demand for multiple sports use on too few fields presents a challenging dilemma. Intense turf management and maintenance of high quality turf in continuous acceptable playable condition are constant demands placed on all sports turf managers. A multipronged approach is needed to ensure that an athletic field will meet the demands of high traffic, multiple use, and minimal abuse/injury. This chapter provides general management practices for most sports fields regardless of the specific grass species used, but with appropriate cultural practices for seashore paspalum.

Seashore paspalum has a number of sports-related attributes that should be considered when choosing a turf species for athletic fields:

- It has very good wear and soil compaction (traffic) tolerances.
- The grass is adapted to a wide range of soil conditions and variable quality irrigation water; while paspalum requires less N than bermudagrass, it responds to additional N for rapid recovery and injury repair
- It has the appropriate growth habit to tolerate mowing heights that are used in various sports venues.
- Paspalum is persistent under prolonged cloudy (reduced light intensity) and wet conditions.
- Paspalum has a longer growing season in the fall than bermudagrass.
- Paspalum has a soft, cushiony feel and dense canopy.

While paspalum can tolerate many climatic, soil, pest, and man-made stresses, good management is essential to maximizing its characteristics and sports turf performance.

12.1. SITE SELECTION

Many athletic fields are constructed in less-than-favorable microenvironments; i.e., low areas next to creeks or streams, areas adjacent to or transitioning into environmentally sensitive sites, or wetland areas with periodic or constant problems with high water tables. These sites often have poor soil profiles for high intensity sports use, with heavy clay content and low organic matter. If the clays are nonexpanding (kaolinitic or Al/Fe oxides) with high bulk density, growing acceptable turf that is subjected to high traffic and compaction is a challenge. If poor quality recycled water or brackish ocean water is used for irrigation, or if saltwater intrusion becomes a problem, the growth rate of the turf may decrease to the point of unacceptable quality, recoverability, and playability, regardless of management level. While seashore paspalum can tolerate adverse site conditions, selection of better sites will result in better turf at lower cost. After site selection, careful field construction, proper selection of turfgrass species, cultivar, and overseeding cultivar, and aggressive management strategies must be implemented to develop and sustain high quality paspalum (or other species) sports turf.

12.2. SOIL PROFILE AND SURFACE STABILIZATION METHODS

Athletic field construction often conveniently involves utilization of on-site soil, which is principally an economic decision, but one that can prove costly for long-term grass performance. Soil profiles dominated by finer-textured composites of clay and silt coupled with poor drainage are highly susceptible to compaction. Managing sports turf on these sites with high traffic is very challenging, since the number of sports events (that can be held before severe deterioration) is limited. Managers require a high degree of sports management expertise and adequate budgets to handle increasing costs and the multiple demands on the athletic fields.

Soil modification with properly selected construction sand and proper drainage is the first step in providing high quality sports turf performance. The modified soil should be 80–90% sand to ensure adequate drainage (Christians, 1998) and the soil matrix for high-intensity-use playing fields should include 75–80% medium-sized (0.25 to 0.50 mm) sand (Watson et al., 1992).

If a thin layer (4–5 in.) of sand is applied and tilled into the top of the clay layer, the fine clay particles will migrate and fill the macropore spaces around the sand particles, resulting in a highly prone-to-compaction playing surface. Drainage must be improved and an aggressive aeration program must be implemented to maintain acceptable sports turf with this type of soil profile.

If 100% sand is capped (15–25 in.) on top of a compacted clay subbase, the sand will not readily compact, but water-holding capacity will be poor, the surface will rapidly dry out, and irrigation costs will be much higher (Christians, 1998). During rainy periods, water may pond above the compacted base and produce excessively wet conditions. A 100% sand profile can also be unstable and may not provide the firm playing surface needed for long-term sports play. As a result of these problems, several proprietary athletic field construction or surface stabilization methods have been developed to provide some standardization on sand-based profiles and to foster water conservation. These methods are summarized in this section and have potential use when growing seashore paspalum or other species on sports fields.

USGA Type Field (USGA Green Section Staff, 1993)

The existing soil is removed and the subgrade is leveled to match the final surface grade. Perforated drainage tile is placed on 20-ft centers on top of the compacted clay subgrade and covered with a 4-in. layer of pea gravel. A 12-in. layer of sand (80–90%) plus peat (10–20%) is placed over the gravel. The sand is carefully selected to provide good stability, drainage, compaction resistance, and adequate water-holding capacity. Soccer fields are usually flat, but football fields usually have a 0- to 10-in. crown (1% slope) in the center of the field to ensure surface drainage. Using a sand-peat-based soil profile with good internal drainage (8–20 in. hr^{-1}), a slope of 0.8 to 1.0% should be sufficient (Christians, 1998). Planting such a profile with sod that has a fine soil texture is a common mistake that compromises the entire construction technique.

Prescription Athletic Turf (PAT®) (Daniel et al., 1974; West, 1997)

The existing 16–22 in. of soil are removed. Subgrade is leveled and covered with a plastic barrier. Perforated drainage pipes are placed on the plastic, interconnected, and attached to a push-pull pump system. A polyethylene holding tank for water pulled off the field is buried off to the side of the playing surface. The Motz Group (Cincinnati, Ohio) has the license for the PAT system and they developed a precise Sand Conduit System® that encompasses a 12-in. root-zone sand profile with very strict particle size specifications and the following physical performance criteria (Christians, 1998).

: 88–100% total sand

60–80%	coarse sand (0.50–1.00 mm)	Fineness modulus: 1.5–2.5
—	medium sand (0.25–0.50 mm)	Uniformity coefficient: 2.5–3.5
5–20%	fine sand (0.10–0.25 mm)	Capillary porosity: 15–25%
5–10%	very fine sand (0.05–0.25 mm)	Air-filled porosity: 15–30%
0–10%	very coarse sand (1.00–2.00 mm)	Total porosity: 35–55%

Saturated hydraulic conductivity: 5–35 in. hr^{-1}
(no more than 10% fine gravel + very coarse sand; no more than 15% very fine sand/silt/clay)

Graviturf (Christians, 1998)

Soil profile is a sand + peat layer over a pea gravel drainage zone, which allows water to be gravity-drained from either a pitched subgrade or flat-field without pumps. An optional heating system (Wirsbo®) can be installed 6–12 in. below the surface on 8- to 10-in. centers to maintain constant temperature in cold climates or when warm season grasses are planted in northern areas.

Sports Grass® (Christians, 1998)

Combining the advantages of natural turf with the durability of the artificial surface, this synthetic turf encompasses the establishment of natural turf loosely woven among polypropylene grass fibers. The root-zone sand profile must meet specific particle size standards:

≥ 75% 0.25 to 1.00 mm sand
< 1% very fine sand (0.1 mm)
< 2% very coarse sand (1.0 mm)

The profile mix must generally meet USGA specifications. Installation: Sports Grass Inc., McLean, Virginia.

VHAF is another fabric system with needle-punched polypropylene blades woven into a porous backing. The fabric distributes weight evenly and the polypropylene blades enhance wear tolerance. The fabric is laid over the prepared seedbed, topdressed with root-zone mix that integrates into the fabric and blades, and is then seeded or sprigged. Some maintenance procedures are limited by intact fabrics, but high pressure water cultivation can be used (Adams and Gibbs, 1989; Dury, 1985).

SubAir® System (Christians, 1998)

Slotted tile system placed under a 4-in. gravel base and attached to a blower system used for warming, cooling, aerification, or water removal. The soil profile is a 12-in. sand-peat medium conforming to USGA standards. Installation: SubAir Inc., Deep River, Connecticut.

Cambridge System (Christians, 1998)

Also called ByPass Drainage System. Reconstruction or new construction on native soils with poor drainage. Trenches (6–8 in. wide) are cut 20 in. deep in the existing field. Drainage tile (4–6 in. diameter) is placed in the bottom of the trench, which is backfilled with coarse stone or pea gravel to within 6 in. of the playing surface, and capped (up to 6 in.) with sand to the surface. Slit trenches ($^5/_8$-in. wide, 9 in. deep) are cut at right angles to the drainage trenches (on 12–40 in. centers) and filled with sand. Additional sand-filled slits are cut at right angles to the 9-in. deep slits so they intersect and allow drainage from the area. The entire field is topdressed with sand and a rigid scheduling of topdressing must be done for the life of the field. Cost savings is 40–50% over complete reconstruction. Installation: Turf Services Inc., Spring Lake, Michigan.

Nelton Advanced Turf® System (Beard and Sifers, 1989, 1990; Christians, 1998)

An extruded polypropylene reflex mesh (2-by-4-in. pieces) is incorporated into a 6-in. deep layer of the root profile medium at a rate of 9 lb yd^{-3} using a specially designed reverse tilling device. The mesh material provides a three-dimensional, interlocking matrix that stabilizes the sandy root-zone (Beard and Sifers, 1993). A 0.75-in. layer of topdressing sand helps to smooth the surface prior to turfgrass establishment. Installation: The Tensar Corporation, Morrow, Georgia and Thomas Bros. Grass, Granbury, Texas. StrathAyr squares (**SquAyrs**) is a related system where Reflex® mesh elements are incorporated into a 4-in.-deep sod that is cut into 4-by-4 ft squares. Worn segments can be removed and reset with these new squares (called BAyr Root Turf or soil-free turfgrass sod). Installation: Manderley Corp., Nepean, Ontario, Canada (Anonymous, 1999a).

TurfGrids (Christians, 1998)

Green polypropylene 1.5 in. fibers incorporated into the upper 4 in. of a sand-based field (rate: 1 lb/12 ft²) or 6 lb/ton of sand mixed off-site. **Fibresand**® is another single fiber material used in England (Baker and Richards, 1995). **Fibermaster**® (manufactured by Fibermesh® Co., Chattanooga, Tennessee) is a similar amendment. Reinforcement fibers at 0.2 to 0.3% (w/w) also increase penetration resistance and shear (traction resistance) (Adams, 1997). **Loksand**® is a precisely crimped polypropylene fiber that creates greater stability, impact resilience, and durability on sports fields (Plasticisers, Ltd., New Zealand).

Crumb Rubber (Hartwiger, 1995; Rogers and Vanini, 1995; Rogers et al., 1998ab; Vanini et al., 1999)

Recycled tires that can be used for sand profile stabilization (Rebound®) or as a topdressing amendment (Crown III®, Rebound®) to reduce wear injury and provide surface resiliency (Landry, 1998e). Maximum layer thickness for topdressing ranges from 0.25 to 0.75 in., with not more than 0.25-in. applied per application. If the turfgrass is mowed at ⁵/₈ in., use ¹/₂–³/₄ in. of crumb rubber (1200–1500 lb/1000 ft²). Sources: Enviro-Cycle Inc., Norcross, Georgia; Jaitire Industries Inc., Denver, Colorado.

Enkaturf is a permanent, three-dimensional nylon mesh matting of 0.72-in. thickness that is laid on prepared soil, topdressed with 1-in. root-zone mix where it integrates into the open meshes with about 0.20 in. left on top, and is then seeded, sprigged, or sodded. This supposedly produces a resilient foundation with very high shear/mechanical stability, reduces soil compaction, promotes better root growth, and distributes weight more evenly. This system prohibits the use of standard cultivation techniques except for high pressure water injection, is undesirable if the surface grass becomes sheared off, and becomes less effective with continuous topdressing applications. **Tensar®** mat is another three-dimensional web with four layers of polypropylene mesh fused together every 30–35 mm (Baker, 1997).

Grass Master system uses green, plastic fibers inserted into a prepared seed bed at 0.80 × 0.80-in. grids (2 × 2 cm) so that 3–4% of the fiber blades constitute the turf area. The plastic fiber blades are inserted just below the cutting height of the grass. As turfgrass roots intertwine with the vertical fibers, wear tolerance and surface stability are improved. New fibers can be inserted as needed and normal maintenance can be practiced.

Dupont Shredded Carpet (McNitt, 1998)

Recycled product added at 3% (v/v) rate to reduce soil bulk density, lower surface hardness, reduce divot length, and resist compaction as wear increases.

Nike Light and Heavies (McNitt, 1998)

Recycled product used to reduce soil bulk density and provide greater wear resistance.

Inturf (Anonymous, 1999b)

Integrated Turf Modules for moveable sports system use.

SuperTiles (Anonymous, 1999c)

Grass tiles grown in plastic module trays using recycled, shredded carpet reinforcement in a sand-based root-zone. Instantly playable, rotatable, and replaceable. Can be installed on asphalt, artificial turf, or other firm bases. Distributor: Hummer Sports Turf.

Advanced Turf System (Anonymous, 1999d)

Modular plastic (polyethylene) turf tray. Systematrix, Ltd., United Kingdom.

Integrated Turf Management System® (Anonymous, 1999e)

High density polyethylene plastic module, 14.5 ft² of turfed area that is 6 in. deep, weighing 750–1000 lb/module. Instantly playable, rotatable, and replaceable. Can be installed on asphalt, artificial turf, or other firm bases. GreenTech, Richmond, Virginia.

Zeoponic Turf Root Zone System (Allen and Andrews, 1997; Andrews et al., 1999ab)

Developed and patented by NASA, this unique growth medium combines zeolite—specifically clinoptilolite, which is an aluminosilicate noted for its rigid crystal structure and is derived from volcanic ash sediments—and synthetic apatite, a calcium hydroxy phosphate, which was developed to provide P and trace elements. The clinoptilolite provides high CEC (>100 meq/100 g compared to sands at 2–3 meq/100 g), high porosity, favorable moisture retention, and rigid structure. The combination gives the root-zone mix physical and chemical properties, holds a long-lasting reservoir of nutrients, and delivers a balanced diet of slowly released plant nutrients through a combination of chemical dissolution and ion exchange reactions. Zeolite particles maintain or improve drainage and infiltration, provide aeration, withstand intense traffic and compaction, accelerate turf establishment and root mass development, and reduce leaching losses to the environment. A 10% zeoponic amendment in a sand-based root can reduce nutrient loss by 65–95+%. (Product: ZeoPro®; ZeoponiX, Inc., Louisville, Colorado).

12.3. ATHLETIC FIELD MANAGEMENT

Sports turf should be firm (providing good footing and stability), resilient (cushioning falls and reducing injury), dense (providing consistent ball roll or bounce), uniform (an even playing surface), persistent (lasting the entire season), deep-rooted (resisting divots or tears), wear-tolerant (withstanding injury from pressure, abrasion, or tearing/shearing), compaction-resistant, and rapid-draining. Primary playing surface problems (such as poor site selection, inappropriate soil profile, number of games played) require long-term management strategies to alleviate or minimize damage to the turfgrass. Secondary problems such as low water infiltration and percolation (i.e., standing water, waterlogged conditions, low soil oxygen, poor rooting, hard or unstable surfaces, and black layer) require immediate management practices to minimize turfgrass injury or field surface disruption.

Overall management strategies to address soil physical problems include: (1) partial/complete soil modification, (2) soil cultivation [aeration: hollow tine or cores, solid tines, slicing blades, spiking, shatter coring, spoons, high pressure liquid pulse injectors (Rogers and Jobson, 1993) and shallow vs. deep], (3) surface or subsurface drainage (Adams et al., 1983; Canaway and Baker, 1993; Gibbs et al., 1993ab; McAuliffe, 1989), (4) irrigation management (neither too wet or too dry), (5) chemical soil conditioners (gypsum, polymers, wetting agents, bio-products), (6) soil gas/temperature alteration (subaeration, fans, heating, cooling), and (7) surface stabilization materials (SportsGrass®, Netlon Advanced Turf System®, Turf Grids/Fibresand, crumb rubber, Enkaturf, or Grass Master). The difference in soil texture provides unique problems and changes the management strategy.

Fine-textured soils high in clay and silt content lack sufficient macropores (>0.12 mm diameter) for effective water infiltration and percolation, gas (O_2, CO_2) exchange, and channels for root growth. These soils notoriously have high soil strength (at field capacity or when dry) that impedes turfgrass root penetration and causes low resiliency. Soil compaction can either be caused by a thin surface layer (0–3 in.) or a subsurface layer (4–12 in.). The presence of layers may result from a soil-compacted surface zone, from thatch buildup, from distinct texture changes (fines migrating, organic matter precipitation), or algae scum. Salt-related problems such as saline soils/water (total soluble salts), sodic soils (Na-enhanced soil structural deterioration), or caliche layers at the surface (impervious, hard zone) will enhance soil surface physical problems. Excess water at the surface (restricted infiltration) is subject to increasing surface compaction. Low percolation rate, high water tables, seepage or lack of runoff, and poor contouring (creating low spots) escalate the compaction problem. Low water content from rapid runoff due to slopes, nonuniform irrigation, shallow rooting, and a shallow root-zone mix contribute to the physical problems. Uneven or unstable playing surfaces cause problems due to excess traffic when saturated, high pressure or concentrated traffic (must redirect the traffic, use pneumatic tires, use soil stabilizers), frost heaving, or thin turf with few roots.

Coarse-textured soils (high in sand) lack micropores (<0.12 mm diameter) for efficient moisture retention and have low soil strength at field capacity or when drier, which is needed for surface stability. Surface soil physical problems are caused by high concentrations of very coarse sands that have a deep profile and are low in organic matter. Some of these sands are hydrophobic and repel water. Saline soils high in total soluble salts cause salt-induced drought on the turfgrass. Layers can occur if fine-textured materials are located in the surface 0–2 in., if a zone of high organic matter content or thatch is located in the surface 0–2 in., or if algae scum is present. Excess water problems at the surface may be caused by high water tables, a perched water table, from sodic sands, from a seepage area, or from adjacent runoff areas. A hard sandy surface could result from low organic matter content (including thatch or matting), from using sands with a wide particle size distribution, or from sands containing an excess of fines. A soft sandy surface can result from using sand with a narrow particle size distribution or with rounded sand particles, from a poor or limited turfgrass root system, from low organic matter content, from excess moisture at the surface, and from a soil surface that is too dry.

Surface stability problems are normally a combination of (a) wear injury on the turfgrass from physical abrasion, shearing forces, pressure, or tearing, and (b) soil compaction. These stresses result in turf biomass losses, including the root system and thatch. These injuries are accentuated during wet periods and on poorly drained soils. Surface instability is a major problem on all root-zone mixes during grass establishment (see Section 12.2 on surface stabilization techniques).

Several criteria can be used to maximize surface stability and traction on sports fields:

a. Carefully select sand particle uniformity, size, gradation, and shape.
b. Incorporate organic matter (1–3% by weight) uniformly into the entire sand profile during establishment.
c. Use a root-zone mix with rapid drainage characteristics.
d. Install good surface and subsurface drainage.
e. Maximize turfgrass root growth since fibrous roots are the primary soil stabilizing agent.
f. Use proper fertilization and mowing, maintain high shoot density and turf biomass to resist wear injury, and provide sufficient protective cushion against compactive forces.
g. Use wear-tolerant grass cultivars and manage for maximum wear tolerance.

h. Avoid extremes in dryness or wetness by carefully scheduling irrigation.
i. Develop a topdressing program that controls thatch, creates a mat-thatch with intermingled sand or soil, maintains a level playing surface, and amends the soil texture on the surface when needed.
j. Limit thatch to less than 0.50 in.
k. Use soil stabilization materials when needed (see Section 12.2).
l. Avoid excess N fertilization that increases turf leaf growth and enhances color at the expense of root, stolon, and rhizome development.

Cultivation (McAuliffe et al., 1993; Rieke and Murphy, 1989; Wieko et al., 1993)

Aerate. Aerate. Aerate. Soil compaction is the biggest problem on high use sports fields. Deep tine (>4 in. deep) aeration or high pressure water injection are effective in alleviating subsurface compaction and should be performed at least twice per year on fields subjected to or prone to excess compaction (prior to the start of the season and immediately after the end of the season). Surface (<4 in.) aeration with hollow- or solid-tines should be performed every 2–3 weeks during the sports season, except during exceptional high-temperature-stress periods or when other climatic stresses are present. Regularly scheduled spiking, slicing, or shatter coring will aid water infiltration, temporarily reduce surface hardness, and enhance overseeding establishment (Hayes, 1989; Landry, 1993, 1995abc, 1997ab, 1998abc, 1999; Landry and Murphy, 1997). Spiking could increase infiltration rates up to 10 mm (0.4 in.) h^{-1}, depending on soil profiles (Hayes, 1989). Using a deep aeration procedure within two weeks of a shallow depth aeration can increase the effectiveness of the overall cultivation program throughout the entire soil profile (Landry, 1998b).

Aeration methods that loosen the soil by vibration or shattering should be timed when moisture levels are slightly below field capacity (i.e., 24 hours after rainfall or irrigation). Aeration methods that cause minimal loosening (spoon-type tines) should be applied when moisture levels are near field capacity. Procedures that bring soil to the surface (core tines) must be scheduled when sports play will not be disrupted, due to the need for a recovery period and root regeneration. Topdressing with a proper-sized sand following core aeration will keep the holes open, enhance fertilizer, water, and air movements to the turfgrass roots, and minimize surface sealing. If core aerating in hot, dry, windy weather, schedule irrigation to compensate for moisture loss and minimize additional injury to the grass surrounding the core holes (Hayes, 1989; Landry, 1998b). If the sports field has a sodic soil problem (Na^+-induced soil structural deterioration, poor aeration, poor drainage), aggressive surface and subsurface cultivation programs beyond that required for normal soil compaction will be needed (Carrow and Duncan, 1998). Amendments such as gypsum can also be incorporated into the cultivation program to reduce the problem.

Irrigation

Except in arid regions, where salt problems exist, or when maintaining overseeded cool-season grasses, 1 in. of water per week should be adequate for most paspalum sports fields (1 in. of water will wet a clay soil to the 4 in. depth, a loam soil to 8 in., and a sandy soil to 15 in.) (Landry, 1994). Maximize the time between irrigation and sports field use—at least 24 to 48 hours to minimize compaction. The higher the surface moisture content during play, the greater the compaction problems (Landry, 1997b).

Irrigation scheduling with good quality effluent or with potable water will be based on the soil profile. With sand + peat soils, a single nighttime application per week should be sufficient to maintain acceptable turf performance if a deep, healthy turfgrass root system is present. Frequent, short-duration, shallow irrigations with potable water should be avoided since this practice promotes shallow rooting and a soft surface, and decreases drought tolerance in paspalum. On sandy soils with no organic matter, one-half inch water applied twice per week is generally adequate. With heavy clay profiles, irrigate to the point of runoff, allow the water to thoroughly infiltrate the soil (possibly 3–4 hours), then either repeat the cycle or wait until the next night to maximize water uptake efficiency and to supply the total weekly volume that is needed (Landry, 1997b), based on climatic conditions. If possible, always irrigate with sufficient volume to wet the soil to the level of deep turfgrass rooting. Excessive irrigation may leach valuable nutrients from the rhizosphere before the turf roots can absorb them.

When using poor quality effluent or brackish ocean water for irrigation, higher volumes and more frequent irrigation scheduling will be needed to minimize salt buildup. Depending on the level of total soluble salts and presence or absence of carbonates/bicarbonates/sulfates, the water may need to be pretreated (gypsum, acid) to minimize adverse Na^+ effects (Carrow and Duncan, 1998) or to form gypsum (if excess sulfates are present) prior to application on the turf. The strategy is to maximize salt movement through the soil profile and away from the turf root system. In general, the higher the buildup of salts in the rhizosphere, the slower the growth rate of the turf. With saline water use on sports turf, nightly irrigation scheduling for 30–45 minutes may be needed to flush the salts through the soil profiles, particularly in areas with windy or high evaporation conditions. Fields using these irrigation sources must have proper drainage to dispose of the salts and a proper area in which to sequester the excess salts. High leaching volumes can cause deficiencies of critical nutrients such as N, P, K, Ca, Mg, Mn, and Fe. Careful monitoring and prescription micro- and macronutrient fertilization applications must be regularly scheduled to maximize sports turf performance.

Fertilization (Gibeault et al., 1999; Landry, 1996b; Landry and Murphy, 1997; Peacock and Dahms, 1998/1999; Tracinski, 1998c)

Water-soluble N sources release on contact with water and immediately become available for turf plant uptake. Inorganic salt sources include ammonium nitrate, ammonium sulfate, monoammonium phosphate, diammonium phosphate, potassium nitrate, calcium nitrate, polymer coated urea, and multicoated urea. A water-soluble organic source is urea.

Water-insoluble N sources must undergo some physical, chemical, or biochemical transformation before they become available. A slowly soluble source is isobutylidenediurea (IBDU). Slow release forms that depend on slow N diffusion include sulfur-coated urea (SCU) coated with polymers (Poly S, Tricote), saran film (V-Cote), ethylene-propylene diene monomer (EPDM or sulfonated rubber), and reactive plastic layer coating or polyurethane membrane (Polyon) (Cisar, 1997). Natural organic sources include sewage sludge, composted manures, feathermeal, soybean meal, or bone meal. These sources and ureaformaldehyde (UF and methylene urea) depend on microbial activity for N-release.

The fertilization program for paspalum parallels a cool-season grass schedule (refer to Section 9.6 for a detailed discussion on paspalum N fertilization programs), with balanced N-P-K applications during the spring and fall, and minimal N applications (0.25 to 0.50 lb N/1000 ft^2) during the summer. N-sources should be used to enhance recovery from injury, and such products as calcium nitrate, with high water solubility, is excellent in conjunction with verticutting for escalating recovery. The rate of sports use and the soil/climate conditions will dictate the volume of N fertilizer used. But, typical **monthly rates** are summarized below:

- mid to late spring @ 0.5 to 1.0 lb N/1000 ft^2
- summer @ 0.33 to 0.50 lb N/1000 ft^2
- early to mid fall @ 0.5 to 1.0 lb N/1000 ft^2
- late fall @ 0 to 0.50 lb N/1000 ft^2
- for salt-affected sites with high leaching needs, use the higher N range; for non-salt-affected sites, use the low to mid range.

The more the field is used, the more frequent the prescription application of fertilizers.

Fall fertilization on the paspalum (September to November in the southern United States) should avoid excess N (>0.50 lb N/1000 ft^2) and overstimulation of the turf, with applications as late as two weeks prior to the expected first frost date. Proper fall fertilization enhances fall color retention, cold temperature hardening, turf density, root growth, winter hardiness, and spring greenup/recovery; medium to high levels of K must also be supplied in 1:1.5 to 1:2.0 N:K$_2$O ratios. At least 2–3 weeks prior to frost, applying K at a rate of 2–3 lb/1000 ft^2 0-0-60 or 4–5 lb/1000 ft^2 0-0-39 can be beneficial, especially if the paspalum is overseeded with a cool-season grass. N fertilization of overseeded paspalum should be kept at minimal amounts until the paspalum is fully dormant from cold temperatures. Excess N at this time will make the paspalum succulent and decrease winter hardiness. Maintenance of a proper nutritional balance in the turf plant is the key to sports turf performance, recovery from injury or excess use, and transitioning into and out of cool-season grass overseeding.

Adequate potassium fertilization is important to maximize wear, salinity, drought, and cold tolerances in paspalum. Multiple K applications during the year, particularly prior to heavy field use, is preferred over only one or two applications. Paspalum is highly efficient in uptake of applied K. For fine-textured soils, annual K needs should be based on a soil test to maintain moderately high to high K concentration ranges. On coarse-textured soils, spoon-feed K with N using 1:1.5 to 1:2.0 $N:K_2O$ ratios. On salt-affected sports fields, increase the K rates by at least 25%, especially if high water volumes are used for leaching.

Phosphorus should be applied at a minimum of 1.0 lb $P_2O_5/1000$ ft^2 (0.22 kg P/100 m^2) during early spring on paspalum sports fields. Based on soil tests, additional applications can be made during both early and late summer, and at the time of any fall overseeding. Most sites require at least 2.0 lb $P_2O_5/1000$ ft^2 annually.

Overseeding (Christians, 1998; Landry, 1993; Tracinski, 1998a; Ruemmele and Wallace, 1998)

Cool-season grass overseeding provides a more attractive and smooth sports playing surface that has more cushion during the winter months than nonseeded paspalum fields. Overseeding can increase the wear tolerance of the overall sports turf canopy and enhance stability and traction during the winter months. A year-round turf maintenance program must be implemented to address (1) compaction problems (aeration), (2) smoothness of playing surface (correcting high and low areas using compatible root zone mixes), (3) removing excess thatch (verticutting or slicing and topdressing), and (4) mowing height adjustment to foster good seed-soil contact in the established paspalum turf.

Schedule overseeding one to three weeks prior to the anticipated first frost date. If field use schedules require an earlier cool-season grass overseeding, consider a preventive fungicide application for fusarium (Table 10.9) or pythium (Heritage®, Alliette®, Banol®, Termec®, Lesan®, Koban®, Subdue®). For later overseeding where soil temperatures might be below the effective germination level, coverage with a tarp or turf blanket will increase the soil temperature and conserve moisture for optimum germination. Optimum temperatures should be: 75°F @ 4-in. depth; or 50°F nighttime air temperature; and/or <70°F average midday air temperature. Soil and night temperatures ≥60–65°F can trigger the resurgence of paspalum growth.

Select cool-season species and cultivars that are adapted to your region and that fulfill the special needs of your site-specific sports field. Improved perennial ryegrasses with endophytes provide insect resistance, improved seedling establishment, rapid tillering, dense growth, improved mowing quality, excellent cosmetic color, and high traffic tolerance. Mowing heights can range from 0.25 to 2.50 in., depending on the type of paspalum sports field. Because of its rapid establishment, perennial ryegrass (PR) is ideally suited for overseeding thinned or damaged sports turf. If PR is mixed with other cool-season grasses, use no more than 20% of this grass in the mixture. Soccer goal mouths can be seeded with 100% PR, and up to 40% PR can be overseeded into other high traffic/heavy wear areas on the sports field.

Turf-type tall fescues (TF) provide excellent wear tolerance on sports fields if they are seeded about a week earlier than perennial ryegrasses. Cultivars have fine-leaf texture, dense and low growth habits, greater persistence, and abiotic/biotic stress tolerances. Mowing height requirements range from 1.5 to 3.0 in. Cool season grass blends often contain 80% TF. Cultivar selection should be based on previous performance in the region and transitioning capability, if this is a necessary component of the management program. Kerb® can be used to transition out overseeded cool-season grasses in paspalum.

Overseeding rates can be found in Table 9.4. Seed can be applied with a broadcast or drop spreader (half rate in two different directions to ensure uniform application) after soil preparation, or using a slit seeder or verticutter that combines soil preparation with the planting process. Seed can be pregerminated by soaking in water a few days before planting in order to ensure rapid establishment. Ideally, a light topdressing will increase the seed-to-soil contact. If topdressing is not an option, a flexible metal or mat drag can be used to ensure contact between the seed and the soil. Light, frequent irrigation should be used during the germination and establishment phases. Intervals between irrigation cycles can be gradually increased and the duration of irrigation application extended to enhance deeper water penetration into the profile and to promote deeper rooting. Allow the new cool-season grass seedlings to grow $^1/_3$-in. higher than the mowing height recommended for the species before beginning the mowing process.

If poor quality effluent or brackish water is used for irrigation in the overseeding germination process, select only the most salt-tolerant cultivars (Table 12.1). Since germinating seeds and young seedling roots are highly sensitive to salt stress even for salt tolerant species, access to or use of reduced salt-laden water resources (possibly through blending) could be beneficial for successful and rapid establishment.

Table 12.1. Salt-Tolerant Cool-Season Grass Cultivars That Can Be Used for Overseeding

Creeping Bentgrass	Kentucky Bluegrass
Seaside	Blacksburg
Seaside II	Livingston
Cobra	Glade
Penneagle	
SR 1020	**Tall Fescue**
Mariner	Tomahawk
	Apache II
Perennial Ryegrass	Alta
Chaparral	
Quickstart	**Weeping Alkaligrass**
Manhattan II	Salty
	Fults
Strong Creeping Red Fescue	
Flyer	**Slender Creeping Red Fescue**
Ensylva	Dawson
Shademaster II	Oasis
	Seabreeze

Topdressing

Use the same texture in the topdressing material as the existing soil to prevent layering. Topdressing over long periods (twice each year for four or more years) on sports fields can improve the soil profile, protect turf seedlings, protect the crown region of the paspalum turf, improve drainage, foster thatch decomposition, and help level uneven surfaces. Light ($1/8$-in. layer or 10.4 ft^3 or 0.4 yd^3/1000 ft^2) frequent applications (every 3–4 weeks) during active growth periods are preferred over less frequent, heavier rates during dormant periods. Consequently, topdressing should be done primarily on the paspalum turf during the summer months rather than on the cool-season overseeded species in the dormant paspalum. Topdressing should be avoided during the spring paspalum greenup period.

Thatch Management (Landry, 1994, 1996a; Waddington, 1992)

Thatch is the layer of living and dead organic plant material between the soil surface and the green leaves of the turf. Roots, stolons, shoots, and crowns can grow into and through this layer. Thatch layers $1/4–1/2$ in. retain moisture, protect grass roots and young seedlings from temperature extremes or high winds, and provide a cushion that protects crowns and stolons from wear damage on sports fields. Since paspalum inherently has a softer, more cushiony feel to the grass compared to bermuda, a thin thatch layer provides extra protection in the playing surface against athletic injuries, skin abrasions, and potential knee/ankle problems.

Thatch layers exceeding 2 in. harbors insect and disease organisms, restricts root development, decreases drought tolerance, and predisposes the turf to injury from temperature extremes. The thatch will form a barrier that reduces water, fertilizer, and pesticide penetration into the soil profile, increases water loss due to runoff and evaporation, becomes puffy and uneven, increases susceptibility to scalping, reduces wear, and increases slipping among sports players. The primary contributor to excess thatch in paspalum sports turf is too much N, especially in conjunction with excess irrigation. Cultural control tactics include vertical mowing, core aeration and topdressing, avoiding excessive fertilization and irrigation, and proper mowing techniques/timing.

12.4. LOW LIGHT INTENSITY TOLERANCE

Because of its ability to retain green color under prolonged reduced light intensity conditions without exhibiting elongated, spindly leaf growth, paspalum has potential use in domed stadiums or other sports stadiums with reduced light problems. The grass can be grown on plastic with a 2-in. root zone base and rolled out in 4–6 ft wide sod strips (like a carpet) in domed stadiums. The grass can be treated with Primo® at 12 liquid ounces/acre and iron 5–6 days in advance of harvest and sod installation. Green color retention can be maintained for 2–4 weeks in a domed stadium. Wear resistance and recoverability from injury are unknown components. How long the turf can remain in the dome before removal has not yet been determined. This paspalum trait also allows the grass to grow quite well under prolonged, cloudy, overcast/hazy/foggy weather conditions, in areas with monsoonal weather patterns, and in areas with >275 days of rainy weather annually.

CHAPTER 13

Lawn and Landscape Use

Paspalum use in landscapes has been limited to mainly coastal venues, salt-affected sites, or areas utilizing poor quality effluent. Saltene is a lawn-type cultivar grown in Western Australia. Some lawn-oriented research has been conducted in Florida (Morton, 1973). Paspalum has been grown in home landscapes in Hawaii. Its potential for use in home lawns, business landscapes, and city parks will increase as water quality and potable water quantity issues escalate in the twenty-first century.

Management (Christians, 1998; Duble, 1996; Watson et al., 1992) will be the key to proper performance of paspalum in landscapes (Knoop, 1997). Because of its inherent multiple stress tolerance, paspalum will have lower maintenance costs than many other warm season grasses. Paspalum does not withstand tree shade conditions very well based on preliminary studies and should not be planted under tree canopies with intense shading. It is comparable to the hybrid bermudagrasses in tree shade tolerance levels, and zoysiagrass and St. Augustinegrass are appropriate grass choices for this particular environmental stress.

13.1. ESTABLISHMENT (refer to Section 9.3)

Paspalum will establish into sands, clays, or wet, boggy mucks. The soil should be tilled and, if possible, organic matter added and incorporated to a depth of 2–4 in. if the percent organic matter is ≤ 3% in order to enhance water-holding capacity. Adjust pH to 5.5 to 8.0 using either lime (acid soils) or sulfur (alkaline soils).

Most lawns and business landscapes will be established using sod or sprigs. Sprigging rates should range from 5–10 bu (1.26 ft^3 = 1 bu)/ 1000 ft^2. On slopes, either hydrosprig or surface-apply the sprigs and cover with a thin layer of straw or a turf blanket (woven plastic cover). Though more expensive initially, sodding of slopes would provide the most effective method for erosion control, and successful establishment will eliminate the need for replanting, which often occurs with grass seed or sprig plantings on slopes.

13.2. MOWING HEIGHTS (refer to Section 9.4)

Cutting heights in home lawns and landscapes should be maintained between 0.5 to 1.0 in. (1.27 to 2.54 cm). In general, the shorter the mowing height, the denser the canopy and fewer problems with weeds. Higher mowing heights produce a grass that is less cosmetically appealing than some other warm-season grasses. A mulching rotary mower with sharp blades is recommended when mowing above 0.75-in., but a reel mower is recommended at less than 0.75-in.

On some sites with prostrate or low-growing seashore paspalum ecotypes, the grass can be used for slope stabilization or for its contrasting texture and color in highlighting the landscape. The natural, moderately dark and "shiny" color of most paspalums is attractive. Ecotypes from the world collection are being assessed for such uses in unmowed situations.

13.3. FERTILIZATION (refer to Section 9.6)

The rule on fertilizer usage in home lawns and landscapes is *minimal* **slow release** *nitrogen* (no more than 1–4 lb actual $N/1000$ ft^2/year) (Table 13.1). Paspalum lawns requiring the higher rate would primarily be found in tropical areas with high rainfall. To minimize thatch buildup and mowing frequency, the N-fertilizer schedule will parallel the same one used for cool-season grasses, with monthly applications during the spring and fall, but minimal amounts or none during the summer months. Typical annual fertilizer schedules might include those in Table 13.1 for the southern United States and for tropical areas.

Potassium (K) and phosphorus (P) needs should be determined by annual soil tests. If the soil tests are not available, K can be applied using an N-carrier with a ratio of 1:1.0 to 1:1.5 ($N:K_2O$). Higher K rates can be applied during the early spring and in the fall (Table 13.1). Phosphorus should be applied at least in the spring at the onset of spring greenup (emergence from winter dormancy). In tropical climates, P and K should be applied several times per year, rather than once, based on rainfall events or monsoonal weather patterns.

Table 13.1. Potential Home Lawn and Landscape Fertilization Programs for Seashore Paspalum in Sub-Tropical and Tropical Climates

Time of Year	lb N/1000 ft² [a]	Suggested Application Times P	K
Subtropical[b]			
Winter			
December	0	—	—
January–March	0	—	—
Spring			
April	0.5–1.0	**	***
May	0–0.50	—	—
Summer			
June	0–0.50	—	*
July	0[c]	—	—
August	0[c]	—	—
Fall			
September	0.50–1.0	**	*
October	0–0.50	—	***
November	0–0.50	—	**
Tropical (12 months)[d]			
Bimonthly schedule	0.33–0.66	3X/yr	4X/yr
Trimonthly schedule	0.50–1.0	3X/yr	4X/yr

[a] The highest N rate in the range would be used if the grass exhibits the onset of N deficiency (yellowing of lower leaves, slow growth, loss of stand density). Otherwise, the low to moderate rate is suggested. 1 lb N/1000 ft² = 0.49 kg N/100 m².
[b] Georgia—southern United States, dormant winter, 50 in. annual rainfall. Use of slow-release N fertilizers is encouraged.
[c] Nitrogen can be applied at <0.50 lb N/1000 ft² if needed based on N deficiency symptoms, or to fill in areas where turf density loss has occurred.
[d] In tropical climates, high N should be avoided prior to the onset of the rainy season, but may be needed after the rainy season.
*, **, *** = Increasing level of importance for application(s) during specific months.

13.4. IRRIGATION (refer to Section 9.8)

Use of light, frequent applications during the first two weeks of establishment is acceptable; then increase the duration between applications and the duration of each application during grow-in to force deeper rooting. Once established, one irrigation (0.5 to 1.0 in.) per week at night in 15–25 minute pulses to avoid runoff if spray heads are used should provide sufficient moisture to maintain the paspalum during the high temperature, high evaporation periods. Irrigation pulses can be repeated every 2 or 3 hours to obtain the desired quantity of water. If rotary heads are used, one long irrigation cycle (30–50 minutes) can be used. On sandy profiles or on heavy clays, the scheduling may need to be extended to two nights per week for 15–25 minutes (spray heads) each night to maximize water conservation/water utilization programs. During severe drought stress conditions, wait until the paspalum starts exhibiting drought stress symptoms during the early morning hours before irrigation application. During the late fall or winter months when the soil becomes exceptionally dry, apply 0.25 to 0.5 in. irrigation water prior to dormancy or severely cold temperatures (45°F or 9°C) to prevent dessication and to maintain winter hardiness.

13.5. CULTIVATION

Home lawns and landscapes should be aerated (3–4 in. deep) at least once per year, especially on sloped sites, preferably during the late spring and in the fall prior to the winter months. This practice will minimize problems with thatch buildup, provide channels for irrigation and rainfall penetration and percolation, and help to maintain sufficient oxygen to the root system. If heavy traffic and/or compaction problems develop, 2–4 aerations may be needed annually if the causes of the excess traffic and compaction cannot be avoided. If the soil pH drops below 5.5, apply lime or gypsum at 1–10 lb/1000 ft^2 during October or November (fall), depending on how low the soil pH has dropped. Even though most paspalum cultivars can withstand soil pHs < 5.0, the lime applications may prove beneficial for microbial activity in soil, especially in enhancing the conversion of $NH_4 \rightarrow NO_3$, in providing more effective uptake of this N source by paspalum, and in promoting thatch decomposition.

CHAPTER 14

Sod and Sprig Production

Paspalum, because of its extensive rhizome and stolon production capability, can effectively and efficiently be grown for sod and sprig uses. The zone of adaptation (30–35° N–S latitudes) will limit production areas to tropical and subtropical regions, with a range of between 1 sod harvest up to 3 sod harvests per year and 2 to 5 sprig harvests possible per year from the same land, depending on cold temperatures. Environmental conditions and management strategies will dictate the productivity of this vegetatively propagated grass.

Management options include:

1. Native mineral soils vs. soilless organic mediums.
2. Sod vs. sprigs vs. both.
3. Market (golf courses, sports field, lawns or landscaping, roadside and municipal parks) and certification.

14.1. SITE SELECTION

A critical initial decision for the paspalum sod producer is the soil type, proximity to and availability of water (including recycled, brackish, or ocean water), and frequency plus duration of cold temperatures < 70°F (21°C). The choice of soil type will be a major factor in determining the cost effectiveness of the sod production operation. Sands, loamy sands, and loam-type native soils are preferred over heavy clay soil because of ease in harvesting for sod or for sprigs. Low drainage throughways and areas plagued by high water tables or periodic flooding can be used when producing paspalum vegetative material since the grass has waterlogging tolerance and can withstand periodic inundation. These areas will be prone to weed contamination. Rocky soil areas and uneven or nonuniform surfaces should be avoided when growing paspalum, because of harvesting problems and sod uniformity requirements. Soil pH should range from 6.0 to 8.0 for maximum production. P and K levels should be in the moderately high to high range for maximum root development and peak sod-forming capacity. Soil preparation prior to establishment must include soil fumigation on land devoid of all other grasses and perennial broadleaf weeds for certification. Soil tillage practices are designed to minimize compaction, but include tillage at a proper depth (4–12 in.) prior to establishment to promote rapid rooting and deep rhizome development as well as to provide a smooth level surface for eventual harvesting.

When alternative water resources are used for irrigation, especially those poor quality sources with salts (brackish), heavy metals, and/or bicarbonates, management for sod production must be intensive. The management strategy must include frequent irrigation applications to provide consistent movement of the salts through the soil profile and prevent salt deposition on the soil surface coupled with periodic (monthly) applications of gypsum where necessary (Carrow and Duncan, 1998) to minimize salt layering from excess bicarbonates or zonal accumulation and soil profile deterioration from excess Na. If ocean water, brackish water, or other salt-laden (25–54 dSm^{-1}) water is used as the irrigation source in the sod production program, growth rate of even the most salt-tolerant paspalum cultivar may be reduced by 50% if salts are not consistently moved through the soil profile and are allowed to accumulate.

Tropical locations with minimal or no freezing temperatures will be able to produce the maximum number of harvests (up to three) annually compared to the more temperate regions. Environments with monsoonal weather patterns and prolonged (3–6 months) cloudy or hazy (reduced light intensity) growing conditions can be considered for sod production, since paspalum is very tolerant of these conditions. The grass performs quite well in climates receiving 275 days of rain per year and will maintain good production in these wet, reduced-soil-oxygen microclimates.

14.2. SOILLESS MEDIUMS

Root impervious technology utilizes an impermeable layer (plastic) to prevent roots and rhizomes from penetrating the soil, forces the roots to grow laterally, ensures a customized uniform product of substantial strength and flexibility with 100% of the root system being harvested, and minimizes problems with nematodes, native soil microflora, weeds, or other on-site contaminants (Anonymous, 1999). The rhizosphere encompasses 1–2 in. of organic and sand-based mediums into which the paspalum sprigs are established. This system requires daily frequent light irrigation applications and a rigid spoon-feeding fertilization schedule for maximum production. If poor quality water is used for irrigation, the underlying plastic barrier must allow for proper drainage to prevent salt accumulation. The area could be contoured to allow salt-laden runoff by surface drainage.

RapidTurf® in Rincon, Georgia (Anonymous, 1999) and Southern Turf® in Alabama, Florida, and Hawaii have patented soilless media systems for growing paspalum sod by this method. Paspalum produced with this system is highly adaptable for use with any of the sports turf modified field construction/renovation systems discussed in Chapter 12.

This technology is becoming increasingly important for international shipments of sod or sprigs for construction of golf courses and sports fields. Sod grown on plastic is easily washed to free the root system of all growing media and to meet the variable quarantine requirements of each importing country. Since the sod was not grown in native soils, biotic concerns (nematodes, weeds, insects, diseases) are minimized and the sod or sprigs can be easily treated with the appropriate pesticides designated by the importing country prior to shipment and upon arrival at the port of entry. Freight charges are reduced since the rooting medium has been removed.

14.3. SOD NETTING

The finer-leaf textured paspalums have more rhizomes and tend to hold together better than the old Adalayd (intermediate texture) or coarse-textured ecotypes. Occasionally, turf netting may need to be established prior to planting paspalum sprigs. Sod wrap may be needed on big roll shipments by trucks over long distances to reduce dessication. A complete "anaerobic" wrap to limit oxygen exchange apparently inhibits high temperature buildup that is caused by high microbial and grass respiration rates.

Products and distribution companies that can be used in the sod operation include:

Radix	Tenax Corporation, Baltimore, MD
SodNet®, Sod Wrap®	Conwed Plastics, Athens, GA and
	Bucyrus Equipment Co., Hillsdale, KS
Tamanet	Tamanet (USA) Inc., Fullerton, CA
Turfnit®	Delmarva Textile Co. Inc., Milford, DE

14.4. HYDROSPRIGGING

Because of its high rate of establishment and high volume of nodes for rooting, paspalum sprigs can be chopped up and run through hydrospriggers for rapid planting. Coral Creek Golf Course on Oahu, Hawaii was successfully established with this planting technique using Salam paspalum (Southern Turf).

A new sprig planter (Sprig Master II®) developed by Grimsley Sprigging Service, Parrott, Georgia, takes sod rolls or sod pieces and breaks them into individual sprigs that are planted 2-in. (50 mm) apart and rolled in one simultaneous operation. The unit is pulled by a small tractor and will plant small areas (>1000 ft²) very efficiently. A larger sprig planting machine is available from either Grimsley Sprigging Service in Georgia or from Southern Turf (Woerner Sports Turf) in Alabama for renovation of sports fields or fairways.

14.5. SOD REGROWTH

Depending on soil depth of previous harvest and management prior to harvest that promotes deep rooting, paspalum harvested for sod may need narrow strips (2–3 in.) left in the field. These strips would need to be rototilled using 2 to 3 different directions to uniformly spread sprig/node volume across the field. The soil profile should be kept moist during the two week reestablishment phase to ensure proper root initiation and beginning growth. Fertilizer formulations for the first month of regrowth should be 1:2:3 or 1:2:4 ratios in order to maintain adequate P and K levels in the soil for rooting. Grow-in, when stolons start extending, can include N fertilizers, especially $Ca(NO_3)_2$ for immediate (within 24 hours) paspalum growth responses. Weekly applications of a to 2 lb/1000 ft² of this highly soluble N source should be adequate for grow-in (2–3 months duration) and also be environmentally sound management.

14.6. SHELF LIFE

Precise research studies have not been conducted on paspalum sprig or sod shelf life after harvest. Practical experiences of some sod companies have shown that sprigs can be shipped internationally in refrigerated (45°F or 7–8°C) containers for five days with good results. In unrefrigerated cardboard boxes, temperatures should be kept below 100°F

(<38°C) if possible, or the boxes wrapped with plastic to create anaerobic conditions, which will minimize heat buildup in the green vegetative material that is packed tightly in an enclosed space (Earl Elsner, personal communication). Shipments can be sent air freight as long as the sprigs are not left in open warehouses with temperatures >80°F (25°C) for more than one day. Spraying with a growth regulator such as Primo® may be beneficial 1–2 days prior to harvest. All sprigs should be planted within five days of shipment into *moist* soil and should be irrigated frequently to minimize drying out for a minimum of 7–10 days.

14.7. MOWING

Mowing height for sod production should be maintained at 1 to 2 in. For sprig production, higher mowing heights are acceptable and will provide a higher node volume than shorter mowing heights. Southern Turf on Oahu, Hawaii maintains their sprig nursery of Salam paspalum at heights greater than 3 in. (75 mm).

14.8. CASE STUDY: ECOSHORES, INC., PORT ORANGE, FLORIDA

Mid-Florida, coastal location. Native sandy soils. Irrigation 2–4 times daily for 5–10 minutes per application, depending on seasons and rainfall (about 90 inches annually). Uses ocean water (25,000–36,000 ppm salts) an average of 3–5 times weekly (300 gal/ac/day) for weed control.

Weekly applications of 5-16-16 at 1 lb/1000 ft^2/application. Applies 8% iron chelate every 7 days. Spikes (3–4 in. deep) and verticuts 1–2 times weekly. Mows once per week at $3/4$ in. height; lightly rolls every 3 weeks after spiking. Application of Cleary's 3336 about one week prior to shipment of sprigs internationally for systemic disease (fusarium) preventive control.

14.9. PESTICIDE USE ON SOD FARMS

Herbicides that are noninjurous to paspalum, and fungicides and insecticides that are labeled for use on sod farms can be found in Table 14.1. Since few chemicals are specifically labeled for *Paspalum vaginatum* use, check each label for their general or specific use category in turf.

Table 14.1. Pesticides Registered for Use on Turfgrass Sod Farms That Are Safe to Use on Seashore Paspalum[a]

Common Name	Trade Name	Distributor
Herbicides		
Bentazon	Basegran	BASF
	Lescogran	Lesco
2,4-D+MCPP+	Trimec Southern	PBI/Gordon
dicamba	Lesco 3-way	Lesco
ethofumesate	Prograss	Lesco, AgEvo
halosulfuron	Manage	Monsanto, Lesco
pendimethalin	Weedgrass	Lesco
	Pre-M, Control	
isoxaben	Gallery	Dow Elanco
dithiopyr	Dimension	Rohm & Haas
oxadiazon	Ronstar G	Rhone Poulenc
glyphosate (Dormant)	Round up	Monsanto
grass		
Fungicides		
azoxystrobin	Heritage	Lesco
fenarimol	Patchwork	Riverdale
forsetyl-a	Prodigy	Lesco
mancozeb	mancozeb	Lesco
	Dithane, Fore	Rohn & Haas
PCNB	Revere	Lesco
	Turfcide, Terraclor	UniRoyal
	Engage	United Hort.
thiophante-methyl	Cavalier	Lesco
vinclozolin	Curalan	BASF
	Touche	Lesco
fenarimol	Rubigan	Dow Elanco
	Rubigan AS	Lesco
aluminum tris	Aliette Signature	Rhone Poulenc
chlorothalonil	Manicure	Lesco
	Terra Thalonil	Terra Int'l
flotolanial	Prostar	Lesco
fosetyl-aluminum	Terra Aliette	Terra Int'l
ipredione	26 GT Flo	Rhone Poulenc
propiconizole	Banner Maxx	Lesco
iproclione	Chipco GT	Lesco
triadimefon	Accost	United Hort.
zerotol	Zerotol	Biosafe Systems

Common Name	Trade Name	Distributor
Insecticides		
acephate	Velocity, Orthene	Valent
	Acephate Pro	Lesco
acephak	Pinpoint	Valent
Bacillus	Xen Tari	Abbott
thuringiensis aizawai		
Bt kurstaki	Dipel	Abbott
bifenthrin	Talstar	FMC
Myrothecium	Ditera	Abbott
verrucaria		
chlorpyrifos	Dursban	Dow Elanco, Lesco
halofenozide	Mach 2	Lesco, Rohmid
pyriproxyfen	Distance	Valent

[a] Since only granular Ronstar® herbicide is specifically labeled for use on *Paspalum vaginatum* turf, check the label for each chemical as to whether it is for general or specific turf use.
Adapted from Anonymous, 1998.

14.10. PASPALUM DISTRIBUTORS

A listing of paspalum sod/sprig growers on a worldwide basis can be found in Table 14.2. The available specific cultivars are listed by location.

14.11. SOD BENEFITS

Erosion control on construction sites and roadside slopes is difficult. Man-made erosion control materials such as wood excelsior, woven-mesh jute fabric, coconut fiber blanket, coconut strand mats and natural products like oat or wheat straw are supposed to dissipate the energy of falling rain, prevent soil particle detachment and erosion (sediment movement), and provide for maximum infiltration of rainfall into the soil profile. Turfgrass sod is the only material that delays the start of runoff, greatly decreases total rainfall runoff volume, has the lowest runoff rates (30%), maintains the highest infiltration rates, and significantly reduces total soil losses (Krenisky et al., 1998). Seashore paspalum could be an alternative grass choice for many sites, including low boggy sites and drainage throughways.

Table 14.2. Distributors of Seashore Paspalum

Adalayd	Vivaio Azara S. Barbara, Cagliari, Sardinia
Adalayd	Vivaio Bindi, Km 21 S.S. Aurelia, Rome, Italy
Adalayd	Pacific Sod, Camarillo, CA
Adalayd	Coastal Turf, Bay City, TX
Salam	Southern Turf, Oahu, HI; Elberta, AL; Punta Gorda, FL; Cairo, Egypt email: drobts@ix.netcom.com web: www. woernersports.com
Durban CC	Superlawn CC., Cramond, Natal SA. email: topcrop@lantic.co.za web: www.superlawn.co.za
Saltene	The Turf Farm, Perth, WA, Australia
Saltene	Wanneroo Turf Farm, Perth, WA, Australia
Salam	Abd El-Ghaffar Farms, Cairo, Egypt
Futurf	Speedeshe, Gilgal Jericho valley, 90674 Israel
Futurf	Levy Brothers, Moshav Yashresh 46, Israel
Futurf	Marvadeshe, Kibbutz Givat Brenner, 60948 Israel
Futurf	Kibbutz Ssammar, Eilot 88815 Israel
Futurf	Deshe Mukhan Gaash 60950 Israel
Sea Isle 1	
Sea Isle 2000	Georgia Seed Development Commission, Athens, GA

Part IV

Basic Principles When Using Alternative Water Resources/Problem Sites

CHAPTER 15

Influence of Irrigation Water Quality on Turfgrass Fertilization

Irrigation water applied to turfgrass sites may come from many sources—**groundwater, surface water, reclaimed (effluent, wastewater) water,** and even seawater. Seawater presents the ultimate management challenge and is discussed in Chapter 16. Chemical constituents in irrigation water can have pronounced effects on turfgrasses, especially when the source is of poor quality. In this chapter, the most common potential nutrient or element problems due to deficiencies, excessive (toxic) levels, or imbalances are addressed.

15.1. SALT-RELATED WATER QUALITY ISSUES

A complete **irrigation water analysis** is essential. If water quality parameters change over a year or season, then sampling and testing must be done more often. Surface water sources and irrigation water from wells with potential for salt-water intrusion are very likely to exhibit variation from wet to dry periods. All irrigation water sources should be tested for the chemical characteristics listed in Tables 15.1 and 15.2.

Most of the chemical characteristics in Table 15.1 pertain to **total salinity problems** (ECw, TDS); potential to cause **sodic soil conditions** with poor soil physical properties (SARw, adj SARw, RSC, SARw-ECw interactions); potential to cause soil accumulation of **specific toxic ions** that may result in excessive shoot uptake with injury or direct root toxicities (Na, Cl, B); or specific ion toxicity to foliage in contact with the irrigation water. Carrow and Duncan (1998) provide an in-depth study on the total salinity, Na^+ permeability hazard, and problems related to specific ions that may be toxic in certain situations. Some of these chemical characteristics of water (Table 15.1) also have an influence on turfgrass fertilization and nutrition; namely:

Table 15.1. Guidelines for Irrigation Water Quality: Total Salinity, Na Permeability Hazard, and Ion Toxicity Problems.

Chemical Characteristics	Degree of Restriction on Use		
	None	Slight to Moderate	Severe
General Water Characteristics			
• pH		———NA———	
• Hardness (grains per gallon)	0–200	200–300	>300
• Bicarbonate (HCO_3) (mg L^{-1})	Depends on RSC Value		
• Carbonate (CO_3) (mg L^{-1})	Depends on RSC Value		
Total Salinity (Impact on Plant Growth)			
• EC_w (dSm^{-1}) <0.7 (electrical conductivity)	0.7–3.0	>3.0	
• TDS (mg L^{-1})[a] <450 (total dissolved salts) (total soluble salts)	450–2000	>2000	
Sodium Hazard (Na Permeability Hazard)			
• SAR_w or adj SAR_w (meq L^{-1}) (2:1 clay) <6 (sodium adsorption ratio) (1:1 clay) <16	6–9 16–24		>9 >24
• RSC (meq L^{-1}) <0 (residual sodium carbonate)	0 to 2.50	>2.50	

• SAR$_w$ and EC$_w$ Relationships on Water Infiltration into Soil.			
SAR$_w$ = 0–3 and EC$_w$ =	>0.7	0.7–0.2	<0.2
SAR$_w$ = 3–6 and EC$_w$ =	>1.2	1.2–0.3	<0.3
SAR$_w$ = 6–12 and EC$_w$ =	>1.9	1.9–0.5	<0.5
SAR$_w$ = 12–20 and EC$_w$ =	>2.9	2.9–1.3	<1.3
SAR$_w$ = 20–40 and EC$_w$ =	>5.0	5.0–2.9	<2.9
Ion Toxicity (Soil Accumulation and Root Toxicity) (Sensitive Plants)[b]			
• Na (mg L^{-1})	0–70	70–210	>210
• Cl (mg L^{-1})	0–70	70–355	>355
• B (mg L^{-1})	<0.7	0.7–3.0	>3.0
Ion Toxicity (Foliage Contact) (Sensitive Plants)[b]			
• Na (mg L^{-1})	0–70	>70	
• Cl (mg L^{-1})	0–90	0–100	>100
• HCO$_3$ (mg L^{-1})	0–90	90–500	>500
(unsightly foliage deposits)			

[a] 1 mg L^{-1} = 1 ppm.

[b] Sensitive trees and shrubs. Turfgrasses can tolerate levels above those noted for trees and shrubs.

Source: Westcot and Ayers (1984) and Eaton (1950).

Table 15.2. Guidelines for Nutrients Contained in Irrigation Water and Quantities That May Be Applied per Foot of Irrigation Water

Nutrient or Element	Nutrient Content in Water in mg L^{-1} (or ppm)				Conversion to lb per 1000 ft^2 of nutrient added for every 12 in. of irrigation water applied
	Low	Normal	High	Very High	
N	<1.1	1.1–11.3	11.3–22.6	>22.6	11.3 ppm N = 0.71 lb N per 1000 ft^2
NO_3^-	<5	5–50	50–100	>100	50 ppm NO_3^- = 0.71 lb N per 1000 ft^2
P	<0.1	0.1–0.4	0.4–0.8	>0.8	0.4 ppm P = 0.057 lb P_2O_5 per 1000 ft^2
PO_4^-	<0.30	0.30–1.21	1.21–2.42	>2.42	1.21 ppm PO_4^- = 0.057 lb P_2O_5 per 1000 ft^2
P_2O_5	<0.23	0.23–0.92	0.92–1.83	>1.83	0.92 ppm P_2O_5 = 0.057 lb P_2O_5 per 1000 ft^2
K	<5	5–20	20–30	>30	20 ppm K = 1.5 lb K_2O per 1000 ft^2
K_2O	<6	6–24	24–36	>36	24 ppm K_2O = 1.5 lb K_2O per 1000 ft^2
Ca	<20	20–60	60–80	>80	60 ppm Ca = 3.75 lb Ca per 1000 ft^2
Mg	<10	10–25	25–35	>35	25 ppm Mg = 1.56 lb Mg per 1000 ft^2
S	<10	10–30	30–60	>60	30 ppm S = 1.87 lb S per 1000 ft^2
SO_4	<30	30–90	90–180	>180	90 ppm SO_4^- = 1.87 lb S per 1000 ft^2
Mn	—	—	>0.2[a]	—	
Fe	—	—	>5.0[a]	—	
Cu	—	—	>0.2[a]	—	
Zn	—	—	>2.0[a]	—	
Mo	—	—	>0.01[a]	—	
Ni	—	—	>0.2[a]	—	

[a] These values are based on potential toxicity problems that may *arise over long-term use* of the irrigation water, especially for sensitive plants in the landscape—turfgrasses can often tolerate higher levels. For fertilization, higher rates than these can be applied as foliar treatment without problems.

Sources: Based on Westcot and Ayers (1984) and Harvandi (1994).

Water pH

The water pH can alter soil surface pH and thatch pH over time. Soil nutrients are most readily available at soil pH 6.0 to 7.5. However, the chemical constituents that cause irrigation water to exhibit a pH outside of this range are more important than pH by itself.

Bicarbonates and Carbonates

High bicarbonates are relatively common in reclaimed water and in some groundwater. While HCO_3^- >500 ppm can cause unsightly, but not harmful, deposits on foliage of plants, HCO_3^- or CO_3^{-2} levels that result in turf nutritional problems are not specific. Instead it is the imbalance of HCO_3^- and CO_3^{-2} with Na^+, Ca^{+2}, and Mg^{+2} that is most important. When $HCO_3^- + CO_3^{-2}$ levels exceed $Ca^{+2} + Mg^{+2}$ levels (in meq L^{-1}), the Ca^{+2} and Mg^{+2} are precipitated as lime in the soil and as scale in irrigation lines. Two problems can arise from excess lime precipitation:

- If Na^+ is moderately high (>150 ppm), removal of soluble Ca and Mg by precipitation into the relatively insoluble carbonate forms will leave Na^+ to dominate the soil CEC sites and potentially create a sodic (soil structural deterioration) condition. High Na^+ on the CEC sites will depress availability of Mg, K, and Ca. Acidification of irrigation water is the normal management option for this situation.
- On sandy soils, the calcite (lime) may start to seal some of the macropores and reduce water infiltration. With light, frequent irrigation, the surface may be the site of sealing while under heavier, less frequent irrigation, a calcite layer may form deeper in the profile at the depth of irrigation water penetration. This problem is only somewhat serious under the combination of high HCO_3/CO_3 + high Ca, Mg + arid climate + sandy soil profile. The sealing can be broken up by a combination of cultivation (aeration) and use of acidic fertilizers or elemental S. Since it is confined primarily to greens, acidifying the irrigation water for a whole golf course would be an expensive option. In contrast, when high Na^+ is present that would be a problem on all areas and for all soil types, irrigation water acidification is more feasible and beneficial.

The RSC (residual sodium carbonate) value is used to determine the potential for either of these problems where RSC = $(HCO_3 + CO_3) - (Ca + Mg)$, in meq L^{-1} (Table 15.1).

Root Toxicities from Na, Cl, B

While the guidelines for root toxicities or soil accumulation of these ions in Table 15.1 are most appropriate for sensitive trees and shrubs, excessive levels of Na^+ can cause turfgrass root deterioration at higher levels than noted in the table.

Excess Na^+ can displace Ca^{+2} in the cell wall membranes of root tissues and cause root deterioration. Turfgrasses with low to moderate salinity tolerance often are susceptible to this type of root injury, which then results in roots that are less effective for nutrient and water uptake. Calcium in a relatively soluble form (not lime) in the root zone corrects this Na toxicity (i.e., in reality, a Ca^{+2} deficiency in the root tissues), especially with leaching to remove the excess Na. Foliar application of Ca is not effective since Ca is the least mobile nutrient and is not translocated from the shoot to root tissues.

High Cl does not cause direct turfgrass root tissue injury except at very high levels that are well above the guidelines in Table 15.1 for more sensitive plants. Instead, Cl inhibits water uptake and, thereby, nutrient uptake. More importantly, high Cl^- may reduce NO_3^- uptake. If the irrigation source has a consistently high Cl^- content, then N rates may need to be increased by 10 to 25%, with NO_3^- forms preferred.

Treatment of reclaimed water may leave excess **residual chlorine** (which is Cl_2), a highly reactive form. At greater than 1 mg L^{-1} residual chlorine, foliage damage can occur. After a few hours in a holding pond, Cl_2 dissipates into the air. Residual chlorine would be listed as a separate item on a reclaimed water quality test since it is not the same as Cl^- ions.

Boron toxicities can be a problem on turfgrasses, especially in arid regions. Injury is expressed as a leaf tip and margin chlorosis. Mowing of turfgrasses aids in reducing B accumulation in tissues but at B soil levels > 6.0 mg kg^+ (saturated paste extract), injury may occur. Kentucky bluegrass is most sensitive at > 2.0 mg kg^{-1}. Irrigation water containing > 3.0 mg L^- B may result in soil accumulation. Except on acid sands, leaching of B is difficult. Boron moves slowly with the soil water and requires three times more leaching fraction than would be needed to reduce an equivalent amount of chloride salinity (Ayers and Westcot, 1989).

Total Salinity and Sodium Permeability Hazard

The presence in the irrigation water of excess total salts or high Na that may induce a sodic condition will necessitate extra water application for leaching. This will result in **leaching of all nutrients** to a greater degree and require higher nutrient availability levels, especially on sandy soils. Fertilizers are not applied at higher rates than normal with each application. But fertilization is more frequent, using a "spoon-feeding" or prescription approach so that annual rates are 10 to 50% higher. Slow release nutrient forms can be incorporated using a spoon-feeding philosophy to aid in maintaining adequate levels.

When high Na^+ content in irrigation water requires appreciable Ca^{+2} to be supplied to replace Na^+ from the CEC sites, **extra Mg and K** will be needed to maintain adequate soil test levels and nutrient balances. Light, more frequent applications are better than heavier but infrequent treatments.

A special case of "leaching" involves ultra-pure water such as from snow-melt sources and after monsoon rains. The $SAR_w - EC_w$ relationships in Table 15.1 indicate when infiltration is restricted by irrigation water that is very low in salts. Gypsum and $CaCl_2$ injection can increase salt content (i.e., EC_w) sufficiently to allow for better infiltration, but these water sources are also likely to cause greater leaching of nutrients over time, without adding appreciable nutrients except Ca, SO_4^{-2}, and Cl^-. Thus, higher fertilization rates may be necessary, particularly on sandy soils.

15.2. NUTRIENT CONTRIBUTION ISSUES

In addition to the chemical characteristics in Table 15.1, a number of nutrients may be present in irrigation water, especially reclaimed water, that can affect turfgrasses and landscape plants (Table 15.2). The quantities of these nutrients have a major influence on the fertilization program. Important considerations with respect to the **macronutrients** (N, P, K, Ca, Mg, S) are included in Table 15.2.

Macronutrients

Nitrogen

The quantity of N added over time in the irrigation source will directly contribute to the needs of turfgrass and other landscape plants receiving irrigation. Thus, supplemental N fertilization must be adjusted accordingly and turfgrasses should be used that can tolerate the levels applied. Some turfgrasses deteriorate rapidly when overfertilized with N, such as red fescues and centipedegrass. On golf greens, high N in the water may produce more growth than desired, especially if the total annual N exceeds 4 to 6 lb N per 1000 ft^2 (*Poa annua* or bentgrass) or 8 to 12 lb N per 1000 ft^2 (bermudagrass). If irrigation water containing even 1.1 ppm N is stored in ponds, algae and aquatic plant growth may flourish. Barley straw is an effective management option (Gaussoin, 1999). Copper sulfate can also be added to ponds to control algae.

Phosphorus

The limits on P in irrigation water are lower than other macronutrients because low P is a limiting factor for algae and aquatic plants. Excessive P that reaches ponds, lakes, or streams can markedly increase growth of these plants. Thus, turfgrasses can easily tolerate annual P additions up to 2.0 lb P$_2$O$_5$ per 1000 ft^2 from irrigation water, but aquatic plants would be greatly stimulated if this P-ladened water reached streams or ponds. The combination of high N plus P would also be most detrimental in causing eutrophication (lack of dissolved O$_2$ in water). If steps are taken to prevent lake or stream water contamination by P from the irrigation source, higher P levels can be tolerated. But, if soil levels of P build up over time, P may reach waterways by leaching or runoff. Buffer strips may be needed for transitioning into environmentally sensitive areas.

Potassium

Since recreational sites require ample K, any K in irrigation water is often viewed as beneficial. If K is high in reclaimed water, adequate Ca and Mg are normally available to prevent any nutrient imbalances, but K will contribute to overall total salinity.

Calcium

Potential problems from high Ca were addressed in the section on "Bicarbonates and Carbonates." Turfgrass managers should be aware of the total Ca added by the water source since groundwater, surface water, reclaimed water, and even rainwater (1 to 8 ppm Ca) all provide Ca. As noted in Table 15.2, 60 ppm Ca would add 3.75 lb Ca per 1000 ft^2 per 12 in. irrigation water (equivalent to 16 lb CaCO$_3$). Thus, rainwater at 8 ppm Ca would add 0.50 lb Ca per 1000 ft^2 (2.2 lb CaCO$_3$ equivalent) per 12 in. rain. Some consultants have recommended foliar Ca or granular Ca fertilization to most turf sites in recent years. This is a questionable practice unless:

- Very high soil Na$^+$ (sodic soil) or Al^{+3} [excessively acid (pH < 4.8)] conditions exist. In both cases, these ions can replace Ca^{+2} from root tissues and soil CEC sites to the point where Ca^{+2} deficiency in the *root* tissues causes root deterioration. Even under these conditions, shoot tissue Ca^{+2} deficiency symptoms have not been documented on turfgrass, which are highly efficient in Ca uptake.
- Unusually high Mg additions or naturally high Mg soil levels may require Ca fertilization. However, the primary response from adding Ca is better soil physical properties since Ca is a better soil colloid aggregating agent than Mg.
- Low pH (< 6.0) soils benefit from lime amendments to adjust pH to within pH 6.0 to 7.5 for better availability of nutrients in general—but, Ca itself is adequate for turfgrasses even at very low pHs until the point of Al^{+3} toxicity arises. However, on acidic soils with pH < 5.5, a rapid greening response after lime or gypsum application is not unusual. This response is due to creating more favorable conditions for *Nitrosomonas* and *Nitrobacter* stimulation, which transform NH$_4^+$ into NO$_3^-$. Many grasses prefer NO$_3^-$ and respond to enhanced NO$_3^-$ availability (i.e., greening response). These soil bacteria activities are limited at low pH primarily because of low Ca and not to low pH itself.

Problems that may occur from applying Ca when not required include (a) the potential to enhance Mg or K deficiencies (two nutrients that can be deficient in turfgrasses), and (b) causing confusion by emphasizing a problem that does not exist except in special cases. Ethical and economical issues may arise when recommending a nutrient amendment that is often added normally by irrigation sources in abundant quantity.

Magnesium

Most often Mg is present in irrigation water at lower levels than Ca. Sometimes Mg content will be relatively high (ocean water or blends with ocean water), which can reduce Ca^{+2} on CEC sites and restrict K availability. In these cases, supplemental Ca may be needed to maintain adequate Ca for soil physical conditions and to counter Na^+ toxicities. Seawater has a high Mg content. So salt water intrusion sites may exhibit this problem. Also, supplemental K will be necessary to maintain ample K nutrition.

More often than excess Mg, low Mg content in irrigation water is a problem, i.e., low Mg caused by the addition of high Ca applications using irrigation water that has too much Na. Another problem of increasing frequency is Mg deficiency induced by application of unneeded Ca on sandy sites. As with Ca, knowledge about Mg content and rates applied in the irrigation water are very useful in avoiding deficiencies or excessive Mg problems.

Sulfur

It is not unusual for SO_4^- content in reclaimed water to be 100 to 200 ppm and groundwater influenced by seawater intrusion may be even higher (seawater contains about 2600 ppm SO_4^-). Sulfur deficiencies may occur with high rainfall. Sandy soils that do not receive SO_4^- from rainfall due to their location relative to industrial activity can be deficient. Normally 2 or 3 lb S per 1000 ft^2 per year is sufficient for turfgrasses and this is often provided by SO_4^{-2} content in N, K, or Ca fertilizers. Irrigation water at 200 ppm SO_4^{-2} would supply 4.2 lb S per 1000 ft^2 per 12 in. water.

The primary problem of high SO_4^{-2} additions onto turfgrass sites occurs with anaerobic conditions, which transform SO_4^{-2} into reduced S. Reduced S can react with reduced forms of Fe and Mn to create FeS and MnS compounds that are contributors to black layer and results in further anaerobic conditions and sealing of soil pores. Thus, a high S level is normally not the initial cause of an anaerobic condition, but it will greatly amplify the condition.

When SO_4^{-2} content is above desirable levels in irrigation water, the application of lime to the soil at low rates can "scrub" SO_4^{-2} from the system. As SO_4^{-2} reacts with Ca from the lime, gypsum ($CaSO_4$) is formed. In this form, S is protected from becoming reduced and is much less soluble. Application of 10 lb $CaCO_3$ per 1000 ft^2 provides about 3.8 lb Ca that can react with 9.1 lb SO_4^{-2}, which is equivalent to 3 lb S per 1000 ft^2. Thus, for every 3 lb elemental S (or the equivalent rate of 9.1 lb SO_4^{-2}) added with irrigation water, 3.8 lb Ca will remove the S through gypsum formation. The Ca can come from the irrigation water itself but if this is not sufficient, lime can be added to the soil surface to remove the remainder.

Micronutrients

In addition to macronutrients in irrigation water, **micronutrients** (Fe, Mn, Cu, Zn, Mo, Ni, B) can affect turfgrass fertilization (Table 15.2). Common interactions and management options include the following:

Iron (Fe)

The 5.0 mg L^{-1} guideline in Table 15.2 for Fe in irrigation water is not related to any potential "toxic level" but to continuous use that could cause (a) precipitation of P and Mo and contribute to deficiency problems for turfgrasses (P) or landscape plants (P or Mo), (b) staining on plants, sidewalks, buildings, and equipment, (c) potential plugging of irrigation pipes by anaerobic Fe sludge deposits, which can be a problem at >1.5 mg L^{-1} Fe, and (d) high, continuous rates of Fe that may induce Mn deficiency or, much less likely, Zn and Cu deficiencies. On heavily leached sands, where Mn content is often low, this may become a problem. At 5.0 mg L^{-1} Fe, 12 in. of irrigation water would add 0.31 lb Fe per 1000 ft^2, while a typical foliar application is 0.025 lb Fe per 1000 ft^2 but in only 3 to 4 gal water per 1000 ft^2. In most instances, Fe concentrations are low and turfgrasses will respond to foliar Fe. When total salinity is high, Fe plus a cytokinin as a foliar treatment is often beneficial, since salt-stressed plants exhibit low cytokinin activity. Increased cytokinin concentration can enhance root production in salt-stressed turf plants with low to moderate levels of salt tolerance. If possible, excess Fe should be precipitated and filtered out before it enters an irrigation system (Ayers, and Westcot, 1985). Iron can be oxidized to an insoluble form by (1) chlorinating to a residual concentration of 1 ppm chlorine, (2) aerating in an open holding pond, or (3) mechanically injecting air into the water supply.

Manganese (Mn)

Manganese can become toxic to roots of many plants, so use of water high in Mn (0.20 mg L^{-1}) can contribute to this problem, especially on poorly drained, acidic soils. Acidic, anaerobic conditions transform soil Mn into more soluble (i.e., toxic) forms. If water is high in Mn, liming to pH 6.0 to 7.5 and providing good drainage greatly reduces the potential for Mn toxicities. At >1.5 mg L^{-1} Mn in irrigation water, Mn can contribute to sludge formation within irrigation lines. Also, high Mn may inhibit Fe uptake and promote Fe deficiency. Supplemental foliar Fe would prevent this problem.

Copper (Cu), Zinc (Zn), Nickel (Ni)

The irrigation water levels in Table 15.2 are based on potential to develop toxicities on sensitive landscape plants over time. Turfgrasses can tolerate relatively high rates due to mowing of leaf tips where these elements tend to accumulate. Unusually high Cu and Zn could inhibit Fe or Mn uptake and, thereby, induce deficiencies of these nutrients, even on grasses.

Molybdenum (Mo)

Molybdenum toxicity would be very unlikely in turf plants, but livestock feeding on grasses high in Mo can be affected. Mo deficiency can occasionally occur on low pH sites.

Boron (B)

Boron problems were addressed in an earlier section related to Table 15.1.

Other Trace Elements

Reclaimed water may contain excessive levels of some elements. These are reported by Westcot and Ayers (1984) and Snow (1994). These elements would not directly influence turfgrass nutrition but would be of concern for toxicities on some landscape plants.

In summary, chemical constituents in irrigation water will be added to the turfgrass soil on a consistent, long-term basis. Knowledge of the added quantities is essential to make adjustments in the fertilization regimes to avoid excessive amounts and nutritional imbalances, and to minimize environmental concerns. Irrigation water sources with high concentrations of chemicals will cause the most problems.

CHAPTER *16*

Seawater Irrigation: Turfgrass Management for the Ultimate Water Quality Problem

The development of high quality seashore paspalums (*Paspalum vaginatum*) for golf greens, tees, and fairways that have excellent salinity tolerance creates the **opportunity for irrigation with straight seawater** or with seawater as a high percentage of the blended irrigation water (Duncan, 1999). Also, the increasing frequency of **salt water intrusion** into coastal aquifers is resulting in unintentional application of seawater onto golf courses. Carrow and Duncan (1998) provide an in-depth treatment on the assessment and management of salt-affected turfgrass sites with much of the material relevant to areas receiving seawater irrigation. However, the extreme case of poor water quality beyond that presented by Carrow and Duncan (1998) requires additional considerations.

An article in *Scientific American* on "Irrigating Crops with Seawater" highlights some of the potential advantages and pitfalls of this water resource. They note that (a) halophytes (salt-tolerant plants) must be used, and over 2000 to 3000 species of halophytes (including *Paspalum vaginatum* for turfgrass) are available, (b) the practice is most feasible on sandy, well drained coastal sites for long-term sustainability, (c) irrigation must be sufficient to leach salts and prevent dry-down of the surface that can concentrate salts in the root-zone, (d) salts must be removed by drainage to sites that are not impacted negatively by supplementation with this concentrated salt resource, (e) pumping costs are increased due to greater irrigation needs, but are somewhat offset by shallow wells near the coast with minimal water lifting requirements, and (f) potential influences on coastal aquatic sites should be evaluated. These and other topics will be discussed in the context of turfgrasses in the following sections on preconstruction, establishment, and after-establishment issues.

16.1. PRECONSTRUCTION

Mistakes or omissions in the preconstruction planning period will become rapidly apparent and amplified once a grass is planted. Management of a salt-affected site when the irrigation source is seawater is considered the most complex situation a turfgrass manager will confront. Preplanning is essential, especially if fresh water sources could be compromised.

Irrigation Water Quality Assessment

Quality of seawater is relatively consistent by location and over time (Table 16.1), but sometimes can vary, especially in brackish sites. A good water quality test will determine the specific chemical constituents at the irrigation source inlet. However, if water is obtained from a well, rather than through a direct inlet from the ocean, water quality may vary considerably over time. This is especially a problem on salt water intrusion areas where the salt water may encroach and retreat with dry and wet periods, respectively. Intrusion of salt water into a well head can occur rather abruptly. On these sites, a continuous water quality testing program will be necessary to monitor changes over time, while direct seawater irrigation should not exhibit appreciable fluctuations in quality. Also, seawater drawn from wells may be influenced by soil conditions and exhibit higher bicarbonates (HCO_3^-) or different levels of other constituents (i.e., B) than direct seawater.

Grass Selection

Seawater salinity is about an EC_w (electrical conductivity of water) of 54 dSm^{-1} or 34,440 ppm total salts (Table 16.1). Soil salinity is also measured by electrical conductivity and is expressed as EC_e, where the soil surface EC_e normally equilibrates to the irrigation water EC_w under leaching conditions. For many years, Tifway bermudagrass was the grass of choice for sites up to EC_e = of 20 to 25 dSm^{-1}, which is the 50% growth reduction level for this grass. Adalayd seashore paspalum (SP) was the only commercial cultivar of paspalum until recently and it had inferior quality traits compared to Tifway with only marginally better salinity tolerance. Some SP ecotypes originating from Sea Island, Georgia have been moved onto various golf courses in Hawaii with good success under high salinity situations.

Table 16.1. Typical Seawater Quality Analysis and Interpretation of Results

Chemical Measurement	Seawater Test Result[a]	Severity of Problem/Comments[b]
Total Salinity Status (Saline Soil)		
EC_w (dSm^{-1})	54	>3.00 very high for plants[c]
TDS (ppm)	34,486	>2000 very high for plants[c]
Sodium Permeability Hazard (Sodic Soil)		
SAR	57.4	>26 probable on kaolinite, Fe/Al oxides
		>10 probable on sands, 2:1 Clays
RSC	−125.5	<0 acceptable
Toxic Ions (Soil Accumulation for Shoot Uptake and Root Toxicity for Sensitive Plants)		
Na (mg L^{-1})	10,556	>210 severe for sensitive plants
Cl (mg L^{-1})	18,980	>355 severe for sensitive plants
B (mg L^{-1})	0	>3.0 severe for sensitive plants
Toxic Ions (Direct Foliage Injury for Sensitive Plants)		
Na (mg L^{-1})	10,556	>70 moderate
Cl (mg L^{-1})	18,980	>100 moderate
HCO$_3$ (deposits)	146	>500 severe deposition
Other		
HCO$_3$ (mg L^{-1})	146	>500 severe deposition on leaves
CO$_3$ (mg L^{-1})	<1	—
Nutrients		
Ca (mg L^{-1})	420	equals 26.2 lb Ca/1000 ft^2 per 12 in. water
Mg (mg L^{-1})	1304	equals 81.4 lb Mg/1000 ft^2 per 12 in. water
K (mg L^{-1})	390	equals 24.3 lb K/1000 ft^2 per 12 in. water
		equals 29.1 lb K$_2$O/1000 ft^2 per 12 in. water
SO$_4$ (mg L^{-1})	2690	equals 168.0 lb SO$_4$/1000 ft^2 per 12 in. water
		equals 55.4 lb S/1000 ft^2 per 12 in. water

[a] Typical values for seawater.
[b] Based on criteria in Carrow and Duncan (1998).
[c] Only halophytes can tolerate these levels.

The golf green ecotype SP (Sea Isle 2000) and fairway or tee type (Sea Isle 1) from the breeding/genetics program of Dr. R.R. Duncan were selected not only for high quality traits but for very high salinity tolerance (54 dSm^{-1}). By combining inherently high growth rates/vigor under low salinity with high salinity tolerance, these grasses can maintain adequate growth and vigor under the extreme salinity of seawater irrigation. This represents a 2 to $2^1/2$-fold increase in salinity tolerance over what Tifway or Adalayd can tolerate.

Thus, application of seawater will require use of a SP ecotype or cultivar that has salinity tolerance up to seawater. Out of 98 SP ecotypes screened for salinity tolerance, only 15 exhibited sufficient salinity tolerance for seawater irrigation, while 5 demonstrated exceptional salinity tolerance (Sea Isle 2000 was one of these, while Sea Isle 1 was within the top 15 group). This illustrates that selecting an ecotype from nature does not ensure the turf quality or salinity attributes necessary for such extreme water-use situations. (Duncan, 1998).

Besides turfgrass selection, the landscape plants must be halophytes. Landscape specialists that utilize salt-tolerant trees and shrubs and their care should be consulted early in the planning process.

Irrigation System Design

The **number one management requirement on all salt-affected sites is leaching** to remove excess salts and prevent sodium accumulation. Due to the high total salinity (34,440 ppm total salts) and high sodium (Na) content (about 10,600 ppm Na) of straight seawater, a saline-sodic soil can be created very rapidly. Therefore, the leaching requirement (LR) is even greater than for any other salt-affected sites. The LR is the quantity of water required to maintain a net downward movement of salts from the root zone in addition to the grass evapotranspiration (ET) needs. But, the ET must be corrected for efficiency of the irrigation system so that total water needs include LR + ET + correction for irrigation design inefficiency.

Two major points arise from the above facts: (a) the irrigation system must be **very well designed to ensure optimum efficiency** for uniform coverage. Otherwise, the extra water for LR plus lack of uniformity will result in excessively wet areas (overirrigation) if sufficient water is applied to leach all areas and prevent high salt buildup, especially those sites receiving less water. Design criteria must emphasize sprinkler head spacing, nozzle size (fine-textured soils may require low application rates), type of sprinkler head, and correct zoning, and (b) **ensure flexible scheduling.** Pulse irrigation is essential on any soils with low infiltration, percolation, or drainage characteristics. Pulse irrigation applies water to the turf just short of runoff, then allows for a period for infiltration/percolation, followed by repeated cycles. Since high Na buildup causes soil structural breakdown and may seal even sandy soils, a pulse approach is necessary on most sites.

Salt Disposal

Table 16.1 lists the quantities of certain salts added per foot of seawater irrigation. The 34,486 ppm total salts in ocean water is equivalent to 2153 lb salt per 1000 ft^2 per foot of seawater applied. Even a very salt-tolerant grass such as seashore paspalum will not be able to tolerate extreme salt buildup on a long-term basis without proper drainage throughout the rhizosphere. Thus, leaching from the root zone is essential, but consistent removal from the soil below the root zone is also necessary. Thus, deep sands are strongly preferred if seawater irrigation is to be applied.

With seawater irrigation, the potential need for disposal of leached salts must be considered in the design/planning stage to avoid either (a) salt accumulation below the root zone in a much more concentrated form, and/or (b) leaching or seepage of the salts into a potable water source or off-site area. Deep-tile lines (3 to 5 feet) may be required with outlet into the ocean in most cases. Since seawater is high in salts and leaching is required on a permanent basis, the long-term (i.e., 2 to 10 years) fate of salts is a serious environmental concern.

When salt leaching into a potable water aquifer is a potential problem, a well-designed drainage system to intercept salt-enriched drainage water is essential. Climates with periodic heavy rainfalls or rainy seasons following dry periods are most prone to salt leaching, especially on sandy soils. Drains on these sites must be sufficiently spaced to easily intercept vertical and lateral drainage waters. Also, installation at a 3 foot depth would assist in better salt removal versus deeper tile lines spaced further apart. On some extreme salt-sensitive sites, sand topsoil may need to be removed to a depth of 3 feet, a more impervious soil layer added to reduce water percolation rate, followed by addition of the sand topsoil and tile drainage above the soil cap layer.

Interception of salt-enriched drainage water is easier in semiarid or arid climates where the water moves more slowly through the profile. This slow movement allows more opportunity for water to reach tile lines. In these instances, deeper tile lines spaced further apart may be sufficient to protect potable groundwater supplies.

If fresh water lenses are located under the construction site, a carefully designed drainage system must be developed to minimize salt water movement into the fresh water zones and to remove the excess salts safely and efficiently away from the sensitive sites. High sand profiles will be much more difficult and expensive in designing proper drainage to minimize topical and soil profile salt water intrusion in these areas than soils with clay and silt components.

Additional Maintenance Costs

Other points to consider in the planning stage involve treatment of saline-sodic soil conditions when using seawater, which will require (a) considerable **chemical applications** (such as gypsum or acid amendments) at high rates on a continuous basis; (b) ongoing extensive surface and subsurface **cultivation programs** (*thus, the equipment*) to maintain water movement within soils for effective salt leaching. Typically, the longevity of a cultivation operation is reduced by one-half on high Na sites, thereby, increasing cultivation frequency; and (c) the **turf manager** must be well-trained to maintain high quality turf under these complex conditions. Successful turfgrass management using seawater or poor quality effluent requires (1) aggressiveness, (2) proactive (rather than reactive) decisions, and (3) flexibility to site-specific problems. Thus, initial plans should include budgeting for the enhanced management needs in terms of chemicals, equipment, and personnel. Some of these costs will be offset by fewer pest problems and a less expensive water source, but "sticker price" shock can occur when these issues are not considered.

In terms of cultivation equipment, deep-tine cultivation will be essential to enhance leaching (Verti-drain, Soil Reliever, Aerway Slicers, Deepdrill). Yeager-Twose Turf Conditioner can apply high gypsum rates at depths of 7 to 8 in. (80 to 90 lb per 1000 ft^2), which would be very beneficial with the high Na rates applied by seawater irrigation for maintaining adequate water percolation. This unit is less effective as a deep cultivation procedure than other units, but has excellent chemical injection capabilities. Deep-drill units can also be used to add gypsum in vertical channels.

Seawater Treatment

Where good quality water is limited along coastal areas, **desalinization** can be used to create high quality water (California Coastal Commission, 1999). The assumption in this chapter is that desalinization has been eliminated as an expensive option and straight seawater will be used. On many turfgrass sites with poor water quality from groundwater or wastewater sources, treatment of irrigation water is often beneficial, especially using acidification to remove excess bicarbonates (HCO_3^-) that can precipitate Ca and Mg out of the water as lime, thereby leaving Na without adequate counterions. This treatment is not necessary in seawater due to the relatively low HCO_3^- content. However, if the water is pumped from ground wells near the ocean or blended with other effluent sources, higher HCO_3^- may be observed and this water will benefit from acidification for HCO_3^- removal.

While acidification of seawater is not usually necessary for HCO_3^- removal, acidification can be a means of adding H_2SO_4 or N-phuric acid (urea sulfuric acid) to aid in formation of gypsum ($CaSO_4$) in the soil by reaction with surface applied lime ($CaCO_3$). The relatively soluble $CaSO_4$ provides Ca^{+2} to replace Na^+ on soil cation exchange sites (CEC) and to form Na_2SO_4, which can be leached. Since considerable Ca^{+2} must be applied by various means, this becomes one amendment method for utilizing the SO_4^{-2} in the water.

Another means of applying Ca^{+2} ions is to use a gypsum injector linked with the irrigation system. Finely powdered gypsum and some soluble Ca sources [$CaCl_2$, $Ca(NO_3)_2$] can be added by these means. Neither of these injection/irrigation water treatment systems are essential for seawater use but with the high Na^+ inputs, all potential means of applying or creating gypsum should be carefully considered. Carrow and Duncan (1998) provide considerable information on various chemical amendment and treatment options via the irrigation water or as direct soil applications.

Dual Water Sources

Sometimes another irrigation source of better quality will allow (a) for blending with seawater to dilute the total salts and high Na^+ levels, (b) for use to irrigate golf greens by means of dual irrigation lines, or (c) for use during periods of intense leaching. Any of these options may seem costly, but reduced requirements for gypsum can help offset the initial expense.

Since a good quality water source will be required for drinking purposes and for other industrial needs, care should be taken not to contaminate the potable water source with leached salts from seawater or poor quality effluent. A groundwater aquifer of good water quality could potentially be contaminated by salt water intrusion due to excessive water removal from the good source, or from leachate transported salt movement from above. Proper drainage, depending on soil texture, can be effectively used to minimize or prevent fresh water contamination.

Fertigation

Fertilization will be discussed in greater detail later. But, irrigation to promote leaching coupled with the use of sandy soils support the use of fertigation. Thus, the equipment for a good fertigation system is another preestablishment consideration. Highly soluble sources of fertilizer should be used (refer to Table 18.1).

Sand Capping

Leaching of salts in a sand profile is much easier than in a finer-textured soil (containing appreciable silt and clay) and requires less water to attain leaching. The "ideal" soil for seawater irrigation would be a deep sand. If the existing soil is fine-textured and has poor soil physical properties—especially low infiltration and percolation rates—sand capping can help. The application of a 6- to 12-in. sand layer (cap) over the existing soil will (a) allow for more effective leaching in the root zone, and (b) help maintain water infiltration by reducing surface soil compaction.

The underlying soil should be tilled prior to applying the sand cap so that water and roots will easily enter this layer. Especially if the underlying soil has appreciable silt and clay, application of 2 in. of sand followed by tilling into the top 1 or 2 in. of soil should be considered. The remaining sand would then be added on top of this tilled zone.

Sometimes soil is dredged from an ocean bay and added as topsoil for the turfgrass area. This creates a very serious situation even if a good quality water source is available since the soil will be an extreme saline-sodic soil with high total salts and high Na with considerable structural deterioration. Leaving this soil as the topsoil when seawater is used for irrigation presents a nearly impossible situation for turfgrass establishment and long-term reduction of total salts and Na.

If soil dredged from the ocean must be used along with seawater irrigation, then the following practices are strongly suggested prior to turfgrass establishment: (a) apply 200 to 600 lb gypsum per 1000 ft^2 (higher rate for heavier soils) to the surface of the soil and till it into the top 6 in., (b) apply another 200 lb gypsum per 1000 ft^2 to the surface along with 2 in. of sand and till into the top 1 or 2 in. of soil, and (c) then add at least 6 in. of remaining sand cap.

Other Considerations

Obviously, when seawater irrigation is practical, considerable effort and cost are required to prevent turfgrass management and pollution problems. The 1962 EPA drinking water standard is <500 mg L^{-1} of total soluble salts (or total suspended solids). Seawater contains about 34,400 mg L^{-1} salt; therefore, contamination of good groundwater aquifers is very possible. Monitoring wells to determine water quality changes by depth and at salt/fresh water interfaces (boundaries) are important.

Newport (1977) and Todd (1997) listed several methods for controlling salt water intrusion in coastal aquifers. However, these methods refer to salt water intrusion from lateral or upward movement of salts rather than the downward (and possibly some lateral movement in the surface zone) movement from irrigation applications. They suggest:

1. reduce pumping
2. relocation of irrigation wells
3. directly recharge the good, surface aquifer
4. recharge fresh water wells at the boundary of the coastal salt water intrusion area
5. create a trough parallel to the coast by excavating encroaching salt water from wells
6. extracting seawater before it reaches potable wells
7. extraction/injection combinations
8. constructing impermeable subsurface barriers.

Methods 3 through 5 rely on creation of a fresh water barrier to block seawater intrusion. Methods 6 and 7 are extraction methods. These considerations illustrate that prevention of salt water intrusion, whether by seawater irrigation or subsurface intrusion, is possible but costly and requires considerable preconstruction planning and long-term management.

16.2. ESTABLISHMENT

All plants, even halophytes, are more sensitive to salt problems during early root growth and establishment. Precautions at this stage can minimize expensive replanting. Primary considerations include (a) reduction of total salts for establishment, (b) alleviation of Na-induced soil physical problems in the surface zone, (c) maintenance of adequate moisture, and (d) initial fertilization.

Since seawater has a total salinity level of $EC_w = 54$ dSm^{-1}, total salts in the soil surface will equilibrate lower than 54 dSm^{-1} only (a) after a heavy rainfall or prolonged rainy period, (b) by use of a better quality water for establishment, or (c) by blending a better quality water with the seawater. Preventing the soil surface EC_e from increasing above 54 dSm^{-1} when seawater is the sole source of irrigation water will require during establishment and on a continuing basis:

- a continuous program of applying sufficient water to maintain net downward movement of salts out of the surface root zone.
- maintaining moist soil conditions between irrigation events so that salts do not concentrate in the soil solution or rise by capillary action from below the surface zone. This requires more frequent irrigation but with sufficient water to facilitate leaching. Light, frequent irrigation at establishment or on a mature turf with seawater without a sufficient quantity for leaching will result in rapid salt buildup in the surface and ultimately turfgrass failure.

If the initial salinity level in the soil surface is greater than $EC_e = 54$ dSm^{-1} before turfgrass establishment, repeated application of seawater on a frequent basis and with volume enough to achieve salt leaching will be needed. This can be achieved 1 or 2 weeks prior to establishment, followed by just enough drying of the soil surface to support equipment for establishment. Excessive drying of the soil surface can cause resalinization of the surface. If sand capping has been practiced, the soil surface should have a lower salinity level, as well as initially be unaffected by high Na levels. This makes establishment much easier.

In terms of a potential sodic condition (i.e., high Na causing soil structural deterioration and, therefore, low water infiltration/percolation) at the surface, aggressive treatment with gypsum is recommended whether a sodic situation exists before establishment or not. This is because the high Na content of seawater can quickly create a sodic condition (seawater has an SAR_w = 57, Tables 9.2, 15.1, 16.1).

Without a sand cap and where the soil is heavier than a sandy loam, mixing of 400 to 1000 lb gypsum per 1000 ft^2 into the surface 4 to 6 in. is recommended—this is in addition to any gypsum applied below the sand cap layer. Another 100 to 200 lb gypsum per 1000 ft^2 should be surface-applied. Where a sand cap or sandy soil is present, 50 to 75% of these rates can be used.

Adequate P (2 to 3 lb P_2O_5 per 1000 ft^2) should be surface-applied at planting to promote establishment. Other nutrients can be incorporated according to soil test results and considering nutrients added by seawater irrigation. Due to the leaching conditions, a spoon-feeding approach for all required nutrients will be best. Frequency of application will be more often with rates of nutrients applied over time at 1.5 to 2.0X that used on seawater irrigated sites compared to similar areas irrigated with other water sources. Obviously a well-designed irrigation system where fertigation can be practiced would be very beneficial. Additional fertilization concerns for establishment and on mature turf are addressed in the next section.

16.3. POSTESTABLISHMENT/MATURE TURF

Implications of Nutrients Ratios

a. **All of these salts** contribute to high total salts, but especially Na^+ and Cl^- ions. Chloride is easily leached as long as adequate water is applied.

b. **The high quantity of Na^+** will rapidly cause a severe sodic condition (i.e., soil structural deterioration) unless adequate Ca^{+2} ions are added to replace Na^+ on the CEC sites and sufficient water is added to leach the Na. The equivalent of 27.35 meq Ca^{+2} (28.66 meq Na^+ minus 1.31 meq Ca^{+2} already present) must be added for every 12 in. seawater irrigation (Table 16.2). This is equal to 547 lb of elemental Ca^{+2} (1 meq wt of Ca = 20) per 1000 ft^2 or 2378 lb per 1000 ft^2 of **gypsum** (i.e., 23% Ca content). Thus, seawater irrigation will obviously require large quantities of amendment on a continuous basis to prevent a severe sodic condition. If a sodic condition is allowed to develop, water infiltration/percolation/drainage will be dramatically reduced; thereby, total salts will build up. One means of reducing high gypsum or gypsum substitute costs is to select sites with deep sands that are "ideal" for seawater irrigation. As long as the sands are several feet deep and well-drained, the above gyp-

Table 16.2. Nutrient and Element Content of Seawater Results in These Quantities Applied per 12 Inches of Seawater Irrigation

Ion	lb per 1000 ft^2	meq per 1000 ft^2	Percent of Cations
Ca^{+2}	26.2	1.31[a]	3.5
Mg^{+2}	81.4	6.67	17.9
K$^+$	24.3	0.62	0.8
Na$^+$	659	28.66	76.9
SO$_4^{-2}$	168	3.50	—
Cl$^-$	1185	33.48	—
HCO$_3^-$	9	0.15	—

[a] Milliequivalent (meq) basis or chemical equivalent basis.

sum rate can be reduced by 50 to 70%. Such sands must not contain more than 2 or 3% silt and clay so that their CEC sites are relatively low (<2 or 3 meq per 100 g) and dispersion of the fines will not seal pores. These sites would also require less intensive cultivation. The only other means of reducing amendment rates is to use better quality irrigation water. Sand-capped sites will still require the higher gypsum applications to maintain nonsodic conditions in the underlying soil. Long-term amendment costs as well as costs associated with the items discussed in Section 16.1 on "Preconstruction" illustrate that a careful cost analysis should be accomplished before attempting seawater irrigation. Desalinization costs versus seawater irrigation costs should be compared with both options balanced against expected revenues.

c. Some of the 2378 lb gypsum per 1000 ft^2 per 12 in. seawater irrigation may be provided through other Ca sources. One Ca source would be surface-applied lime (CaCO$_3$) to react with any SO$_4^{-2}$ in the seawater to form gypsum over time. Approximately, 70 lb CaCO$_3$ per 1000 ft^2 per 12 in. seawater irrigation will react with the 168 lb of SO$_4^{-2}$ added. If the irrigation water is acidified with additional H$_2$SO$_4$, then sufficient lime can be added to react with the total SO$_4^{-2}$ in the treated water. It is beneficial to remove the SO$_4^{-2}$ from the soil system, not only to use it to form gypsum but to avoid excess SO$_4^{-2}$ that may revert to reduced S under poor aeration. Reduced S can react with Fe and Mn under low aeration to form a black layer and greatly restrict water movement through the soil. Another Ca source should be Ca (NO$_3$)$_2$ as the routine N-carrier. High Cl$^-$ can suppress NO$_3^{-2}$ uptake. So addition of N in the NO$_3^{-2}$ form is preferred. Also, seashore paspalum has a strong preference for NO_3^{-2} versus NH_4^+ for N uptake. The Ca in Ca $(NO_3)_2$ is very soluble and active as a replacement ion for Na^+. A third Ca source can be $CaCl_2$ placed through an injector system, since it is highly soluble.

d. The **high Mg content** relative to Ca in seawater (Ca:Mg is 1:5.1) will not be a problem with the large quantities of Ca applied as an amendment to replace Na^+. In fact, some additional Mg^{+2} may be required if Mg on the CEC sites become <10% or the Mg soil test reveals a low quantity. Magnesium is not an effective ion for soil structure formation. It can replace Na^+ on the CEC sites, but Mg^{+2} has a much larger ion radius than Ca^{+2}, which limits its effectiveness to bring together colloidal particles for aggregation. When extra Mg^{+2} is needed as a nutrient, dolomitic lime can be used to provide a "slow release" Mg fertilizer or a soluble Mg source can be applied by fertigation.

e. While appreciable **K** (29.1 lb K_2O per 1000 ft^2 per 12 in. seawater irrigation) is being added with seawater, K^+ constitutes <1% of the cations. In addition, high Na^+ suppresses K^+ uptake of most plants. Seashore paspalum has a high affinity for K uptake regardless of the Na^+ level, which is one of the mechanisms allowing it to exhibit high salinity tolerance. Nevertheless, a routine spoon-feeding program for K^+ will be required with preference for KNO_3 or K_2SO_4. On sand-capped sites or those with deep, well-drained sands, the addition of 5% by weight of a medium to coarse (0.25 to 1.00 mm diameter) zeolite will greatly aid in maintaining adequate K since zeolite preferentially holds K^+ ions. The selective retention of K^+ versus Na^+ or Mg^{+2} is due to charge density and hydrated ionic sizes of these ions being larger than K^+. High total salts (salinity) reduces the growth rate of even very salt-tolerant seashore paspalums, which can potentially increase wear injury. Maintenance of adequate K^+ nutrition will improve wear tolerance.

f. Ample SO_4^- **for plant nutritional needs** should be available from the seawater even when surface-applied lime is used to convert SO_4^- into gypsum.

g. Adequate Ca^{+2} **to meet plant nutritional requirements** and to prevent Na^+ replacement of Ca^{+2} within root tissues (i.e., Na^+ root toxicity) will be available from the Ca sources applied to replace Na^+ ions on soil CEC sites.

In addition to the influence of seawater on turfgrass nutrition from chemicals in the seawater or chemicals added to replace Na^+ on soil CEC sites, the high leaching requirement will **enhance leaching of all nutrients**. Implications from the greater leaching requirement are:

- all nutrients will need to be applied at a higher quantity than on similar sites with good water quality. An approximation for N-P-K is 1.5 to 2X *annual* rates.
- However, nutrients should not be applied at 1.5 to 2X rates per application but spoon-fed at normal application rates and more frequently. Spoon-feeding does not need to be solely water-soluble carriers applied by fertigation, even though fertigation will be very useful where seawater irrigation is practiced. Slow release granular materials can also be applied in a spoon-feeding manner—medium to low rates of nutrients on a relatively frequent basis. In fact, slow release fertilizers applied in this manner can be the "base" fertilization with fertigation used to supplement nutrition.
- The micronutrients Fe and Mn may require extra attention with foliar applications at 0.025 and 0.013 lb per 1000 ft^2 of Fe and Mn, respectively, every 2 to 3 weeks and additional granular applications several times per year. A good micronutrient package fertilizer should be applied at the recommended rate but more frequently than normal (i.e., 1.5 to 2X more frequent).

Overseeding

Overseeding with another species during winter months on seawater-irrigated areas is greatly limited due to the lower salt tolerance of the overseeding grasses and to the continuous high salinity level within seawater. Rough bluegrass (*Poa trivialis*) should not be used. Refer to Table 12.1 for a listing of salt-tolerant grass cultivars to try on a limited trial area at your specific location.

Landscape Plants

Only very salt-tolerant trees and shrubs should be established where seawater irrigation is used, especially if they are located within the irrigation zones. The "Toxic Ions" data in Table 15.1 for "root toxicity/ shoot uptake" and "foliage injury" are primarily applicable for selection of trees and shrubs rather than being a concern for seashore paspalum or other salt-tolerant turfgrasses.

16.4. SUMMARY

While seawater irrigation is a potential option due to the availability of seashore paspalum turfgrass that can tolerate seawater under optimum management, selection of this option requires careful evaluation of pre-construction requirements, establishment procedures, and post-establishment management. Lack of adequate attention to any of these issues may result in rapid accumulation of total salinity and sodium to levels well above the already extreme levels in seawater and above the tolerance limits of any turfgrass.

CHAPTER 17

Fertilization of Excessively Acid (pH 5.0) Soils

Excessively acid soils (pH <5.0) are common in humid climates, especially where annual rainfall is sufficient to cause leaching of basic cations (Ca, Mg, K). At a pH <5.0, soil cation exchange sites (CEC) are increasingly occupied by H^+ and Al^{+3} ions, and Mn becomes more soluble. Thus, at pH <5.0 nutritional problems include (a) potential nutrient deficiencies (N, P, K, Mg, Ca, S, B, Mo), and (b) possible toxicities to plant roots from Al and Mn. Some microorganisms are also adversely affected by excess Al, Mn, and H levels. These toxicities are much more likely to arise on fine-textured soils than on leached sands. Sands contain much less Al than fine-textured soil types since the Al is associated with clay minerals. Soluble Mn can be leached from an acid sand rather than accumulate in the root zone and eventually even result in a deficiency. Also, a waterlogged condition is less likely on a sand, which can increase soluble Mn.

Four turfgrass field situations can occur where excessive acid pH is the primary problem:

- the "acid soil complex" is the most prevalent and important problem
- excessive acidity induced by overapplication of S or acidic N-carriers
- acidic thatch
- acid sulfate soils.

17.1. ACID SOIL COMPLEX

A "complex" of nutrient deficiencies, element toxicities, and high soil strength often occurs together where the high soil strength arises from clays, particularly kaolinitic, Fe/Al oxides, and allophanes—all nonexpanding clays. This complex has been called the **"acid soil complex"** and is **the major soil chemical constraint on plants in humid climates**, affecting over one-half of the land area. Within the United States, such soils are primarily found in the Southeast (Piedmont; i.e., red clay zone), Northeast, Northwest, and on acid mine spoils.

In the United States, management programs have focused on correcting moderate soil pH problems (pH >5.0, no toxicities, fewer deficiencies) by liming to alter pH in the surface 4 to 6 inch zone. The acid soil complex presents a greater challenge than moderately acid pH because (a) potential deficiencies are more frequent and severe, (b) the toxicities and high soil strength limit rooting of many plants, (c) it is normally a problem throughout the whole soil profile, and management approaches must be targeted accordingly rather than only at the surface, (d) the higher quantities of amendments required to alleviate the chemical constraints coupled with availability problems in some regions increase economic considerations and influence management decisions, (e) high amendment application rates may induce additional nutrient imbalances, (f) the low pH can adversely affect microorganism populations involved in N-transformations from NH_4^+ to NO_3^- (the preferred N-form for uptake) and organic matter decomposition, both of which influence overall turf nutritional programs, and (g) the problem takes a long time to alleviate and will recur. Thus, proper fertilization is essential to minimize plant problems while the soil chemical constraints are being corrected.

Liming Practices

Excessively acid soils will have a high lime requirement not only because of the initially low pH, but in order to alleviate toxicities and nutrient deficiencies throughout the root zone instead of just the surface few inches. The four options include:

1. Deep mixing of lime prior to establishment. The major concern with this practice is to avoid bringing any excessively fine-textured layer, such as a heavy B horizon, to the surface. Tillage aids in reducing high soil strength problems.

2. Using a combination of surface application and subsurface injection of lime. The Yeager-Twose Turf Conditioner can inject 75 to 90 lb lime per 1000 ft² at a 7 to 8 in. depth.

3. Using acidifying N fertilizers (Table 9.2) with lime to increase Ca^{+2} solubility and movement into the lower root zone. The acidifying

fertilizers include ammonium nitrate, urea, ammonium sulfate, diammonium phosphate, and monoammonium phosphate. The basic reactions for the acidic fertilizer $NH_4 NO_3$ are:

$$NH_4 NO_3 + O_2 \rightarrow 2 HNO_3 + H_2O \text{ (i.e., nitrification process)}$$

$$2HNO_3 + CaCO_3 \rightarrow Ca(NO_3)_2 + CO_2 + H_2O$$

Three benefits arise from these reactions (a) a soluble Ca^{+2} form is created, (b) the N is all transformed into the NO_3^- form preferred by grasses for uptake, and (c) when the NO_3^- is absorbed, OH^- ions are exchanged from the roots to allow formation of $Ca(OH)_2$, another more soluble Ca-carrier.

If the acidic N-carrier $(NH_4)_2SO_4$ is used, the reaction is:

$$(NH_4)_2SO_4 + CaCO_3 \rightarrow CaSO_4 + 2NH_3 + H_2O$$

While a more soluble Ca compound (gypsum, $CaSO_4$) is formed, N volatilization potential as NH_3 gas is increased. To minimize this problem, the $(NH_4)_2SO_4$ fertilizer should be watered into the turfgrass soil and not left on the surface. As the NH_4 is converted to NO_3^- by the nitrification process, a net release of H^+ contributes to further soil acidification. This is compensated for by a rapid release and mobilization of Ca^{+2} to increase pH.

The above reactions illustrate how acidifying fertilizers can be used to enhance Ca mobility into the deeper root zone. However, when acidity is only moderate, acidifying fertilizers are avoided since deep penetration of Ca is of less concern due to the absence of toxicity problems.

4. Besides creating soluble Ca compounds with acidifying N-fertilizers, relatively soluble materials can be directly applied as gypsum ($CaSO_4$), $Ca(NO_3)_2$, $CaCl_2$, phosphogypsum, or other less used materials (Sumner, 1995). The effects of these materials are to:

- decrease exchangeable Al^{+3}, an ion toxic to roots
- increase exchangeable Ca^{+2} on the soil CEC
- enhance downward movement of Ca into the root zone
- not alter soil pH to any appreciable degree.

Since pH is not changed, other nutrients remain less available, except for Ca^{+2}. Some soil physical improvements may occur due to the added Ca^{+2}.

pH alteration requires lime amendments, but soluble Ca forms can at least decrease Al^{+3} toxicities and, therefore, enhance rooting until the lime has had time to increase soil pH.

Application of high rates of lime to the soil surface may promote N-volatilization from NH_4^+-containing fertilizer and urea, as illustrated for $(NH_4)_2SO_4$. While the bulk soil would be acidic, the surface where the lime resides would be alkaline, allowing for conversion of NH_4^+ into NH_3, a gas;

$$NH_4^+ \rightarrow NH_3 \text{ (gas)}$$

This reaction is favored at pH >7.0, while at pH <7.0, NH_4^+ is the predominant form. As noted for $(NH_4)_2 SO_4$, irrigating with sufficient water to wash the fertilizer into the soil rather than leaving it on the surface will greatly decrease volatilization.

Nitrogen

Nitrification bacteria responsible for transforming NH_4^+ into NO_3^- are very sensitive to soil pH <5.5, and particularly the lack of sufficient Ca^{+2} at those low pH levels. Grasses that exhibit a strong preference for NO_3^- rather than NH_4^+ for N-uptake often demonstrate only a modest response to applied N under acidic conditions. Even a relatively light lime application of 5 to 10 lb per 1000 ft^2 can dramatically enhance N availability and uptake by these grasses through stimulation of *Nitrosomonas* and *Nitrobacter* activity. Since these organisms are responding to a higher Ca availability and activity rather than a change in pH, this probably explains the rapid turfgrass greening response that can sometimes follow a lime or gypsum treatment to an acid soil. Higher Ca availability may stimulate nitrification organisms by (1) alleviating cellular stress on the organism in association with maintenance of internal cell pH and membrane functions involving conditions where H^+ is high and Ca^{+2} low, (2) possibly reducing Al/Mn toxicities through organic acid chelation, and (3) favoring a larger organism population at a more neutral pH. The first two responses could be more rapid than the latter and may account for quick stimulation of NH_4^+ conversion to NO_3^- for a turfgrass greening effect.

The use of $Ca(NO_3)_2$ as an N-carrier allows for immediate NO_3^- availability without undergoing nitrification, while providing Ca^{+2} for nitrifying bacteria or to alleviate Al^{+3}-induced Ca deficiency in turf roots. Seashore paspalum seems to respond to $Ca(NO_3)_2$ more rapidly than other N-carriers on acid soils. The rapid response is especially apparent at soil temperatures less than 55°F, which would limit the activity of nitrifying bacteria, but it is also evident at higher soil temperatures.

Basic Cations (Mg, K,Ca)

Turfgrass plants grown on excessively acid soils are likely to be deficient in Mg or K due to leaching of these cations. Also, high inputs of Ca are required to increase pH or to alleviate Al/Mn toxicities, which may further induce Mg and K deficiencies.

For Mg, the easiest means of applying high rates is to use dolomitic lime, which contains $MgCO_3$. Not only can high Mg rates be applied, but $MgCO_3$ functions as a "slow release" Mg carrier. Supplemental Mg may still be required from other more soluble Mg sources such as $MgSO_4$.

The high rainfall typical of many acid soil regions makes it difficult to build up K soil levels, especially on sandy sites. Frequent, light to moderate K applications can assist in maintaining adequate levels of this nutrient. On fine-textured soils, soil testing will provide a good guideline for K-fertilization and somewhat higher K-rates per application can be used, compared to sands.

Prior to liming or treatment with more soluble Ca forms, a Ca deficiency may occur within the root tissues that allows for deterioration of the roots; hence, less efficient water and nutrient uptake. High Al^{+3} concentration causes Ca^{+2} to be replaced from root exchange sites and limits Ca^{+2} levels within cell walls of root cells and the plasma membrane. Even under this situation, however, Ca uptake is sufficient for shoot tissues. Soil application of Ca^{+2} must reach the roots in order to alleviate root deficiencies of Ca^{+2} (often presented as Al^{+3} toxicity, which can also have other mechanisms for root injury). Calcium is the least mobile nutrient, so foliar-applied Ca remains within the shoot tissues and is not translocated to the root cells that greatly need Ca.

Phosphorus

Under excessively acid conditions, high levels of soluble Fe and Al forms are present that react quickly with any P in soil solution to form insoluble Fe-P and Al-P compounds. Thus, P deficiency can easily occur.

When high rates of Ca-compounds are added, relatively insoluble Ca-P materials may form to immobilize P. Thus, excessively acid soils often require somewhat higher P rates than similar soils at neutral pH, as well as more frequent applications. Phosphorus at times of establishment, overseeding, or renovation is a very important management consideration on these soils.

Sulfur

Sulfur deficiency is most frequent on sands subjected to high rainfall or excessive irrigation and in locations not receiving industrial input as S from the atmosphere. Sometimes S deficiency is overlooked on these acidic sites because S is used to reduce pH (and thus presumed to be high at low acidity). Adequate S can come from gypsum; phosphogypsum (also a source of P); $(NH_4)_2SO_4$ when applied with lime to form gypsum; S applied with lime to create gypsum; K_2SO_4; $MgSO_4$ or other sources. If soluble forms are used, these should be applied on a light, frequent basis, especially on sites receiving high N, which can enhance the S requirement.

Micronutrients

Boron (B) can be leached from acid sands. If the soil test for B is low, some B can be applied, but care should be taken to avoid overapplication since toxic B is also a potential problem, especially in some salt-affected areas.

Normally, Mn would be adequate and sometimes excessive (toxic) at low pH. Toxic levels of Mn to root systems usually result from a combination of acidic plus anaerobic conditions that result in high soluble Mn levels. Liming plus good aeration from cultivation, drainage, or soil modification will reduce Mn toxicity potential. Leached sands can easily exhibit Mn deficiency since soluble Mn can be leached. Periodic application of soil Mn treatments or foliar Mn amendments can alleviate Mn deficiency.

Theoretically, excessive acidity could result in deficiencies of Cu, Zn, and Mo, but these are very seldom encountered on turfgrasses. Application of a balanced micronutrient "package" fertilizer on a more frequent time schedule than for a similar neutral pH site can help ensure adequate levels of these nutrients.

17.2. EXCESSIVE ACIDITY INDUCED BY S OR ACIDIC N-CARRIERS

While the "acid soil complex" is the most prevalent field problem of excessive acidity, an additional one is a surface zone (0.5 to 1.0 in. thickness) that becomes excessively acid from overapplication of S or acid N-fertilizers. This can expose the lower turfgrass crown, where roots are initiated, to Al/Mn toxicity as well as inhibit root formation from stolon nodes.

Soils containing even 1% free calcium carbonate (i.e., lime) are buffered against a rapid pH change when S or acidic N-carriers are applied. The H^+ ions react with $CaCO_3$ to dissolve it by the reaction:

$$H_2SO_4 + CaCO_3 \rightarrow CaSO_4 + H_2O + CO_2^-$$

This reaction does not change soil pH. After all the lime is dissolved, free H^+ ions are available to exchange Ca^{+2} and other base cations from the soil CEC sites; thereby, reducing pH.

When no free $CaCO_3$ is present to buffer against H^+ ions, soil pH can decrease rapidly, especially on low CEC soils such as sands. Under these conditions, a 4-in.-depth soil sample used for soil testing may reveal only a small decrease in bulk soil pH, while within the surface 0.5 to 1.0 in. the pH may decline to <5.0. This creates the potential for high Al/Mn and even H^+ ions toxicities to injure existing roots at the crown level and to inhibit new root growth.

The primarily nutritional effects are (a) the Al/Mn/H toxicities of excessive S or acidic N-carriers, (b) root injury decreases uptake of all nutrients and water, and (c) a low to moderate application of lime (5 to 10 lb $CaCO_3$ per 1000 ft^2) will correct the problem. Turf managers may apply S as a means to acidify the soil; to create gypsum on sodic soils when S and lime are added; through acidification of irrigation water to remove $HCO_3^-/CO_3^=$ from the water; or directly as a fertilizer to avoid S deficiency. In any of these situations, surface soil pH (within the top 1 inch) should be routinely monitored as well as bulk or average pH over the normal 3 to 4 in. sampling depth used for routine soil testing. Turf managers can request the determination of free $CaCO_3$ content as a special soil test analysis. A soil with even 1% free $CaCO_3$ evenly distributed within the surface 3 inches of soil would contain about 77 lb of free $CaCO_3$ in the surface 1 inch to buffer against a pH decrease.

17.3. ACIDIC THATCH

The same conditions conducive to creating an excessively acid soil surface can also cause an acidic thatch layer (pH <5.0). Crown and roots within the thatch are exposed to the potential for Al/Mn/H toxicities. Also, bacterial populations important for decomposition of organic matter, including the thatch, are greatly suppressed, along with nitrifying bacteria. This can result in thatch accumulation even when the grass may be growing very slowly or from a grass species that does not normally cause thatch buildup, like perennial ryegrass or tall fescue. When turfgrass roots become severely restricted by high Al/Mn/H or after high temperature stress on cool-season grasses, Fe chlorosis may result even at low pH values where it would not normally be expected.

When soil test samples are obtained, the thatch is usually discarded. Whenever there is a possibility of an acidic thatch, the turf manager should send in a thatch sample and request a pH determination. Other conditions favoring acid thatch development could include high rainfall regions where the thatch is "leached," sites receiving S deposition from the atmosphere, and where acidic N-carriers are routinely used. Regardless of the cause, a periodic application of 2 to 4 lb $CaCO_3$ per 1000 ft^2 can maintain thatch pH above 5.5. Frequency of treatment depends on the cause but, in general, thatch pH can change more rapidly than soil or mat (soil plus thatch intermingled together) pH. Any Fe chlorosis induced by this problem is temporary and can be corrected by foliar application. In contrast, alkaline thatch pH often demonstrates more chronic Fe chlorosis symptoms.

17.4. ACID SULFATE SOILS

Acid sulfate soils are sometimes found in coastal and tidal swamps where easily decomposed organic matter and an ample supply of $SO_4^=$ from seawater is present. The $SO_4^=$ becomes reduced to form FeS_2 (**iron pyrite**), which accumulates. Upon drainage, the FeS_2 oxidizes to form H_2SO_4 and cause extreme acidic condition of pH 1.5 to 3.5. All the nutritional deficiencies and toxicities inherent in excessively acid soils (pH 3.5 to 5.0) discussed in the "acid soil complex" are present in acid sulfate soils, but are accentuated. Additionally, a severe sodic condition occurs that complicates leaching of Na and Al. Treatment is similar to the "acid soil complex" but much higher rates of lime are the preferred treatment. "Ripe" acid sulfate soils are ones that have been drained with an irreversible loss of water so they become firm and weathering/oxidizing/leaching has occurred to less than 3 feet. These can be reclaimed with rates of lime as low as 150 lb per 1000 ft² in some cases, versus several times this rate for other problem soils. Since high rates of lime are required, care to avoid Ca^{+2}-induced deficiencies is needed as well as replacement of nutrients that were leached when removing excess Na^+.

In summary, turfgrass field problems where pH is <5.0 are widespread around the world in the form of the acid soil complex; S or acidic N-carrier induced acid pH in the soil surface; acidic thatch; and acid sulfate soils. Each of these present unique fertility problems that arise from the initial condition or from high amendment rates used to correct these conditions. The fertility problems may be in the form of nutrient deficiencies, excessive levels of nutrients/imbalances, or element/nutrient toxicities. Fertilization programs on these sites should be adjusted for these problem areas.

CHAPTER 18

Environmentally Sensitive Sites: Turfgrass Fertilization Considerations

Turfgrasses adjacent to wetlands occur on most golf courses and many other turfgrass sites. The potential for fertilizer contamination of surface and subsurface waters requires certain adjustments and precautions in fertilization practices. Three major issues influencing fertilizer movement or chemistry must be addressed; namely, factors affecting fertilizer runoff, leaching, and anaerobic conditions.

18.1. RUNOFF ISSUES

Fertilizers may be carried off the turfgrass and into nearby waters by dissolution into solution, as fertilizer particles, or as fertilizer associated with sediment. Thus, the physical and chemical nature of the carrier as well as timing of application relative to rainfall may affect runoff potential. However, the dominant site factors influencing runoff are (a) a combination of quantity and velocity of the water moving across the turfgrass surface, (b) nature of the turfgrass stand such as shoot density, mowing height, and the presence or absence of a thatch or mat layer, and (c) soil aspects, especially slope, infiltration rate, and initial soil moisture where a drier soil will exhibit a higher initial infiltration rate. Some soil types with shrinkswell clays will crack when dry, which causes a high infiltration rate until the cracks seal.

Adjustments in cultural practices can create site conditions that reduce runoff of all fertilizers. Examples include (a) altering soil characteristics by cultivation, sand topdressing heavy soils to increase infiltration, or contouring to avoid excessive slopes near water features, (b) adjustments in irrigation scheduling in terms of rate and timing relative to fertilizer application, and (c) enhancing turfgrass interception capabilities by maintaining good shoot density, using a moderate mowing height, and allowing some thatch development of <0.5 in. In addition, common sense approaches during irrigation application periods (such as not applying a fertilizer just ahead of an anticipated heavy rainfall on areas near water features or, not applying fertilizer onto nonturf surfaces such as roads, cart paths, sidewalks, or bare soil areas) are essential. Fertilizer intended for turfgrass areas should never be spread in a manner that allows particles to directly enter the water.

Nitrogen

Nitrogen, especially as nitrate (NO_3^-), is one nutrient of concern for runoff since it can stimulate growth of algae or plant growth in streams and lakes. Excessive algae growth results in oxygen depletion in the water. Nitrate contamination of domestic water supplies increases the risk of methemoglobinemia, or "blue baby disease," with 10 mg L^{-1} NO_3^--N as the maximum allowable limit for drinking water.

Fertilization practices that would limit N runoff are particularly important on turfgrass areas near water bodies and on sites with steep slopes. The buffer areas immediately adjacent to water should be managed as unique or separate turfgrass areas, often at a higher mowing height. Fertilization practices that can assist in reducing N runoff are:

- Do not apply N-fertilizers prior to expected rainfall events on these sites.
- Use only the minimal quantity of N to maintain an adequate turfgrass cover, but a thin (less dense) stand can enhance runoff.
- Use a "spoon-feeding" approach where lower N-rates are applied at any one application. This can be with granular (slow release or quick release) or foliar applications.
- Irrigate lightly (0.10 to 0.25 in. water) to move any soluble N into the soil surface and "settle" particles into the turfgrass sward.
- Time N-applications during seasons when the grass is actively growing and not dormant to minimize N loading in the soil.
- If clippings accumulate to the point where they may be washed into waterways, they should be removed and properly discarded. Also, avoid clipping disposal or piles where they could be physically washed into water, or where leachates from piles could reach water bodies. Use a mulching mower.

Table 18.1. Solubility of Fertilizers Used in Preparing Liquid Fertilizer Solutions

Fertilizer	Parts Soluble in 100 Parts Cold Water	Pounds per Gallon[a]
Ammonium nitrate - NH_4NO_3	118	9.8
Ammonium sulfate - $(NH_4)_2SO_4$	71	5.9
Ammonium chloride - NH_4Cl	30	2.5
Calcium nitrate - $Ca(NO_3)_2 \cdot 4H_2O$	266	22.1
Diammonium phosphate - $(NH_4)_2HPO_4$	43	3.6
Monoammonium phosphate - $NH_{42}H_2PO_4$	23	1.9
Nitrate of soda - $NaNO_3$	73	6.0
Potassium chloride - KCL	35	2.9
Potassium nitrate - KNO_3	13	1.1
Potassium sulfate - K_2SO_4	12	1.0
Urea - NH_2CONH_2	78	6.5
Single superphos - $Ca(H_2PO_4)_2 \cdot H_2O \cdot CaSO_4$	2	0.2
Treble superphos - $Ca(H_2PO_4)_2 \cdot H_2O$	4	0.3
Sodium chloride - NaCl	36	3.0
Calcium chloride - $CaCl_2 \cdot 6H_2O$	279	23.2
Borax - $Na_2B_4O_7 \cdot 10H_2O$	1	0.1
Copper sulfate - $CuSO_4 \cdot 5H_2O$	32	2.7
Ferrous sulfate - $FeSO_4 \cdot 7H_2O$	16	1.3
Magnesium sulfate - $MgSO_4 \cdot 7H_2O$	71	5.9
Sodium molybdate - $Na_2MoO_4 \cdot 2H_2O$	56	4.6
Zinc sulfate - $ZnSO_4 \cdot 7H_2O$	75	6.2
Manganese sulfate - $MnSO_4 \cdot 4H_2O$	105	8.7

[a] 1 gallon = 3.785 L; 1 pound = 454 grams.

- Any granular N-carriers should be of sufficient particle density so as not to be easily carried by water from the point of application. High density particles that easily integrate into the turfgrass stand are ideal.
- Water solubility of specific fertilizers should be considered (Table 18.1), since highly soluble forms are prone to movement with leaching volumes of irrigation water or high rainfall events.

Phosphorus

Phosphorus contamination of surface waters is an environmental concern because P is normally the limiting factor controlling algae and aquatic plant growth. Soluble P can rapidly cause eutrophication of water bodies and oxygen depletion over time. Since P is very insoluble once it is applied to the soil, runoff occurs primarily as fertilizer particles or P absorbed onto sediment that is carried along with water movement. Thus, P fertilization should be timed so that site conditions (soil moisture, turfgrass, water applications) are suitable to minimizing sediment or fertilizer particle movement.

18.2. LEACHING ISSUES

As with runoff, the two nutrients of most concern for leaching into groundwaters are N and P. Whether directly applied as NO_3^- or from NO_3^- formed during nitrification, the NO_3^- molecule is as mobile as a water molecule in the soil. It is not retained on soil cation exchange sites and, in fact, it is repelled by the negatively charged CEC sites. However, turfgrasses and other plants, as well as microorganisms, take up NO_3^- and incorporate it into amino acids.

Leaching of NO_3^- can be reduced by several means and these practices are especially important on sandy soils with high percolation rates. A spoon-feeding approach, where only light N-rates are applied as the plant needs N, will greatly reduce leaching. The spoon-feeding philosophy can be used with liquid (foliar, fertigation/drench), water-soluble granulars, or slow release N-carriers. Regardless of the carrier, the idea is to maintain relatively low NO_3^- concentration at all times so that when heavy rainfalls occur, leaching losses are still minimal. When higher N-rates must be applied, slow release N-fertilizer can be used to maintain a low, more controlled N-release pattern. In all instances, N-rates should not exceed the turf plant's need for the specific site.

Irrigation practices can influence leaching potential. Some turfgrass managers use fertigation, where nutrients are added through the irrigation system. This is a drench application, rather than a foliar feeding operation (which uses 1–5 gallons of water per 1000 ft^2), where nutrients are added to the soil. If a heavy irrigation is planned, N could be leached by the fertigation application. When irrigation is applied even without fertigation, NO_3^- can leach beyond the root zone if excessive water is applied, especially on sands.

When N is in the NH_4^+ form, it can be retained by CEC sites. Thus, soils with higher CEC can retain more NH_4^+. Sometimes, the root zone mix may have CEC values of < 4.0 meq per 100 g. High application rates of even the NH_4^+ form may leach under heavy water applications on these soils due to a limited number of CEC sites. Enhancement of CEC will aid in limiting NH_4^+ leaching as well as other cations. Incorporation of zeolite is especially effective for increasing CEC. Also, organic matter addition and maintaining soil pH >6.5 aids CEC enhancement.

Phosphorus does not easily leach since any soluble P rapidly reacts with Fe, Al, or Ca to form insoluble compounds. However, continuous application of high P can induce P leaching over time, especially on sand soils. These often have limited Fe, Al, or Ca levels relative to soils with more clay content. Since turfgrasses are rather efficient in taking up P, fertilizer additions should be based on plant need. Also, adequate P within the surface 1 or 2 inches is sufficient for turfgrasses in contrast to requiring P throughout the root zone. On high sand content root zone mixes, particularly if they have shallow drainage lines, some P leaching may occur as colloidal particles migrating in the water phase. This is usually only a problem during the establishment phase or whenever there is little grass cover and percolation rates are high. With a grass cover, roots fill many of the surface macropores and reduce the rate of water movement (percolation), even during heavy rains.

Regardless of the nutrient, one important means of limiting leaching losses is to maintain a deep, viable root system. Grasses are efficient in taking up nutrients as long as the root system is present and healthy. Such a root system can be achieved by a combination of (a) selecting grasses that are adapted to the climatic and edaphic (soil) stresses at the site, (b) using cultural practices to maintain a photosynthetically active shoot system. Turfgrasses need green, leaf tissue area for photosynthesis that produces the food (carbohydrates) to grow and maintain roots, which are low in priority for carbohydrate allocation when food is limited. Mowing height is the primary factor influencing leaf area, while nutrient deficiencies (N, Fe, Mg, Mg, S) may reduce chlorophyll activity (i.e., cause chlorosis) and limit photosynthesis. Also, light is required for photosynthesis, so shaded turf cannot develop a vigorous root system, and (c) using cultural practices to alleviate root-limiting soil stresses. These include soil physical (low O_2, high soil strength, high soil temperatures), soil chemical (acid soil complex, salt toxicity, nutrient deficiencies), and soil biological (insects, nematodes, diseases) stresses.

18.3. ANAEROBIC CONDITIONS AND MOWED TURFGRASS AREAS

It is not unusual for many sites to contain *waterlogged* or *low aeration* (low soil O_2) areas where mowed turfgrasses is present. Some of the most common causes of poor soil aeration conditions are:

- high water table resulting in saturation of the root zone, especially near water features.
- Low spots that accumulate water such as "pocket areas" on greens that are not surface-drained off the green.
- compacted soils exhibit waterlogging in low areas but even level compacted sites can retain excess soil moisture at the expense of soil aeration.
- seepage areas where water rises to the surface.
- perched water tables due to a layer that slows or impedes drainage, thereby ponding water above the layer.
- soils containing too many fines (clay, silt) or organic matter may retain excess moisture due to a high content of micropores but few macropores. These soils are often prone to soil compaction, which further reduces aeration.
- sites subjected to periodic flooding.
- soils whose structure has been destroyed by high Na content.

Some of these situations may cover large acreage, while others are confined to relatively small areas, but many of these are adjacent to water features. Also, it is not unusual for more than one of the above factors to be present on the same site. The long-term management goal is to remove the underlying cause for poor soil aeration on excess moisture. Specific management practices depend on the particular problem but often include cultivation, soil modification, or drainage techniques.

Until the primary factor causing low aeration is corrected, turfgrass managers must deal with the adverse effects that occur in the soil and turfgrass plant. Limited soil oxygen can range from (a) *hypoxia* conditions with varying degrees of oxygen stress or depletion, to (b) *anoxia*, where the O_2 molecule is not present. The general term *anaerobic* includes both conditions while *aerobic* indicates that O_2 is not limited. Low aeration problems may be a chronic problem in soils with few macropores, high water tables, perched water tables from an undesirable layer problem, or simply a low area. In the case of flooding, an acute, rapid anaerobic condition results.

Lack of O_2 causes adverse soil chemical, turfgrass plant, and soil microorganism responses. The magnitude of a particular response depends on many conditions, such as: degree of low O_2 stress, soil temperatures, soil pH, type of grass, longevity of O_2 stress, and other aspects.

Soil chemical and biochemical (chemical reactions involving microorganisms) reactions of C, N, S, Fe, and Mn often are oxidation and reduction in nature. An *oxidation-reduction reaction* involves the transfer of electrons from one molecule or ion to another, where an *electron acceptor* is called an oxidizing agent while an *electron donor* is a reducing agent. Oxygen is the strongest electron acceptor generally present in soils.

When soil O_2 starts to become limited, other electron acceptors become important in chemical and biochemical soil reactions. However, turfgrasses and other higher plants can only use O_2 as an electron acceptor in their respiration processes. While other electron acceptors can be used by certain soil microorganism populations under limited aeration, the energy production is much less.

Thus, as soil O_2 becomes limited, several important changes are induced in soils that influence fertilization:

- Soil microorganism populations shift from primarily aerobic and facultative anaerobic organisms to facultative anaerobic and strict anaerobic organisms. These utilize different electron acceptors than O_2 and alternative energy sources to organic matter. Thus, new sets of biologically induced reactions are initiated as well as accumulation from end products of these reactions.
- Important biochemical reactions that are initiated under various degrees of anaerobic conditions are listed in Table 18.2. The chemical forms produced under reducing (low O_2) conditions are in the right-hand side of the reaction. The general time frame for reactions to be initiated or completed after initiation of waterlogging at 25°C (77°F) is listed in Table 18.2 but these vary greatly with severity of reducing conditions, temperature, pH and other factors.
- Some of these reducing compounds can combine to create even worse aeration conditions in the future such as formation of FeS and MnS precipitates that contribute to plugging soil pores and the black coloration in *black layer*.
- Anaerobic conditions and anaerobic respiration by soil microorganisms and plant roots can cause certain chemicals to accumulate, such as organic acids (acetic, butyric, formic lactic, and others), ethylene, ethanol, phenolic substances, methane, and others. Some of these can be root toxins. Carbon dioxide (CO_2) also accumulates to a much higher percentage (i.e., 1 to 10% or more).

Table 18.2. Soil Chemical and Biochemical Reactions That Occur Under Anaerobic Conditions and the Time for Reactions to Occur

Reactions		Time After Flooding for Chemical Change to Appear in Soil (days)
$O_2 + 4H^+ + 4e^- \rightarrow 2H_2O$	aerobic	—
$Fe^{3+} + e^- \rightarrow Fe^{2+}$ (onset of reaction)		4–22
$NO_3^- + 2H^+ + 2e^- \rightarrow NO_2^- + H_2O$ (onset of denitrification process)		—
$Mn^{4+} + 4e^- \rightarrow Mn^{2+}$ (onset of Mn^{2+} formation)		1–12
Absence of free O_2		1–10
$SO_4^{-2} + 10H^+ + 8e^- \rightarrow H_2S + 4H_2O$ (onset of sulfate reduction)		5–20
NO_3^- conversion to N_2 completed		4–16
Mn^{4+} conversion to Mn^{2+} completed		—
Fe^{3+} conversion to Fe^{2+} completed		—
SO_4^{2-} conversion to S^{2-} completed		—
CO_2 conversion CH_4 completed	anoxic	>100

Soil fertility and plant nutrition are influenced by many of these anaerobic-induced, soil chemical and biochemical changes. Primary nutritional affects are (a) alternating the chemical form of nutrients into less available forms (N, S) or into a more available form (Fe, Mn) with the latter increasing to toxic levels in some cases, (b) creating a more hostile environment for root viability and persistence through lack of O_2 and root toxins, and (c) loss of soil N as N_2 gas.

In most cases, these adverse soil chemical conditions are improved by enhancing soil physical properties, especially by the creation of macropores for water movement, gas exchange, and root growth channels. Macroporosity is enhanced by cultivation procedures or soil modification. Additional excess water must be removed through surface and subsurface drainage methods.

18.4. CONSTRUCTED WETLANDS

Grasses, such as seashore paspalum, that grow in anaerobic soils and along the edge of water can remove unwanted nutrients or elements (see Chapter 19, Bioremediation and Reclamation) directly from the water or the soil solution. This ability can be useful in *constructed wetlands* designed to remove nutrients and contaminants from wastewater (Hammer, 1989; and Wood et al., 1999). For example, rinse water from equipment cleaning after fertilization or pesticide application may be channeled into a constructed wetland. Seashore paspalum would be expected to be efficient in N and P removal in such systems that may also use other plants. Plants can be harvested to remove constituents from the wetland on a periodic basis.

18.5. BUFFERS

Riparian buffers are simply a zone of vegetation that functions to remove nutrients and sediment from flowing groundwater before they reach an adjacent stream, river, or lake (Bowman 1999). By adjusting mowing heights when coming off a fairway and transitioning into a wetland or environmentally sensitive site, seashore paspalum can effectively reduce surface runoff and possible cascading of nutrients off the golf course or recreational field (Cole et al., 1997). Fine-textured paspalums can be mowed up to 2.5 to 3.0 in. for the initial buffer zone filtration (Beard, 1998). Coarse-textured paspalums or well-adapted native vegetation can be planted in an unmowed, low maintenance final buffer strip immediately adjacent to the wetland sites. Some coarse paspalums will reach heights of 24–30 in. with a very thick canopy that is exceptionally effective in removing nutrients and sediment. Buffer strips should be made as wide as possible, depending on slope, size of watershed, and chemical properties (water solubility, absorption coefficient) of the pesticides and fertilizers used at the site (Beard, 1998; Walker and Branham, 1992).

Because of its deep rooting capability, paspalum would also be effective in removing nitrates or other chemicals from lateral, subsurface groundwater flows, both through direct absorption/uptake and through enhancement of denitrification and other chemical processes. Paspalum will also function in this capacity in saturated soil conditions when other warm-season grasses, such as bermudagrass, tend to lose their root systems.

CHAPTER 19

Bioremediation and Reclamation

Plant bioremediation can involve many different ways of naturally cleaning up environmental or man-made problems. Grasses can be used to clean up contaminated soils. Riparian vegetation (buffer strips) will intercept nonpoint source pollution (McCutcheon, 1998). Created wetlands can be designed to remove dissolved contaminants from industrial effluents, surface waters, or groundwaters pumped to the surface (Dushenkov et al., 1995; Medina and McCutcheon, 1996).

Phytoremediation of soil or water uses green plants to degrade, assimilate, metabolize, or detoxify metals and organic chemicals (McCutcheon and Wolfe, 1998). Types of green remediation include:

1. Phytoaccumulation, phytoextraction, hyperaccumulation (Kumar et al., 1995).
   Metals and organic chemicals are absorbed with water or by cation pumps, sorption, or other mechanisms. Examples of hyperaccumulator or metal scavenger plants include *Thlaspi* (pennycress) for Cd, Zn, Pb, and Ryegrass (Ni) (Brown et al., 1995; Comis, 1995).
2. Rhizofiltration (Dushenkov et al., 1995)
   Contaminant uptake through the root system
3. Phytostabilization
   Plants control soil gases, pH, and redox conditions in the soil and mine tailing ponds that change speciation.
4. Phytovolatilization
   Volatile organic compounds are taken up; metal species are changed and are transpired into the air.
5. Phytostimulation, rhizosphere bioremediation, or plant-assisted bioremediation (Anderson et al., 1993).
   Roots provide the habitat to retard chemical movement. Dead roots "house" the anaerobes while live roots pump oxygen to them. Exudates stimulate enzyme production and

transformation/co-metabolic degradation via soil bacteria, mycorrhizal fungi, and microbes.
6. Phytodegradation or phytotransformation (Schnoor, 1998)
    Reductive or oxidative (growth or senescence) enzymes metabolize or detoxify certain compounds biochemically. Key enzymes: dehalogenase, nitroreductase, peroxidase, laccase, nitrilase, phosphatase (McCutcheon and Wolfe, 1998).

Several different species of plants have been used to phytoremediate organic contaminants (Schnoor, 1998):

- *phreatophytes,* which establish roots deep into the groundwater table (*Salix* family-hybrid poplar, cottonwoods, willow)
- grasses that produce a fibrous root system, which retards chemical movement and holds the soil in place
- legumes for nitrogen enrichment of poor soils (clover, alfalfa)
- aquatic plants in created wetlands that will degrade contaminants in sediments and water.

Seashore paspalum has a long history of use for bioremediation of contaminated or unproductive soils, beginning in South Africa and spreading eventually to salt-affected areas around the world (especially Australia). Since the grass evolved on sand dunes, it was naturally used for sand dune stabilization and coastal erosion control. Later, it was used in soil conservation programs and to rehabilitate flood-prone areas plagued by wet, saline-seepage problems or by physically degraded soils.

Seashore paspalum was used as a hyperaccumulator on iron ore tailings with elevated levels of Mn, Cu, and Fe (Wong et al., 1983), on kimberlite mine tailings in South Africa (Miles and Tainton, 1979), and on phytotoxic mining wastes in Zimbabwe (Hill, 1972, 1978ab). It has been used for rehabilization of structureless soils (Theron et al., 1972), coastal sand dune stabilization (Batianoff and McDonald, 1980; Craig, 1974, 1976; Ferguson, 1951; Rose and Lorber, 1976), and reclamation of high saline problem areas in a desert (Le Houerou, 1977).

Because of its adaptation to aquatic biotopes, seashore paspalum has been valuable in reclamation of flood-prone areas (Colman and Wilson, 1960; Chaudhri et al., 1969; Vanden Berghen, 1982) and wet saline seepage sites [Gross, 1952; Glenhill, 1963; Logan, 1958; Malcolm, 1962, 1977, 1986; McPhie, 1973; salt land reclamation in West Australia (1967);

Straatmans, 1954]. It has been used to reclaim highly alkaline soils in Argentina (Ragonese and Covas, 1947) and in various soil conservation programs (Cameron, 1954, 1959; Mitchell, 1965; Soil Conservation Authority, 1963).

In the United States, the grass has been evaluated along with common bermudagrass for revegetation of bauxite residue spoil areas in the Port Lavaca-Corpus Christi, Texas areas (Lloyd Hossner, personal communication). Additional research with this species involves remediation of TCEs (trichloroethylene) and phytoextraction of cesium and strontium from soils and sediments at the U.S. Department of Energy site on the Savannah River (Domy Adriano, personal communication) (Hoyt and Adriano, 1979).

References

Note: References are grouped together by topic. Some references are not cited in the text, but provide an additional source for information.

Chapter 1. Introduction

Carrow, R.N. and R.R. Duncan. 1998. *Salt-Affected Turfgrass Sites: Assessment and Management.* Ann Arbor Press, Chelsea, MI.

Duncan, R.R. 1999a. Environmental compatibility of seashore paspalum (saltwater couch) for golf courses and other recreational uses. I. Breeding and genetics. *Int'l Turfgrass Soc. Res. J.* 8(2):1208–1215.

Duncan, R.R. 1999b. Environmental compatibility of seashore paspalum (saltwater couch) for golf courses and other recreational uses. II. Management protocols. *Int'l Turfgrass Soc. Res. J.* 8(2):1216–1230.

Morton, J.F. 1973. Salt-tolerant siltgrass (*Paspalum vaginatum* Sw.). *Proc. FL State Hort. Soc.* 86:482–490.

U.S. Golf Association. 1994. *Wastewater Reuse for Golf Course Irrigation.* Lewis Publishers, Boca Raton, FL.

Chapter 2. Nomeclature

Acevedo de Vargas, R. 1944. Contribucion al conocimiento del genero *Paspalum* en Chile. *Bol. Museum Nacional de Historica Nature* 21:121–135.

Alderson, J. and W.C. Sharp. 1995. *Grass varieties in the United States.* USDA Handbook 170. Lewis Publishers, Boca Raton, FL.

Bosser, J. 1969. *Graminees des Pasturages et des cultures A Madagascar.* Ostrom, Paris, France. p. 397.

Chase, A. 1929. The North American species of *Paspalum. Cont. U.S. Natl. Herb.* 28:1–310.

Echarte, A.M. and A.M. Clausen. 1993. Morphological affinities between *Paspalum distichum* sensu lato and *P. vaginatum* (Poaceae). *BOL. Soc. Argentina Botany* 29(3–4):143–152.

Fosberg, F.R. 1977. *Paspalum distichum* again. *Taxon* 26:201–202.

Guedes, M. 1976. The case for *Paspalum distichum* and against futile name changes. *Taxon* 25(4):512–513 (nomenclature).

Guedes, M. 1981. Against rejecting the name *Paspalum distichum* L: comment on proposal 528. *Taxon* 30:301.

Hafliger, E. and H. Scholz. 1980. *Panicoid grass weeds.* Ciba-Geigy, Ltd. Basel, Switzerland. p. 108.

Hitchcock, A.S. 1971. *Manual of the Grasses of the United States.* 2nd ed. Revised by A. Chase. Dover Publ. Inc., New York. pp. 603, 933.

Hitchcock, A.S. and A. Chase. 1917. *Grasses of the West Indies.* In Contribution from U.S. Nat'l Herbarium 18(7):261–471. Smithsonian Institute, U.S. Nat'l Museum. Washington DC Govt. Print. Office.

Loxton, A.E. 1974. The taxonomy of *Paspalum paspaloides* and *Paspalum vaginatum* as requested in South Africa. *Bothalia* 11(3):243–245.

Loxton, A.E. 1977. *Paspalum vaginatum* subsp. *nanum.* A new status. *J. So. Africa. Bot.* 43:93–95.

Mejia, M.M. 1984. *Scientific and common names of tropical forage species.* CIAT, Cali, Columbia. p. 28.

Morton, J.F. 1973. Salt-tolerant siltgrass (*Paspalum vaginatum* Sw.). *Proc. FL State Hort. Soc.* 86:482–490.

Renvoize, S.A. and W.D. Clayton. 1980. Proposal to reject the name *Paspalum distichum* L. *System. Natural. Ed.* 10(2):855, 1759 and *Taxon* 29:339.

Report of the Committee for Spermatophyta. 1983. Proposal 528. Rejection of *Paspalum distichum* L. (*Gramineae*). *Taxon* 32:281.

Schulz, A.G. 1962. Plantas forraijeras indigenas del Chaco. Nota preliminar. *Estacion Experimentale Agricultura Colonia Benitez Foll.* N° 4.

Skerman, P.J. and F. Riveros. 1990. *Tropical grasses.* Food & Agric. Organization of the United Nations. pp. 119, 128, 130, 565–568.

Webster. R.D. 1987. *The Australian Paniceae (Poaceae).* J. Cramer. Berlin-Stuttgart, Germany. pp. 173–174, 181–182.

Chapter 3. Taxonomy

Alderson, J. and W.C. Sharp. 1995. *Grass varieties in the United States.* USDA Handbook 170. Lewis Publishers, Boca Raton, FL.

Barnard, C. 1969. *Herbage plant species.* Austral. Herbage Plant Reg. Authority, CSIRO, Australian Division of Plant Industries, Canberra, Australia.

Barreto, I.L. 1957. The *Paspalum* species with two conjugate recemes in Rio Grande do Sul (Brazil). *Rev. Argentina Agron.* 24:89–117.

Bashaw, E.C., A.W. Hovin, and E.C. Holt. 1970. Apomixis, its evolutionary significance and utilization in plant breeding. pp. 245–248. In *Proc. XI Int'l Grassland Congress.* Univ. Queensland Press, Australia.

Beehag, G.W. 1986. Paspalum turfgrass. *Bowling Greenkeeper* 20(11):20–21.

Bor, N.L. 1960. *The Grasses of Burma, Ceylon, India, and Pakistan (excluding Bambuseae).* Int'l Series Monog., Permagon Press, Oxford, UK.

Bovo, O.A., L.A. Mroginski, and C. Quarin. 1988. Paspalum spp. pp. 495–503. In Y.P.S. Bajaj (Ed.). *Biotechnology in Agriculture and Forestry.* Vol. 6, *Crops II.* Springer-Verlag, Berlin.

Burson, B.L 1981a. Genome relations among four diploid *Paspalum* species. *Bot. Gaz.* 142:592–596.

Burson, B.L. 1981b. Cytogenetic relationships between *Paspalum jurgensii, P. intermedum, P. vaginatum,* and *P. setaceum* var. *ciliatifolium. Crop Sci.* 21:515–519.

Burson, B.L. 1983. Phylogenetic investigations of *Paspalum dilatatum* and related species. pp. 170–173. In J.A. Smith and V.W. Hays (Eds.). *Proc. XIV Int'l Grassland Congress.* Lexington, KY. June 15–24, 1981. Westview Press, Boulder, CO.

Burson, B.L. and H.W. Bennett. 1972. Cytogenetics of *Paspalum urvillei* X *P. juergensii* and *P. urvillei* X *P. vaginatum* hybrids. *Crop Sci.* 12:105–108.

Burson, B.L., H.-S. Lee, and H.W. Bennett. 1973. Genome relations between tetraploid *Paspalum dilatatum* and four diploid *Paspalum species. Crop Sci.* 13:739–743.

Carpenter, J.A. 1958. Production and use of seed in seashore paspalum. *J. Australian Inst. Agric. Sci.* 24:252–256.

Chapman, G.P. 1992. Grass evolution and domestication. Cambridge University Press, Cambridge, UK.

Chapman, G.P. and W.E. Peat. 1992. *An introduction to grasses (including the bamboos and cereals).* CAB Int'l., Wallingford, UK.

Chase, A. 1929. *The North American Species of Paspalum.* Contrib. U.S. Nat'l Herbarium 28:1–310.

Chase, A. 1951. *Manual of the Grasses of the United States.* USDA Miscellaneous pub. No. 200. Vol. 2, 2nd ed. pp. 928–929, 933.

Clayton, W.D. and S.A. Renvoize. 1986. Genera Graminum, grasses of the world. *Kew Bulletin,* Add. Ser. 13:1–389.

Echarte, A.M. and A.M. Clausen. 1993. Morphological affinities between *Paspalum distichum* sensu lato and *P. vaginatum* (Poaceae). *BDL Soc. Argentina Botany* 29(3–4):143–152.

Echarte, A.M., A.M. Clausen, and C.A. Sala. 1992. Chromosome numbers and morphological variability in *Paspalum distichum* (Poaceae) in Buenos Aires province (Argentina). *Darwiniana* 31:185–197.

Ellis, R.P. 1974. Comparative leaf anatomy of *Paspalum paspaloides* and *P. vaginatum. Bothalia* 11:235–241. Also *Herb. Abstr.* 45:3142.

Espinoza, F. and C.L. Quarin. 1997. Cytoembryology of *Paspalum chaseanum* and sexual diploid biotypes of two apomictic *Paspalum* species. *Austral. J. Botany* 45:871–877.

Fedorov, A. 1974. *Chromosome members of flowering plants.* Koenigstein, Fed. Repub. Germany. Otto Koeltz Science Pub.

Hafliger, E. and H. Scholtz. 1980. *Panicoid grass weeds.* Ciba Geigy, Ltd., Basel, Switzerland.

Hitchcock, A.S. 1971. *Manual of the Grasses of the United States.* 2nd ed. revised by A. Chase. Dover Publ. Inc., New York.

Hitchcock, A.S. and A. Chase. 1917. *Grasses of the West Indies.* In Contribution from U.S. Nat'l Herbarium 18(7):261–471. Smithsonian Institute, U.S. Nat'l Museum. Washington DC Government Printing Office.

Llaurado, M. 1984. El genero *Paspalum* L.A. Catalunya. *Bulletin Inst. Catalana Historical Nature, Session Botany* 51:101–108.

Loxton, A.E. 1974. The taxonomy of *Paspalum paspaloides* and *P. vaginatum* as represented in South Africa. *Bothalia* 11:243–245. Also *Herb. Abstr.* 45:3158.

Morton, J.F. 1973. Salt-tolerant siltgrass (*Paspalum vaginatum* Swartz). *Proc. FL State Hort. Soc.* 86:482–490.

Norrmann, G.A., C.L. Quarin, and B.L. Burson. 1989. Cytogenetics and reproductive behavior of different chromosome races in six *Paspalum* species. *J. Heredity* 80:24–28.

Okoli, B.E. 1982. IOPB chromosome number reports LXXIV. *Taxon* 31:127.

Pitman, M.W., B.L. Burson, and E.C. Bashaw. 1987. Phylogenetic relationships among *Paspalum* species with different base chromosome numbers. *Botanical Gazette* 148:130–135.

Quarin, C.L. 1992. The nature of apomixis and its origin in panicoid grasses. *Apomixis Newsletter* 5:8–15.

Quarin, C. and B.L. Burson. 1983. Cytogenetic relations among *Paspalum notatum* var. *saurae*, *P. pumilum*, *P. indecorum*, and *P. vaginatum*. *Botanical Gazette* 144:433–438.

Quarin, C.L. and B.L. Burson. 1991. Cytology of sexual and apomictic *Paspalum* species. *Cytologia* 56:223–228.

Silveus, W.A. 1933. *Texas grasses.* The Clegg Co., San Antonio, TX.

Skerman, P.J. and F. Riveros. 1990. *Tropical Grasses.* Food & Agric. Organization of the United Nations. #23, Rome, Italy.

Sleper, D.A., K.H. Asay, and J.F. Pedersen. 1989. *Contributions from Breeding Forage and Turf Grasses.* CSSA Spec. Pub. 15. Crop Sci. Soc. Amer. Madison, WI.

Valls, J.F.M. 1987. Recursos geneticos de especies de *Paspalum* no Brasil. pp. 3–13. In J.F.M. Valls (Ed.) *Encontro Internacional sobre Melhoramento de Paspalum.* Annals Institute de Zootecnia. Nova Odessa, Brasil.

Vegetti, A.C. 1987. Typological analysis of inflorescence in *Paspalum* Poaceae. *Kurtziana* 19:155–160.

Watson, L. and M.J. Dallwitz. 1992. *The Grass Genera of the World.* CAB Int'l., Wallingford, UK.

Webster, R.D. 1987. *The Australian Paniceae (Poacea).* J. Cramer, Berlin, Germany.

Wipff, J.K. 1995. A biosystemic study of selected facultative apomictic species of *Pennisetum* (Poaceae:Paniceae) and their hybrids. Dissertation: Texas A & M University, College Station, TX.

Chapter 4. History

Anonymous. 1982. Grass experiment a hit at Alden Pines, *Fort Myers News-Press.* January 10, 1982.

Beard, J.B, S.M. Batten, S.R. Reed, K.S. Kim, and S.D. Griggs. 1982. A preliminary assessment of Adalayd *Paspalum vaginatum* for turfgrass characteristics and adaptation to Texas conditions. *Texas Turfgrass Research-1982.* PR-4039. pp. 33–34, 43.

Beard, J.B, S.I. Sifers, and S.D. Grigg. 1991a. Genetic diversity in low temperature hardiness among 35 major warm-season turfgrass genotypes. *Texas Turfgrass Research-1991.* PR-4898. pp. 56–58.

Beard, J.B, S.I. Sifers, and M.H. Hall. 1991b. Cutting height and nitrogen fertility requirements of Adalayd seashore paspalum (*Paspalum vaginatum*)—1988–1989. *Texas Turfgrass Research-1991.* PR-4921. pp. 107–109.

Beard, J.B, S.I. Sifers, and W.G. Menn. 1991c. Cultural strategies for seashore paspalum. *Grounds Maintenance* August: 32, 62.

Beehag, G.W. 1986. Paspalum turfgrass. *Bowling Greenkeeper* 20(11):20–21.

Bor, N.L. 1960. *The Grasses of Burma, Crylon, India, and Pakistan (excluding Bambuseae).* Int'l. Series Monog., Pergamon Press, Oxford, UK.

Bovo, O.A., L.A. Mroginski, and C. Quarin. 1988. *Paspalum* spp. pp. 495–503. In Y.P.S. Bajaj (Ed.). *Biotechnology in Agriculture and Forestry,* Vol. 6, Crops II. Springer-Verlag, Berlin, Germany.

Burt, E.O. 1963. Summary of South Florida Turf Research. *Proc. Univ. FL Turfgrass Manage. Conf.* 11: 164.

Busey, P. 1977. Turfgrasses for the 1980's. *Proc. FL State Hort. Soc.* 90:111–114.

Campbell, W.F. 1979. Futurf: A new turfgrass for Utah's Dixie. *Utah Sci.* June: 32–33.

Carrow, R.N. and R.R. Duncan. 1998. *Salt-Affected Turfgrass Sites: Assessment and Management.* Ann Arbor Press, Chelsea, MI.

Chapman, G.P. 1992. *Grass Evolution and Domestication.* Cambridge University Press, UK.

Chapman, G.P. and W.E. Peat. 1992. *An Introduction to the Grasses.* CAB Int'l., Wallingford, Oxon, UK.

Chase, A. 1929. The North American species of Paspalum. *Contrib. Nat'l Herb.* 28:1–310.

Chippendall, L.K.A. 1955. A guide to identification of grasses in South Africa. In D. Meredith (Ed.). *The Grasses & Pastures of South Africa Parov. (Cape Province),* South Africa Central News Agency.

Colman, R.L. and G.P.M. Wilson. 1960. The effects of floods on pasture plants. *Agric. Gazette, NSW* 71:337–347.

Cope, T.A. 1985. A key to the grasses of the Arabian Peninsula. *Arab Gulf J. Scientific Res. Spec. Pub. #1.* Arab Bur, Educ. for Gulf States. Riyadhg, Saudi Arabia.

Craig, R.M. 1974. Coastal dune vegetation. *Proc. FL. State Hort. Soc.* 87:548–552.

Craig, R.M. 1976. Grasses for coastal dune areas. *Proc. FL. State Hort. Soc.* 89:353–355.

Dirven, J.G.P. 1963a. The nutritive value of the indigenous grasses of Surinam. *Netherlands J. Agric. Sci.* 11:295–307.

Dirven, J.G.P. 1963b. The protein content of Surinam roughages. Surinam Paramaribo, *Agric. Exp. Stn. Bull.* 82.

Duble, R.L. 1988. Seashore paspalum. *Southern Turfgrass,* Spring. pp. 12–13.

Dudeck, A.E. and C.H. Peacock. 1985. Effects of salinity on seashore paspalum turfgrasses. *Agron. J.* 77:47–50.

Echarte, A.M., A.M. Clausen, and C.A. Sala. 1992. Chromosome numbers and morphological variability in *Paspalum distichum* (Poaceae) in Buenos Aires province (Argentina). *Darwiniana* 31:185–197.

Edwards, A.W.A. and O.E.C. Ekundayo. 1981. Biomass analysis of mangrove swamp successional species. *Int'l J. Ecol. Environ. Sci.* 7:1–10.

Everist, S.L. 1974. *Poisonous plants of Australia.* Angus & Robertson, Sydney, Australia.

Everist, S.L. 1975. Under-exploited tropical plants with promising economic value. *U.S. Nat'l Acad. Sci.* 9.

Facelli, J.M., R.J.C. Leon, and V.A. Deregibus. 1989. Community structure in grazed and ungrazed grassland sites in the Flooding Pampa, Argentina. *Amer. Midland Naturalist* 121:125–133.

Fisher, M.J. and P.J. Skerman. 1986. Salt tolerant forage plants for summer rainfall areas. *Reclam. Reveg. Res.* 5:263–284.

Fosberg, F.R., M.-H. Sachet, and R. Oliver. 1987. A geographical checklist of the Micronesian monocotyledonae. *Micronesia* 20(1–2):19–129.

Garland, K. and J.S. Duff 1981. *Saltland in Victoria*. Victorian Irrig. Res. & Promot. Org.

Gibeault, V.A., M.K. Leonard, and J.M. Henry. 1988. Seashore paspalum scalping study. *Calif. Turfgrass Cult.* 38(3–4):1–3.

Gibeault, V.A., J.L. Meyer, R. Autio, and R. Strohman. 1989. Turfgrass alternatives with low water needs. *Calif. Agric.* 43:20–22.

Gray, L.C. 1933. *History of Agriculture in the Southern United States to 1860*. Vol. I. Carnegie Institute, Washington DC.

Haflinger, E. and H. Scholtz. 1980. Panicoid Grass Weeds. Ciba Geigy, Ltd., Basel, Switzerland.

Harivandi, M.A. and V.A. Gibeault. 1983. Fertilizing seashore paspalum. *Calif. Turfgrass Cult.* 33:8–10.

Harivandi, M.A., W. Davis, V.A. Gibeault, M. Henry, J. Van Dam, and L. Wu. 1984. Selecting the best turfgrass. *Calif. Turfgrass Cult.* 34:17–18.

Harivandi, M.A., C.L. Elmore, and J.M. Henry. 1987. An evaluation of herbicides on seashore paspalum. *Calif. Turfgrass Cult.* 17(1–2):2–5.

Hattersley, P.W. 1992. Significance of intra-C_4 photosynthetic pathway variation in grasses of arid and semi-arid regions. pp. 181–212. In G.P. Chapman (Ed.) *Desertified Grasslands, Their Biology and Management.* Academic Press, London, UK.

Henry, M. 1981. Adalayd—A new turfgrass species. *The Florida Green.* Fall:25–27.

Henry, M., V.A. Gibeault, V.B. Younger, and S. Spaulding. 1979. *Paspalum vaginatum* 'Adalayd' and 'Futurf.' *California Turfgrass* 29:9–12.

Hill, J.C.R. 1978a. The use of range plants in the stabilization of phytotoxic mining wastes. pp. 707–711. In D.N. Hyder (Ed.). *Proc. 1st Int'l Rangeland Congress.* Denver, CO, 14–18 Aug. 1978. Soc. Range Mgmt. Dep. Bot. Rhodesia Univ., Salisbury, Rhodesia.

Hill, J.C.R. 1978b. A root growth study used to examine the suitability of two grasses for stabilizing toxic mine wastes. Dept. Conserv. Exten. Salisbury, Zimbabwe. *Proc. Grassland Soc. South Africa* 13:129–133.

Horn, C.C. 1963. Progress Report. *Proc. Univ. FL Turfgrass Manage. Conf.* 11:169.

Ibrahim, K.M. and C.H.S. Kabuye. 1988. *An Illustrated Manual of Kenya Grasses.* FAO. Rome, Italy.

Joy, R.J. and P.P. Rotar. 1991. 'Tropic Shore' seashore paspalum *Paspalum vaginatum* Sw. *University of Hawaii Research Extension Series* 122. pp. 1–4.

Judd, B.I. 1979. *Handbook of Tropical Forage Grasses.* Garland STPM Press, New York.

Lazarides, M. 1980. *The Tropical Grasses of Southeast Asia (Excluding Bamboos).* A.R. Gantner Verlag K.G., Germany.

Maddaloni, J. 1986. Forage production on saline and alkaline soils in the humid region of Argentina. *Reclam. Reveg. Res.* 5:11–16.

Malcolm, C.V. 1962. *Paspalum vaginatum* for salty seepages. J. Dept. Agric. West. Austr. 3:615–616.

Malcolm, C.V. 1986. Production from salt affected soils. *Reclam. Reveg. Res.* 5:343–361.

Marcum, K.B. and C.L. Murdoch. 1994. Salinity tolerance mechanisms of six C$_4$ turfgrasses. *J. Amer. Soc. Hort. Sci.* 119:779–784.

McTaggart, A. 1940. Plant introduction. In *Grassland Investigations in Australia. Herbage Publication Series Bulletin* 29:18–21. Imperial Bureau Pasture Forage Crops. Aberystwyth, UK.

Morey, D. 1994. Golf in Hawaii. The best of the best. *Southern Golf* 25(5):16–19.

Morton, J.F. 1973. Salt-tolerant siltgrass (*Paspalum vaginatum Swartz*). *Florida State Hort. Soc. Proc.* 86:482–490.

National Academy of Sciences. 1975. *Underexploited tropical plants with promising economic value.* Washington DC.

O'Kelly, J.C. and H.P. Reich. 1976. The fatty acid composition of tropical grasses. *J. Agric. Sci. UK* 86:427–429.

Peacock, C.H. and A.E. Dudeck. 1985. Physiological and growth responses of seashore paspalum to salinity. *HortSci.* 20:111–112.

Rinciman, H.V. 1986. Forage production from salt affected wasteland in Australia. *Reclamation Reveg. Res.* 5:17–29.

Rose, S.A. and M.D. Lorber. 1976. Sand dune stabilization and revegetation in Brevard county. *Proc. FL State Hort. Soc.* 89:346–348.

Roseveare, G.M. 1948. *The Grasslands of Latin America.* Bulletin 3b. Imperial Bureau Pastures & Field Crops. William Lewis Printers, Ltd., Cardiff, Aberystwyth, UK.

Skerman, P.J. and F. Riveros. 1990. *Tropical Grasses.* Plant Prod. & Protect. Series #23. Food & Agric. Organization of the United Nations. Rome, Italy.

Smalley, R.R. 1962. Turf research in South Florida in 1961–62. *Proc. Univ. FL Turfgrass Manage. Conf.* 10:217.

Swaine, M.D, D.U.V. Okali, J.B. Hall, and J.M. Lock. 1979. Zonation of a coastal grassland in Ghana, West Africa. *Folia Geobotanica et Phytotaxonomica* 14:11–27.

Theron, E.P., R. Ludorf, and A. Jones. 1972. Notes on the value of *Paspalum vaginatum* Sw. as a pasture grass for saline and structureless soils. *Proc. Grassland Soc. South Africa* 7:126–129.

Trumble, H.C. 1940. *Grass Investigations at the Waite Agricultural Research Institute,* University of Adelaide. pp. 57–60.

Vermeulen, P.H. 1992. The best choice may not always be your favorite. *USGA Green Section Record* 30(1):1–5.

Webster, R.D. 1987. *The Australian Paniceae (Poaceae).* J. Cramer, Berlin, Germany. pp. 173–174, 181–182.

Chapter 5. Genetics

Brown, S.M., S.E. Mitchell, C.A. Jester, Z.W. Liu, S. Kresovich, and R.R. Duncan. 1998. DNA typing (profiling) of seashore paspalum (*Paspalum vaginatum* Swartz) ecotypes and cultivars. pp. 39–51. In M.B. Sticklen and M.P. Kenna (Eds.). *Turfgrass Biotechnology: Cell and Molecular Genetic Approaches to Turfgrass Improvement.* Ann Arbor Press, Chelsea, MI.

Burson, B.L. 1981. Cytogenetic relations between *Paspalum jurgensii* and *P. intermedum*, *P. vaginatum*, and *P. setaceum* var. *ciliatifolium*. *Crop Sci.* 21:515–519.

Burson, B.L. 1985. Cytology of *Paspalum chacoense* and *P. durifolium* and their relationship to *P. dilatatum*. *Bot. Gaz.* 146:124–129.

Busey, P. 1977. Turfgrasses for the 1980's. *Proc. FL State Hort. Soc.* 90:111–114.

Cardona, C.A. 1996. Development of a tissue culture protocol and low temperature tolerance assessment of *Paspalum vaginatum* Sw. Ph.D. Dissertation. University of Georgia, Athens.

Cardona, C.A., R.R. Duncan, and O. Lindstrom. 1997a. Low temperature tolerance assessment in paspalum. *Crop Sci.* 37:1283–1291.

Cardona, C.A. and R.R. Duncan. 1997b. Callus induction and high efficiency plant regeneration via somatic embryogenesis in paspalum. *Crop Sci.* 37:1297–1302.

Cardona, C.A. and R.R. Duncan. 1998. In vitro culture, somoclonal variation, and transformation strategies with paspalum turf ecotypes. pp. 229–236. In M.B. Sticklen and M.P. Kenna (Eds.). *Turfgrass Biotechnology: Cell and Molecular Genetic Approaches to Turfgrass Improvement.* Ann Arbor Press, Chelsea, MI.

Carpenter, J.A. 1958. Production and use of seed in seashore paspalum. *J. Austral. Instit. Agric. Sci.* 24:252–256.

Clausen, A.M., S.I. Alonso, M.C. Nuciari, A.M. Echarte, and M. Pollio. 1989. *FAO/IBPGR Plant Genetic Resources Newsletter* 78/79:31.

Duncan, R.R. 1999. Environmental compatibility of seashore paspalum (saltwater couch) for golf courses and other recreational uses. I. Breeding and genetics. *Int'l Turfgrass Soc. Res. J.* 8(II):1208–1215.

Jarret, R.L., P. Ozias-Akins, S. Phatak, R. Nadimpalli, R. Duncan, and S. Hilliard. 1995. DNA contents in *Paspalum* spp. determined by flow cytometry. *Genetic Resour. Crop Eval.* 42:237–242.

Jarret, R.L., Z.W. Liu, and R.W. Webster. 1998. Genetic diversity among *Paspalum* spp. as determined by RFLPs. *Euphytica* 104:119–125.

Joy, R.J. and P.P. Rotar. 1984. 'Tropic Lalo' paspalum *Paspalum hieronymii* Hack. *Univ. Hawaii Res. Extn. Series* 046. College Trop. Agric. Human Resources, Honolulu, HI.

Liu, Z.W., R.L. Jarret, R.R. Duncan, and S. Kresovich. 1994. Genetic relationships and variation of ecotypes of seashore paspalum (*Paspalum vaginatum* Swartz) determined by random amplified polymorphic DNA (RAPD) markers. *Genome* 37:1011–1017.

Liu, Z.W., R.L. Jarret, S. Kresovich, and R.R. Duncan. 1995. Characterization and analysis of simple sequence repeat (SSR) loci in seashore paspalum (*Paspalum vaginatum* Swartz). *Theor. Appl. Genet.* 91:47–52.

Malcolm, C.V. 1983. Wheatbelt salinity. A review of the land problem in Southwest Australia. *Tech. Bull.* #52. Dept. Agric. W. Austral., Perth.

Malcolm, C.V. and I.A.F. Liang. 1969. *Paspalum vaginatum*—for salty seepages and lawns. *J. Agric. West. Austral.* 11:474–475.

M'Ribu, H.K. and K.W. Hilu. 1996. Application of random amplified polymorphic DNA to study genetic diversity in *Paspalum scrobiculatum* L. (Kodo millet, Poaceae). *Genetic Resour. Crop Eval.* 43:203–210.

Ortiz, J.P.A., S.C. Pessino, O. Leblanc, M.D. Hayward, and C.L. Quarin. 1997. Genetic fingerprinting for determining the mode of reproduction in *Paspalum notatum*, a subtropical apomictic forage grass. *Theor. Appl. Genet.* 95:850–856.

Pupilli, F., M.E. Caceres, C.L. Quarin, and S. Arcioni. 1997. Segregation analysis of RFLP markers reveals a tetrasomic inheritance in apomictic *Paspalum simplex*. *Genome* 40:822–828.

Quarin, C. and B.L. Burson. 1983. Cytogenetic relations among *Paspalum notatum* var. *saurae*, *P. pumilum*, *P. indecorum*, and *P. vaginatum*. *Bot. Gaz.* 144:433–438.

Ramirez, G.C. and A.M. Romero. 1978. The Pacific as a transporting agent on the Chilean coast. *Ecologia* 3:19–30.

Raynal, G. 1996. Presence en France de *Claviceps paspali* Stev. et Hall sur *Paspalum distichum* L. et de L'ergotisme correspondant sur du Betail. *Cryptogamie Mycol.* 17(1): 21–31.

Skerman, P.J. and F. Riveros. 1990. *Tropical Grasses*. FAO Plant Prod. Series #23. Rome, Italy.

Chapter 6. Breeding for Multiple Environmental Stresses

Akashi, R. and T. Adachi. 1992. Somatic embryogenesis and plant regeneration from cultured immature inflorescences of *Paspalum dilatatum* Poir. *Plant Sci.* 82:213–218.

Akashi, R., A. Hashimoto, and T. Adachi. 1993. Plant regeneration from seed-derived embryogenic callus and cell suspension cultures of bahiagrass (*Paspalum notatum*). *Plant Sci.* 90:73–80.

Bovo, O.A. and L.A. Mroginski. 1985. Tissue culture in *Paspalum* (*Gramineae*). Plant regeneration from cultured inflorescences. *J. Plant Physiol.* 124:481–492.

Bovo, O.A. and L.A. Mroginski. 1989. Somatic embryogenesis and plant regeneration from cultured mature and immature embryos of *Paspalum notatum* (*Gramineae*). *Plant Sci.* 65:217–223.

Bovo, O.A. and C.L. Quarin. 1993. Obtencion deplantas de *Paspalum almum* (*Gramineae*) a partir del cultivo *in-vitro* de ovarios jovenes. *Phyton* 43:29–34.

Brown, S.M., S.E. Mitchell, C.A. Jester, Z.W. Liu, S. Kresovich, and R.R. Duncan. 1998. DNA typing (profiling) of seashore paspalum (*Paspalum vaginatum* Swartz) ecotypes and cultivars. pp. 39–51. In M.B. Sticklen and M.P. Kenna (Eds). *Turfgrass Biotechnology: Cell and Molecular Genetic Approaches to Turfgrass Improvement*. Ann Arbor Press, Chelsea, MI.

Burson, B.L. and C.R. Tischler. 1993. Regeneration and somaclonal variation in apomictic *Paspalum dilatatum* Poir. *Euphytica* 67:71–78.

Cardona, C.A. 1996. Development of a tissue culture protocol and low temperature tolerance assessment in *Paspalum vaginatum* Sw. University of Georgia Ph.D. Dissertation.

Cardona, C.A. and R.R. Duncan. 1997. Callus induction and high efficiency plant regeneration via somatic embryogenesis in paspalum. *Crop Sci.* 37:1297–1302.

Cardona, C.A. and R.R. Duncan. 1998. In vitro culture, somaclonal variation, and transformation strategies with paspalum turf ecotypes. pp. 229–236. In M.B.

Sticklen and M.P. Kenna (Eds.). *Turfgrass Biotechnology: Cell and Molecular Genetic Approaches to Turfgrass Improvement.* Ann Arbor Press, Chelsea, MI.

Carrow, R.N. and R.R. Duncan. 1996. Breeding priorities and approaches for edaphic and climatic constraints on turfgrasses. pp. 64–76. In R.R. Duncan (Ed.). *Proc. 34th Grass Breeders Work Planning Conference.* Sept. 16–17, 1996. University of Georgia, Griffin, GA.

Colosi, J.C. and B.A. Schaal. 1993. Tissue grinding with ball bearings and vortex mixer for DNA extraction. *Nucleic Acids Res.* 21:1051–1052.

Davies, L.J. and D. Cohen. 1992. Phenotypic variation in somaclones of *Paspalum dilatatum* and their seedling offspring. *Can. J. Plant Sci.* 72:773–784.

Duncan, R.R. 1996. Breeding turf-type paspalums and tall fescues for the SE. pp. 83–86. In R.R. Duncan (Ed.). *Proc. 34th Grass Breeders Work Planning Conference.* Sept. 16–17, 1996. University of Georgia, Griffin, GA.

Duncan, R.R. and R.N. Carrow. 1998. Genetic tolerance enhancement of warm and cool season grasses for multiple abiotic: Edaphic stresses. pp. 34–41. In G.E. Brink (Ed.) *Proc. 54th South. Pasture & Forage Crop Impv. Conf.,* April 27–29, 1998. Lafayette, LA.

Liu, Z.W., R.L. Jarret, R.R. Duncan, and S. Kresovich. 1994. Genetic relationships and variation of ecotypes seashore paspalum (*Paspalum vaginatum* Swartz) determined by random amplified polymorphic DNA (RAPD) markers. *Genome* 37:1011–1017.

Liu, Z.W., R.L. Jarret, S. Kresovich, and R.R. Duncan. 1995. Characterization and analysis of simple sequence repeat (SSR) loci in seashore pasplaum (*Paspalum vaginatum* Swartz). *Theoretical Appl. Genet.* 91:47–52.

Marousky, F.J. and S.H. West. 1990. Somatic embryogenesis and plant regeneration from cultured mature caryopses of bahiagrass (*Paspalum notatum* Fluegge). *Plant Cell Tissue Organ Cult.* 20:125–129.

Nayak, P. and S.K. Sen. 1991. Plant regeneration through somatic embryogenesis from suspension culture-derived protoplasts of *Paspalum scrobiculatum* L. *Plant Cell Rep.* 10:362–365.

Shatters, R.G. Jr., R. Wheeler, and S.H. West. 1994. Somatic embryogenesis and plant regeneration from callus cultures of 'Tifton 9' bahiagrass. *Crop Sci.* 34:1378–1384.

Chapter 7. Paspalum Abiotic/Edaphic Stress Resistance

Aronson, L.J., A.J. Gold, and R.J. Hull. 1987. Cool-season turfgrass responses to drought stress. *Crop Sci.* 27: 1261–1266.

Bassiri Rad, H. and M.M. Caldwell. 1992. Temporal changes in root growth and ^{15}N uptake and water relations of two tussock grass species recovering from water stress. *Physiol. Plant.* 86:525–531.

Beard, J.B. 1976. *Turfgrass: Science and Culture.* Prentice Hall, Englewood Cliffs, NJ.

Beard, J.B. 1989. Turfgrass water stress: drought resistance components, physiological mechanisms, and species-genotype diversity. pp. 23–28. In H. Takatoh (Ed.) *Proc. 6th Int'l Turf. Res. Conf.,* Japanese Soc. Turfgrass Sci., Tokyo, Japan.

Beard, J.B., S.M. Batten, S.R. Reed, K.S. Kim, and S.D. Griggs. 1982. A preliminary assessment of Adalayd *Paspalum vaginatum* for turfgrass characteristics and adaptation to Texas conditions. *Texas Turfgrass Research-1982.* PR-4039. pp. 33–34.

Beard, J.B, S.I. Sifers, and S.D. Griggs. 1991a. Genetic diversity in low temperature hardiness among 35 major warm-season turfgrass genotypes. *Texas Turfgrass Research-1991.* PR-408. pp. 56–58.

Beard, J.B, S.I. Sifers, and M.H. Hall. 1991b. Cutting height and nitrogen fertility requirements of Adalayd seashore paspalum (*Paspalum vaginatum*)—1988–1989. *Texas Turfgrass Research-1991.* PR-4921. pp. 107–109.

Beard, J.B, S.I. Sifers, and W.G. Menn. 1991c. Cultural strategies for seashore paspalum. *Grounds Maintenance* August: 32, 62.

Brady, D.J., C.L. Wenzel, I.R.P. Fillery, and P.J. Gregory. 1995. Root growth and nitrate uptake by wheat (*Triticum aestivum L.*) following wetting of dry surface soil. *J. Exp. Bot.* 286:557–564.

Campbell, W.F. 1979. Futurf: A new grass for Utah's Dixie. *Utah Sci.* June: 32–33.

Cardona, C.A., R.R. Duncan, and O. Lindstrom. 1997. Low temperature tolerance assessment in paspalum. *Crop Sci.* 37:1283–1291.

Cardona, C.A. and R.R. Duncan. 1998. In vitro culture, somaclonal variation, and transformation strategies with paspalum turf ecotypes. pp. 229–236. In M.B. Sticklen and M.P. Kenna (Eds.). *Turfgrass Biotechnology: Cell and Molecular Genetic Approaches to Turfgrass Improvement.* Ann Arbor Press, Chelsea, MI.

Carrow, R.N. 1996a. Drought avoidance characteristics of diverse tall fescue cultivars. *Crop Sci.* 36:371–377.

Carrow, R.N. 1996b. Drought resistance aspects of turfgrasses in the Southeast: Root-shoot responses. *Crop Sci.* 36:687–694.

Carrow, R.N. and R.R. Duncan. 1998. *Salt-Affected Turfgrass Sites: Assessment and Management.* Ann Arbor Press, Chelsea, MI.

Carrow, R.N. and A.M. Petrovic. 1992. Effects of traffic on turfgrasses. pp. 285–330. In D. Waddington, R.N. Carrow, and R.C. Shearman (Eds.). *Turfgrass Agron. Monogr. No. 32.* ASA, CSSA, Madison, WI.

Carrow, R.N., R.C. Shearman, and J.R. Watson. 1990. Turfgrass. pp. 889–919. In B.A. Stewart and D.R. Nielsen (Eds.). *Irrigation of Agriculture Crops. Agron. Monogr. 30.* ASA, CSSA, and SSSA. Madison, WI.

Casnoff, D.M., R.L. Green, and J.B Beard. 1989. Leaf blade stomatal densities of ten warm-season perennial grasses and their evapotranspiration rates. pp. 129–131. In *Proc. 6th Int'l Turf. Res. Conf.*, Japanese Soc. Turfgrass Sci., Tokyo, Japan.

Chaudhri, I.I., M.Y. Sheikh, and M.M Alam. 1969. Halophytic flora of saline and water-logged areas of West Pakistan plains. *Agric. Pakistan* 20:405–415.

Colman, R.L. and G.P.M. Wilson. 1960. The effects of floods on pasture plants. *Agric. Gaz. N.S.W.* 71:337–347.

Duble, R.L. 1988a. Seashore paspalum *Texas Turfgrass,* Winter, pp. 12–13.

Duble, R.L. 1988b. Seashore paspalum. *Southern Turfgrass* Spring, pp. 12–13.

Duble, R.L. 1989. Seashore paspalum. pp. 86–89. In *Southern Turfgrasses: Their Management and Use.* Tex Scape Inc., College Station, TX.

Dudeck, A.E. and C.H. Peacock. 1985. Effects of salinity on seashore paspalum turfgrasses. *Agron. J.* 77:47–50.

Dudeck, A.E. and C.H. Peacock. 1992. Shade and turfgrass culture. pp. 269–284. In D.V. Waddington, R.N. Carrow, and R.C. Shearman (eds.). *Turfgrass.* Agron. Monogr. No. 32. ASA-CSSA-SSSA, Madison, WI.

Dudeck, A.E. and C.H. Peacock. 1993. Salinity effects on growth and nutrient uptake of selected warm-season turf. *Int'l Turf. Soc. Res. J.* 7:680–686.

Duncan, R.R. 1994. Seashore paspalum may be the grass for the year 2000. *Southern Turf Manage.* 5(1):31–32.

Duncan, R.R. 1997. Paspalum for recreational turf. *Through the Green* July/August: 25, 34.

Duncan, R.R. 1999. Environmental compatibility of seashore paspalum (salt water couch) for golf courses and other recreational uses. II. Management protocols. *Int'l Turf. Soc. Res. J.* 8(2):1216–1230.

Duncan, R.R. and R.N. Carrow. 1998. Genetic tolerance enhancement of warm and cool season grasses for multiple abiotic: edaphic stresses. pp. 34–41. In G.E. Brink (Ed.). *Proc. 54th South. Pasture & Forage Crop Impv. Conf.,* April 27–29, 1998. Lafayette, LA.

Ferguson, D.S. 1951. Construction of coastal bunds in Malaya. *Malay Agric. J.* 34:3–12.

Gibeault, V.A., M.K. Leonard, J.M. Henry, and S.T. Cockerham. 1988. Seashore paspalum scalping study. *Calif. Turf. Culture* 38(3–4):1–3.

Glenhill, D. 1963. The ecology of the Aberdeen Creek mangrove swamp (Sierra Leone). *J. Ecol.* 51:693–703.

Harivandi, M.A. and V.A. Gibeault. 1983. Fertilizing seashore paspalum. *Calif. Turfgrass Cult.* 33:8–10.

Harivandi, M.A., J.D. Butler, and L. Wu. 1992. Salinity in turfgrass culture. pp. 207–229. In D.V. Waddington, R.N. Carrow, and R. Shearman. *Turfgrass.* Agronomy Monograph No. 32. Amer. Soc. Agron., Madison, WI.

Hays, K.L., J.F. Barber, M.P. Kenna, and T.G. McCollum. 1991. Drought avoidance mechanisms of selected bermudagrass genotypes. *Hort Sci.* 26:180–182.

Henry, J.M. and V.A. Gibeault. 1985. *Paspalum vaginatum* winter color management study. *Calif. Turf. Culture* 35(1–4):4–7.

Henry, J.M., V.A Gibeault, V.B. Younger, and S. Spaulding. 1979. *Paspalum vaginatum,* 'Adalayd' and 'Futurf.' *Calif. Turfgrass Culture* 29:9–12.

Henry, J.M. et al. 1982. Turf fertilization study: *Paspalum vaginatum var.* Adalayd. *Western Landscape News,* October: 24, 27–30.

Huang, B. 1997a. Roots and drought resistance. *Golf Course Management* June: 55–59.

Huang, B., R.R. Duncan, and R.N. Carrow. 1997b. Drought-resistance mechanisms of seven warm-season grasses under surface soil drying: I. Shoot response. *Crop Sci.* 37:1858–1863.

Huang, B., R.R. Duncan, and R.N. Carrow. 1997c. Drought-resistance mechanisms of seven warm-season turfgrasses under surface soil drying: II. Root aspects. *Crop Sci.* 37:1863–1869.

Huang, B., R.R. Duncan, and R.N. Carrow. 1997d. Root spatial distribution and activity of four turfgrass species in response to localized drought stress. *Int'l Turf. Soc. Res. J.* 8:681–690.

Ibitayo, O.O., J.D. Butler, and M.J. Burke. 1981. Cold hardiness of bermudagrass and *Paspalum vaginatum* Sw. *HortSci.* 16:638–684.

Le Houerou, H.N. 1977. Biological recovery versus desertification. *Econ. Geogr.* 53:413–420.

Malcolm, C.V. 1977. Saltland and what to do about it. *J. Agric. West. Austral.* 18:127–133.

Marcum, K.B., M.C. Engelke, S.J. Morton, and R.H. White. 1995. Rooting characteristics and associated drought resistance of zoysiagrass. *Agron. J.* 87:534–538.

Miles, N. and N.M. Tainton. 1979. Establishing vegetation on kimberlite mine tailings. 1. Defining the problem and selecting the species. *Proc. Grassland Soc. South Africa* 14:37–41.

Minner, D.D. and J.D. Butler. 1985. Drought tolerance of cool-season turfgrasses. pp. 199–212. In F. Lemaire (Ed.). *Proc. 5th Int'l Turf. Res. Conf.*, Avignan, France. July 1985. Institute National de la Recherche Agronomique, Grenelle, France.

Nobel, P.S. and B. Huang. 1992. Hydraulic and structural changes for lateral roots of two desert succulents in response to soil drying and rewetting. *Int'l J. Plant Sci.* 153:163–170.

Peacock, C.H. and A.E. Dudeck. 1985. Physiological and growth responses of seashore paspalum to salinity. *Hort. Sci.* 20:111–112.

Shearman, R.C. and J.B Beard. 1975. Turfgrass wear tolerance mechanisms. I. Wear tolerance of seven turfgrass species and quantitative methods for determining turfgrass wear injury. *Agron. J.* 67:208–211.

Sifers, S.I., J.B Beard, and M.H. Hall. 1990. Cutting height and nitrogen fertility requirements of Adalayd seashore paspalum-1987. *Texas Turfgrass Research-1990.* PR-4764. pp. 70–71.

Smucker, A.J.M., A. Nunez-Barrios, and J.T. Ritchie. 1991. Root dynamics in drying soil environments. *Belowground Ecol.* 1:1–5.

Straatmans, W. 1954. Reclamation of tidal mud flats in Tonga. *Herb. Abstr.* 25:874. South Pacific Commis. Tech. Paper #53.

Trenholm, L.E., R.N. Carrow, and R.R. Duncan. 1998. Paspalum vs. bermudagrass: Which is more traffic tolerant? *Golf Course Management* July: 61–64.

Trenholm, L.E., R.R. Duncan, and R.N. Carrow. 1999. Wear tolerance, shoot performance, and spectral reflectance of seashore paspalum and bermudagrass. *Crop Sci.* 39:1147–1152.

Trenholm, L.E., R.R. Duncan, and R.N. Carrow. 2000a. The influence of silica on growth, quality, and wear tolerance of seashore paspalum. *Crop Sci.* (in review).

Trenholm, L.E., R.N. Carrow, and R.R. Duncan. 2000b. Wear tolerance, growth, and quality of seashore paspalum in response to nitrogen and potassium. *Crop Sci.* (in review).

Wilson, J.R. 1997. Adaptive responses of grasses to shade: relevance to turfgrasses for low light environments. *Int'l Turf. Soc. Res. J.* 8:575–591.

Wong, C.C. and W.W. Stur. 1996. Persistence of tropical forage grasses in shaded environments. *J. Agric. Sci., Camb.* 126:151–159.

Chapter 8. Paspalum Biotic Stress Resistance

Alfieri, S.A. Jr., K.R. Langdon, J.W. Kimbrough, N.E. El-Gholl, and C. Wehlburg. 1994. *Diseases and Disorders of Plants in Florida.* Bull. #14. FL Dept. Agric. Conserv. Serv., Div. Plant Industry, Gainesville, FL.

Ali, H., D. Backhouse, and L.W. Burgess. 1996. *Fusarium heteroporum* associated with paspalum ergot in eastern Australia. *Australasian Plant Path.* 25:120–125.

Botha, C.J., T.S. Kellerman, and N. Fourie. 1996. A tremorgenic mycotoxicosis in cattle caused by *Paspalum distichum* (L.) infected by *Claviceps paspali. J. South. Afric. Vet. Assoc.* 67(1):36–37.

Braman, S.K. and J.M. Ruter. 1997. Preference of twolined spittlebug for *Ilex* species, hybrids and cultivars. *J. Environ. Hort.* 15(4):211–214.

Brown, H.B. and E.M. Rank. 1915. Forage poisoning due to *Claviceps paspali* on *Paspalum. Miss. Agric. Exp. Stn. Tech. Bull.* 6:3–35.

Cole, R.J., J.W. Dorner, J.A. Lansden, R.H. Cox, C. Pape, B. Cunfer, S.S. Nicholson, and D.M. Bedell. 1977. *Paspalum* staggers: Isolation and identification of tremorgenic metabolites from sclerotia of *Claviceps paspali. J. Agric. Food Chem.* 25:1197–1201.

Cummins, G.B. 1971. *The Rust Fungi of Cereals, Grasses, and Bamboos.* Springer-Verlag. New York.

Duncan, R.R. 1999. Environmental compatibility of seashore paspalum (saltwater couch) for golf courses and other recreational uses. II. Management protocols. *Int'l Turfgrass Soc. Res. J.* 8(2):1216–1230.

Gay, C.N. and R.C. Shattock. 1980. *Fusarium heterosporum* and *Claviceps purpurea* on *Lolium perennne. Trans. Brit. Mycol. Soc.* 74:537–542.

Greber, R.S. 1989. Biological characteristics of grass geminiviruses from eastern Australia. *Ann. Appl. Biol.* 114:471–480.

Johnson-Cicalese, J.M., R.H. Hurley, G.W. Wolfe, and C.R. Funk. 1989. Developing turfgrasses with improved resistance to billbugs. pp. 107–111. *Proc. 6th Int'l Turfgrass Res. Conf.,* Tokyo, Japan.

Langdon, R.F.N. 1963. Paspalum ergot of Australia. *Aust. J. Sci.* 26:55.

Lefebvre, C.L. 1939. Ergot of *Paspalum. Phytopath.* 29:365–367.

Matosic, S., M. Mehak, L. Ercegovic, N. Brajkovic, and J. Suskovic. 1998. Effect of surfactants on the production of ergot-alkaloids by immobilized mycelia of C*laviceps paspali. World J. Microbiol. Biotech.* 14:447–450.

Morton, J.M. 1973. Salt-tolerant silt grass (*Paspalum vaginatum* Sw.). *Florida State Hort. Soc. Proc.* 86:482–490.

Overstreet, C. 1999. Nematode problems in turfgrass. Science and management. *Turf South* January: B1, B2, B5.

Preece, T.F., T.R. Pettit, and D.T. Biggs. 1994. *Fusarium heterosporum* growing on ergots (*Claviceps purpurea*) in spikelets of common cordgrass (*Spartina anglica*) in the Isle of Wright. *Mycol.* 8:9–11.

Raynal, G. 1992. Les ergots des graminees: rappels et nouveauete pour la France. *Phytoma-La Defense des Vegetaux* 444:67–69.

Raynal, G. 1996. Presence en France de *Clavieps paspali* Stev. et Hall sur *Paspalum distichum* L. et de L'ergotisme correspondant sur du Betail. *Cryptogamie Mycol.* 17(1):21–31.

Smiley, R.W., P.H. Dernoeden, and B.B. Clarke. 1992. *Compendium of Turfgrass Diseases.* APS Press, St. Paul, MN.

Watson, L. and M.J. Dallwitz. 1992. *The Grass Genera of the World.* CAB Int'l., Wallingford, UK.

Wiseman, B.R. and R.R. Duncan. 1996. An evaluation of *Paspalum* spp. leaf samples for antibiotic resistance against *Spodoptera frugiperpda* (J.E. Smith) (Lepidoptera: Noctuidae) larvae. *J. Turf Manag.* 1(4):23–36.

Wong, C.C. and W.W. Stur. 1996. Persistence of tropical forage grasses in shaded environments. *J. Agric. Sci. Camb.* 126:151–159.

Chapter 9. Management of Abiotic/Edaphic Stresses

Beard, J.B. 1998. The benefits of golf course turf. *Golf Course Management.* March: 191–201.

Beard, J.B, S.M. Batten, S.R. Reed, K.S. Kim, and S.D. Griggs. 1982. A preliminary assessment of Adalayd *Paspalum vaginatum* for turfgrass characteristics and adaptation to Texas conditions. *Texas Turfgrass Research-1982.* PR-4039. pp. 33–34, 43.

Beard, J.B, S.I. Sifers, and S.D. Griggs. 1991a. Genetic diversity in low temperature hardiness among 35 major warm-season turfgrass genotypes. *Texas Turfgrass Research-1991.* PR-4898. pp. 56–58.

Beard, J.B., S.I. Sifers, and M.H. Hall. 1991b. Cutting height and nitrogen fertility requirements of Adalayd seashore paspalum (*Paspalum vaginatum*)—1988–1989. *Texas Turfgrass Research-1991.* PR-4921. pp. 107–109.

Beard, J.B, S.I. Sifers, and W.G. Menn. 1991c. Cultural strategies for seashore paspalum. *Grounds Maintenance* August: 32, 62.

Carrow, R.N. and R.R. Duncan. 1998a. Performance of several seashore paspalum ecotypes and three bermudagrasses. *GTA Today* 13(1):18–19.

Carrow, R.N. and R.R. Duncan. 1998b. *Salt-Affected Turfgrass Sites: Assessment and Management.* Ann Arbor Press, Chelsea, MI.

de Fatima Ferreira, M. and I.F.M. Valio. 1992. Effects of light and carbohydrate content on rooting of rhizome cuttings of *Paspalum vaginatum* Swartz. (Gramineae). *J. Plant Physiol.* 139:727–730.

Diesburg, K. 1999. A new growth regulator for golf course turfgrass. *Golf Course Management* April: 49–51.

Dubey, R.S. and M. Pessarakli. 1995. Physiological mechanisms of nitrogen absorption and assimilation in plants under stressful conditions. pp. 605–626. In M. Pessarakli (Ed). *Handbook of Plant And Crop Physiology.* Marcel Dekker, Inc., New York.

Duble, R.L. 1988a. Seashore paspalum. *Texas Turfgrass* Winter: 12–13.

Duble, R.L. 1988b. Seashore paspalum. *Southern Turfgrass* Spring: 12–13.

Duble, R.L. 1989. Seashore paspalum. pp. 86–89. In *Southern Turfgrasses: Their Management and Use.* Tex Scape Inc., College Station, TX.

Duble, R.L. 1996. Seashore paspalum. pp. 81–83. In *Southern Turfgrasses: Their Management and Use in the Southern Zone.* Texas A&M University Press, College Station, TX.

Duncan, R.R. 1994. Seashore paspalum may be grass for the year 2000. *Southern Turf Management* 5(1):31–32.

Duncan, R.R.. 1996a. The environmentally sound turfgrass of the future—seashore paspalum can withstand the test. *USGA Green Section Record* 34(1):9–11.

Duncan, R.R. 1996b. Seashore paspalum: the next-generation turf for golf courses. *Golf Course Management* April: 49–51.

Duncan, R.R. 1997a. Seashore paspalum responds to demands of stewardship. *Golf Course Management* February: 49–51.

Duncan, R.R. 1997b. Paspalum for recreational turf. *Through the Green* (Ga GCSA) July/August: 25, 34.

Duncan, R.R. 1997c. Best management strategies for paspalum sod/stolen production and establishment. *TPI Turf News* 21(6):37–38. November/December.

Duncan, R.R. 1998a. 21st century lawn/landscape care: paradox vs. paradigm. In *Nat'l Proc. Pest Control Assoc. Conf.,* October 31, 1998. Nashville, TN.

Duncan, R.R. 1998b. Keys to success with paspalum on golf courses. *Golf Course Management* February: 58–60.

Duncan, R.R. 1998c. Paspalum—An alternative environmentally friendly warm-season grass. *Georgia Green Industry Assoc. J.* 9(3):38, 40, 42.

Duncan, R.R. 1999. Environmental compatibility of seashore paspalum (saltwater couch) for golf courses and other recreational uses. II. Management protocols. *Int'l Turf. Soc. Res. J.* 8(2):1216–1230.

Engelke, M.C. 1985. Survival of selected *Digitaria* spp. and 'Adalayd' seashore paspalum at TAES-Dallas 1983–1985. *Texas Turfgrass Research-1985.* TAES PR-4333. p. 72.

Fender, D. 1998. The importance of turfgrass sod in landscape ordinances. *TPI Turf News* January/February: 45–56.

Gibeault, V.A., M.K. Leonard, J.M. Henry, and S.T. Cockerham. 1988. Seashore paspalum scalping study. *Calif. Turfgrass Culture* 38(3–4):1–3.

Gibeault, V.A., J.L. Meyer, R. Autio, and R. Strohman. 1989. Turfgrass alternatives with low water needs. *Calif. Agric.* 43:20–22.

Goatly, J.M., Jr., V.L. Maddox, and R.M. Watkins. 1996. Growth regulation of bahiagrass (*Paspalum notatum* Fluegge) with imazaquin and AC 263, 22. *Hort. Sci.* 31:396–399.

Harivandi, M.A. and V.A. Gibeault. 1983. Fertilizing seashore paspalum. *Calif. Turfgrass Culture* 33:8–10.

Harivandi, M.A., W. Davis, V.A. Gibeault, M. Henry, J. Van Dam, and L. Wu. 1984. Selecting the best turfgrass. *Calif. Turfgrass Culture* 34:17–18.

Hartwiger, C. 1995. Lay down some rubber. *USGA Green Section Record* May: 19–20.

Henry, J.M. et al. 1982. Turf fertilization study. *Paspalum vaginatum* var. Adalayd. *Western Landscaping News* 24:27–30. October.

Henry, J.M. and V.A. Gibeault. 1985. Paspalum vaginatum winter color management study. *Calif. Turfgrass Culture* 35:4–7.

Henry, M., V.A. Gibeault, V.B. Younger, and Stan Spaulding. 1979. *Paspalum vaginatum* 'Adalayd' and 'Futurf'. *Calif. Turfgrass* 29: 9–12.

Henry, M. 1981. Adalayd—A new turfgrass species. *The Florida Green* Fall: 25–27.

Huang, B., R.R. Duncan, and R.N. Carrow. 1997a. Drought-resistance of seven warm-season turfgrasses under surface soil drying. I. Shoot response. *Crop Sci.* 37:1858–1863.

Huang, B., R.R. Duncan, and R.N. Carrow. 1997b. Drought-resistance of seven warm-season turfgrasses under surface soil drying. II. Root aspects. *Crop Sci.* 37:1863–1869.

Leslie, M. 1995. Top dressing breakthrough: crumb rubber. *Golf Course News* 7(7):1,25.

Marcum, K.B. and C.L. Murdoch. 1990. Growth responses, ion relations, and osmotic adaptations of eleven C_4 turfgrasses to salinity. *Agron. J.* 82: 892–896.

Marcum, K.B. and C.L. Murdoch. 1994. Salinity tolerance mechanisms of six C_4 turfgrasses. *J. Amer. Soc. Hort. Sci.* 119:779–784.

McDonald, K.A. 1995. Where the rubber hits the turf. *Chron. Higher Educ.* June: A10.

Morey, D. 1994. Golf in Hawaii. The best of the best. *Southern Golf* 25 (5):16–19.

Morton, J.F. 1973. Salt-tolerant siltgrass (*Paspalum vaginatum* Sw.) *Proc. FL State Hort. Soc.* 86:482–490.

Nelson, L.S., K.D. Getsinger, and K.T. Luu. 1993. Effect of chemical treatments on bahiagrass (*Paspalum notatum*) suppression. *Weed Tech.* 7:127–133.

Rogers, J.N. and J.T. Vanini. 1994. Topdressing with crumb rubber from used tires on athletic fields and other high-traffic turf areas. pp. 234–240. In *Ann. Michigan Turfgrass Conf. Proc.*

Rogers, J.N., III and T. Vanini. 1995. Grounds for study: Used as top-dressing, crumb rubber appears to benefit athletic fields. *Athletic Business* May: 9.

Rogers, J.N., III., J.T. Vanini, and J.R. Crum. 1998a. Simulated traffic on turfgrass topdressed with crumb rubber. *Turfgrass Trends* 7(7):11–14.

Rogers, J.N. III., J.T. Vanini, and J.R. Crum. 1998b. Simulated traffic on turfgrass topdressed with crumb rubber. *Agron. J.* 90:215–221.

Shiels, G. 1998. Benefits of top dressing with crumb rubber. *Turf Management* June: 24.

Sifers, S.I., J.B Beard, K.S. Kim, and J.R. Walker. 1987. An assessment of cutting height and nitrogen fertility requirements of seashore paspalum. *Texas Turfgrass Research-1986.* TAES PR-4529. p. 43.

Sifers, S.I., J.B Beard, K.S. Kim, and J.R. Walker. 1988. An assessment of cutting height and nitrogen fertility requirements of Adalayd seashore paspalum. *Texas Turfgrass Research-1987.* TAES PR-4671. pp. 33–34.

Sifers, S.I., J.B Beard, and M.H. Hall. 1989. An assessment of cutting height and nitrogen fertility requirements of Adalayd seashore paspalum. *Texas Turfgrass Research-1990.* TAES PR-4764. pp. 70–71.

Sifers, S.I., J.B Beard, and M.H. Hall. 1990. Cutting height and nitrogen fertility requirements of Adalayd seashore paspalum-1987. *Texas Turfgrass Research-1990.* TAES PR-4764. pp. 70–71.

Trenholm, L.E., R.N. Carrow, and R.R. Duncan. 1998. Paspalum vs. bermudagrass: Which is more traffic tolerant? *Golf Course Management* July: 61–64.

Trenholm, L.E., R.N. Carrow, and R.R. Duncan. 1999. Mechanisms of wear tolerance in seashore paspalum and bermudagrass. *Crop Sci.* (in review)

Trenholm, L.E., R.R. Duncan, and R.N. Carrow. 2000. The influence of silica on growth, quality, and wear tolerance of seashore paspalum. *Crop Sci.* (in review).

U.S. Golf Association. 1994. *Wastewater Reuse for Golf Course Irrigation.* Lewis Publishers, Chelsea, MI.

Vermeulen, P.H. 1992. The best choice may not always be your favorite. *USGA Green Section Record* 30(1):1–5.

Workman, B. 1998. Using effluent water to irrigate golf courses. *Through the Green* July/August: 11, 29–30.

Chapter 10. Management of Biotic Stresses

Akanda, R.U., J.J. Mullahey, C.C. Dowler, and D.G. Shilling. 1997. Influence of postemergence herbicides on tropical soda apple (*Solanum viarum*) and bahiagrass (*Paspalum notatum*). *Weed Tech.* 11:656–661.

Anonymous. 1999. Pesticide flip charts (turf). *Sports Turf* 15(3):33–38.

Brandenburg, R. and A. Cooke. 1998/1999. Integrated fire ant management. *North Carolina Turfgrass* 16(7):24, 26, 28.

Carrow, R.N. and R.R. Duncan. 1998. *Salt-Affected Turfgrass Sites: Assessment and Management.* Ann Arbor Press, Chelsea, MI.

Couillard, A.-A. and G. Wiecko. 1998. A saline solution: seawater as a selective herbicide. *Golf Course Management* May: 54–57.

Cudney, D.W., V.A. Gibeault, C.L. Elmore, and J.S. Reints. 1995. Sensitivity of seashore paspalum to postemergence herbicides. *Calif. Turfgrass Culture* 45:22–23.

Davis, S.D., R.R. Duncan, and B.J. Johnson. 1997. Suppression of seashore paspalum in bermudagrass with herbicides. *J. Environ. Hort.* 15(4):187–190.

DeFrank, J. 1992. Report on the response of newly planted seashore paspalum to oxadiazon. *Misc. Rep. University of Hawaii-Manoa.*

Dernoeden, P.H. 1998. The new generation of fungicides of microbial origin. *TurFax®* 6(1):2,5.

Duble, R.L. 1989. Seashore paspalum. pp. 86–89. In *Southern Turfgrasses: Their Management and Use.* Tex Scape Inc. College Station, TX.

Duble, R.L. 1996. Seashore paspalum. pp. 81–83. In *Southern Turfgrasses: Their Management and Use in the Southern Zone.* Texas A&M University Press, College Station, TX.

Duncan, R.R. 1998. Seashore paspalum herbicide management. *USGA Green Section Record* 36(2):17–19.

Duncan, R.R. 1999. Environmental compatibility of seashore paspalum (saltwater couch) for golf courses and other recreational uses. II. Management protocols. *Int'l Turfgrass Soc. Res. J.* 8(2):1216–1230.

Elliott, M.L. 1997. Surface algae on golf course putting greens and tees. *Turfgrass Trends* 6(6):1–4.

Elliott, M.L. 1998. Use of fungicides to control blue-green algae on bermudagrass putting-green surfaces. *Crop Protection* 17(8):631–637.

Fry, J. and H. Jiang. 1998. Plant growth regulators may help reduce water use. *Golf Course Management* November: 58–61.

Goatly, J.M., Jr., V.L. Maddox, and R.M. Watkins. 1996. Growth regulation of bahiagrass (*Paspalum notatum* Fluegge) with imazaquin and AC 263, 222. *Hort. Sci.* 31:396–399.

Harivandi, M.A., C.L. Elmore, and J.M. Henry. 1987. An evaluation of herbicides on seashore paspalum. *Calif. Turfgrass Culture* 27(1–2):2–5.

Hodges, C.F. and D.A. Campbell. 1998. Gaseous hydrocarbons associated with black layer induced by the interaction of cyanobacteria and *Desulfovibrio desulfuricans.* *Plant Soil* 205:77–83.

James, T.K. and A. Rahman. 1997. Control of couch (*Elytrigia repens*) and mercer grass (*Paspalum distichum*) in maize with nicosulfuron. *Proc. 50th N.Z. Plant Protection Conf.* pp. 467–471.

Johnson, B.J. and R.R. Duncan. 1997. Tolerance of four seashore paspalum (*Paspalum vaginatum*) cultivars to postemergence herbicides. *Weed Technol.* 11:689–692.

Johnson, B.J. and R.R. Duncan. 1998a. Tolerance of seashore paspalum cultivars to preemergence herbicides. *J. Environ. Hort.* 16(2):76–78.

Johnson, B.J. and R.R. Duncan. 1998b. Influence of herbicides on establishment of eight seashore paspalum cultivars. *J. Environ. Hort.* 16(2):79–81.

Kalmbacher, R.S., D.L. Colvin, F.G. Martin, and A.E. Kretschmer, Jr. 1996. Reaction of Suerte *Paspalum atratum* to herbicides. *Soil Crop Sci. Soc. Florida Proc.* 55:110–115.

Landry, G. Jr., T. Murphy, B. Sparks, W. Hudson, and E. Brown 1998. *Turfgrass Pest Control Recommendations for Professionals.* Univ. Georgia Coop. Ext. Service, GA Turfgrass Assoc., Acworth, GA.

McCarty, L.B. and D.L. Colvin. 1988. Bahiagrass turf weed control guide. *Turfgrass Clippings* 1(5):1–5. IFAS, University of Florida, Gainesville, FL.

McCarty, L.B. and T.R. Murphy. 1994. Control of turfgrass weeds. pp. 209–256. In *Turf Weeds and Their Control.* ASA-CSSA, Madison, WI.

Menn, W.G. and J.B. Beard. 1984. Effect of eleven herbicides on establishment of *Paspalum vaginatum* Swartz. *Progress Rep. 4338. Texas Turfgrass Res.-1985.* pp. 183–189. Also *Turfax* III (6):4–6 (1995).

Morton, J.F. 1973. Salt-tolerant siltgrass (*Paspalum vaginatum* Sw.). *Proc. FL State Hort. Soc.* 86:482–490.

Nelson, E.B. 1997. Subsurface algae in turfgrass soils: both friend and foe. *Turfgrass Trends* 6(6):5–8.

Nelson, L.S., K.D. Getsinger, and K.T. Luu. 1993. Effect of chemical treatments on bahiagrass (*Paspalum notatum*) suppression. *Weed Tech.* 7:127–133.

Overstreet, C. 1999. Nematode problems in turfgrass: science and management. *Turf South* January: B1–B2, B5.

Potter, D.A. 1998. Understanding halofenozide (Mach 2®) and imidacloprid (Merit®) soil insecticides. *Turfax*® 6(1):6–7.

Smiley, R.W., P.H. Dernoeden, and B.B. Clarke. 1992. *Compendium of Turfgrass Diseases.* APS Press, St. Paul, MN.

Tavares, J. and J. De Frank. 1992. Herbicides on seashore paspalum (*Paspalum vaginatum* Swartz). Research summary 1992. *Hawaii Landscape Industry News* 6(4):22–23 (August).

Umemoto, S., T. Shingyoji, M. Yasuda, and K. Aoki. 1997. Control of *Curvularia* leaf blight of *Zoysia matrella* by lowering soil pH with acidifying fertilizers and amendments. *Int'l Turfgrass Soc. Res. J.* 8:937–947.

West African Rice Research Station. 1957. Arboricide and herbicide trials. pp. 10–14. *Rep. West. African Rice Res. Stn.,* Rokupr, Sierra Leone.

Chapter 12. Sports Fields

Adams, W.A. 1997. The effect of 'Fibermaster' fibres on the stability and other properties of sand rootzones. *Int'l Turfgrass Soc. Res. J.* 8:15–26.

Adams, W.A. and R.J. Gibbs. 1989. The use of polypropylene fibres (VHAF) for the stabilization of natural turf on sports fields. pp. 237–239. In *Proc. 6th Int'l Turfgrass Res. Conf.,* Tokyo, Japan.

Adams, W.A., R.J. Gibbs, S.W. Baker, and C.D. Lance. 1983. A national survey of winter games pitches in the UK with high quality drainage design. *Int'l Turfgrass Soc. Res. J.* 7:406–412.

Allen, E.A. and R.D. Andrews. 1997. Space age soil mix uses centuries-old zeolites. *Golf Course Management* 65(5):61–66.

Andrews, R., J. Shaw, and J. Murphy. 1999a. Zeoponic Turf Root zone systems. *Sportsturf* 15(4):14–19.

Andrews, R.D., A.J. Koski, J.A. Murphy, and A.M. Petrovic. 1999b. Zeoponic materials allow rapid greens grow-in. *Golf Course Management* 67(2):68–72.

Anonymous. 1999a. The StrathAyer International SportsTurf System and How You Can Join the Team. *TPI TurfNews* 23(1): 25–26, 56.

Anonymous. 1999b. Inturf-Special Applications for New Sports Stadiums, Tennis Courts and Cricket Wickets. *TPI TurfNews* 23(1):26,35.

Anonymous. 1999c. Hummer Sports Turf and the Grass SuperTiles. *TPI TurfNews* 23(1):27.

Anonymous. 1999d. Systematrix, Ltd. Modular Plastic Turf Trays for Sports Fields. *TPI TurfNews* 23 (1): 27–28.

Anonymous. 1999e. The Greentech Integrated Turf Management Sports Field System Using Turf Trays. *TPI TurfNews* 23(1):29–30, 56.

Baker, S.W. 1997. The reinforcement of turfgrass areas using plastics and other synthetic materials: a review. *Int'l Turfgrass Soc. Res. J.* 8:3–13.

Baker, S.W. and P.M. Canaway. 1993. Concepts of playing quality: criteria and measurement. *Int'l Turfgrass Soc. Res. J.* 7:172–181.

Baker, S.W. and C.W. Richards. 1993. The effect of slit tine and hollow tine aeration on the performance of soccer pitches of five construction types. *Int'l Turfgrass Soc. Res. J.* 7:430–436.

Baker, S.W. and C.W. Richards. 1995. The effect of fibre reinforcement on the quality of sand rootzone used for winter games pitches. *J. Sports Turf Res. Inst.* 71:107–117.

Beard, J.B. and S.I. Sifers. 1989. A randomly oriented interlocking mesh element matrices system for sports turf rootzone construction. pp. 253–257. In *Proc. 6th Int'l Turfgrass Res. Conf.* Tokyo, Japan.

Beard, J.B and S.I. Sifers. 1990. Feasibility assessment of randomly oriented interlocking mesh element matrices system for turf rootzones. *Natural and Artificial Playing Fields: Characteristics and Safety Features.* ASTM STP 1073.

Beard, J.B and S.I. Sifers. 1993. Stabilization and enhancement of sand-modified root zones for high traffic sports turfs with mesh elements. *Texas Agric. Exp. Stn.,* Dept. Soil & Crop Sci., Texas A&M University, pub. B-1710. pp. 1-40. College Station, TX.

Canaway, P.M. and S.W. Baker. 1993. Soil and turf properties governing playing quality. *Int'l Turfgrass Soc. Res. J.* 7:192–200.

Carrow, R.N. and R.R. Duncan. 1998. *Salt-Affected Turfgrass Sites: Assessment and Management.* Ann Arbor Press, Chelsea, MI.

Carrow, R.N. and G. Wiecko. 1989. Soil compaction and wear stresses on turfgrasses: future research directions. pp. 37–42. In *Proc. 6th Int'l Turfgrass Res. Conf.,* Tokyo, Japan.

Christians, N. 1998. *Fundamentals of Turfgrass Management.* Ann Arbor Press, Chelsea, MI.

Cisar, J.L. 1997. Turfgrass response to controlled-release urea fertilizers. *Turfgrass Trends* 6(4):13–15.

Cockerham, S.T., V.A. Gibeault, and R.A. Khan. 1993. Alteration of sports field characteristics using management. *Int'l Turfgrass Soc. Res. J.* 7:182–191.

Cockerham, S.T., J.R. Watson, and J.C. Keisling. 1995. The soccer field gauge: Measuring field performance. *Calif. Turfgrass Culture* 45(3–4):13–16.

Cook, A. and S.W. Baker. 1998. Effects of organic amendments on selected physical and chemical properties of rootzones for golf greens. *J. Turfgrass Sci.* 74:2–10.

Daniel, W.H, R.P. Freeborg., and M.J. Robey. 1974. Prescription athletic turf system. pp. 277–280. In E.C. Roberts (Ed.). *Proc. 2nd Int'l Turfgrass Res. Conf.,* Blacksburg, VA. 19–21 June 1973. ASA-CSSA, Madison, WI.

Duncan, R.R. 1999. Paspalum. A new environmental sports turf. *Sports Turf* 15(9):14, 16–17.

Dury, P.L.K. 1985. V.H.A.F. for natural and synthetic turf. *Turf Management* 4(8):15–17.

Gibbs, R.J., W.A. Adams, and S.W. Baker. 1989. Factors affecting the surface stability of a sand rootzone. pp. 189–191. In *Proc. 6th Int'l Turfgrass Res. Conf.,* Tokyo, Japan.

Gibbs, R.J., W.A. Adams, and S.W. Baker. 1993a. Playing quality, performance, and cost-effectiveness of soccer pitches in the UK. *Int'l Turfgrass Soc. Res. J.* 7:212–221.

Gibbs, R.J., W.A. Adams, and S.W. Baker. 1993b. Changes in soil physical properties of different construction methods for soccer pitches under intensive use. *Int'l Turfgrass Soc. Res. J.* 7:413–421.

Gibeault, V., M. Yates, J. Meyer, and M. Leonard. 1999. Movement of nitrogen fertilizer in a turfgrass system. *Sportsturf* 15(1):38–39. Also *Calif. Turfgrass Culture* 48(1–2):1–4.

Hartwiger, C.E. 1995. Lay down some rubber. USGA *Green Section Record* May: 19–20.

Hayes, P. 1989. Sports field, soil and management. pp. 43–48. In *Proc. 6th Int'l Turfgrass Res. Conf.,* Tokyo, Japan.

Hunt, J.A. and S.W. Baker. 1996. The influence of rootzone depth and base construction on moisture retention profiles of sports turf rootzones. *J. Sports Turf Res. Inst.* 72:36–41.

Karlik, J. 1995. Effects of pre-plant incorporation of polymers on turfgrasses. *Calif. Turfgrass Culture* 45(3–4):19–22.

Landry, G. 1993. Success with overseeding warm-season grasses. *Sportsturf* Sept.: 12–14.

Landry, G. Jr. 1994. Turfgrass water management. *Agronomy Fact Sheet, Leaflet 399.* Coop. Ext. Ser., University of Georgia.

Landry, G. 1995a. Aeration strategies to reduce compaction. *Sportsturf* March 11(3):24–26.

Landry, G. 1995b. Sports turf cultivation. pp. 102–103. In F. Perry *Pictorial Guide to Quality Groundskeeping II.* Grounds Maintenance Serv., Orlando, FL.

Landry, G. 1995c. Develop plan to protect high-traffic sports turf. *Turf Landscape Press* Jan.: 23–24.

Landry, G. 1996a. Thatch management for warm season turf. *Sportsturf* 12(6):12–13.

Landry, G. Jr. 1996b. Better education and products enhance sports turf management. *Park/Grounds Management* 11–12:10–12.

Landry, G. 1996c. Fall fertilizer programs. *Sports Turf Manager* Sept./Oct.: 3, 8.

Landry, G. 1997a. Tips for sports turf managers. *Grounds Maintenance* August: C40–C43.

Landry, G. Jr. 1997b. High performance sports turf. *Sports Turf Manager* May/June: 4–5.

Landry, G. 1998a. Remedies for failing fields. *Sports Turf Manager* January/February: 5, 10,15.

Landry, G., Jr. 1998b. Aeration strategies to reduce compaction. *Sports Turf Manager* July/August: 5,14,16.

Landry, G. 1998c. Diagnosing golf course turf problems. *NZ Turf Management J.* 12(4):10,12.

Landry, G. 1998d. Will New Zealand follow in America's footsteps? pp. 9–10. *Proc. 6th NZ Sports Turf Conv.* 28–31 July 1998. Rotorua Conv. Centre, New Zealand.

Landry, G. 1998e. Trends and innovations for sports fields in the USA. p. 114–115. *Proc. 6th NZ Sports Turf Conf.* 28–31 July, 1998. Rotorua Conv. Centre, New Zealand.

Landry, G. 1999. Is soil compaction killing your field? *Sports Turf Manager* 17(2):3, 5.

Landry, G. and T. Murphy. 1997. *Athletic Field Management.* CES, University of Georgia, Athens, GA. Circular 822.

Leboucher, J.P. 1989. Observations on the influence of the nature and grain-size of the different layers making up the substrate for the root-system of golf-courses, greens-turf and sports-ground turf. pp. 267–268. In *Proc. 6th Int'l Turfgrass Res. Conf.,* Tokyo, Japan.

McAuliffe, K.W. 1989. Sportsturf drainage—Bridging the disciplines of engineering and agronomy. pp. 243–245. In *Proc. 6th Int'l Turfgrass Res. Conf.,* Tokyo, Japan.

McAuliffe, K.W., P.E. Rieke, and D.J. Horne. 1993. A study of three physical conditioning treatments on a fine sandy loam golf green. *Int'l Turfgrass Soc. Res. J.* 7:444–450.

McCarty, L.B. (Bert), G. Landry, and L.C. Miller. 1997. *Sports Field Construction.* Turfgrass Slide Monograph, CSSA, Madison, WI.

McNitt, A. 1998. Sports turf research report. *Sportsturf* 14(11):22–23.

McNitt, A.S. 1999. Soil inclusions' impact on soil physical properties and athletic field quality. *Turfgrass Trends* 8(2):12–15.

Minner, D.D. 1998. Research report. *Sportsturf* 14(8):20–21.

Murphy, J.W. T.R.O. Field, and M.J. Hickey. 1993. Age development in sand-based turf. *Int'l Turfgrass Soc. Res. J.* 7:464–468.

Peacock, C.H. and D.S. Dahms. 1998/1999. Nitrogen sources and nitrogen: Sulfur ratios for bermudagrass fertilization. *North Carolina Turfgrass* 16(7):20.

Rieke, P.E. and J.A. Murphy. 1989. Advances in turf cultivation. pp. 49–54. In *Proc. 6th Turfgrass Res. Conf.,* Tokyo, Japan.

Rogers, R.B. and A.J. Jobson. 1993. Turf root-zone high-pressure injection measurement and imaging. *Int'l Turfgrass Soc. Res. J.* 7:993–999.

Rogers, J.N., III and D.V. Waddington. 1993. Present status of quantification of sports turf surface characteristics in North America. *Int'l Turfgrass Soc. Res. J.* 7:231–237.

Rogers, J.N., III and T. Vanini. 1995. Grounds for study. Used as top-dressing, crumb rubber appears to benefit athletic fields. *Athletic Business* May: 9.

Rogers, J.N., III, J.T. Vanini, and J.R. Crum. 1998a. Simulated traffic on turfgrass topdressed with crumb rubber. *Agron. J.* 90:215–221.

Rogers, J.N., III, J.T. Vanini, and J.R. Crum. 1998b. Simulated traffic on turfgrass topdressed with crumb rubber. *Turfgrass Trends* 7(7):11–14.

Ruemmele, B. and V. Wallace. 1998. Choosing cool-season turfgrasses for athletic fields. *Sportsturf* 14(6):5, 9.

Skirde, W. 1989. Problems and research on sports turf areas in West Germany, with particular reference to the deterioration in environmental conditions. pp. 29–35. In *Proc. 6th Int'l Turfgrass Res. Conf.,* Tokyo, Japan.

Tracinski, B. 1998a. Preparing turf for overseeding. *Sportsturf* 14(8):16–18.

Tracinski, B. 1998b. Sports turf research report. *Sportsturf* 14(11):22–23.

Tracinski, B. 1998c. Early- and late-season fertilization. *Sportsturf* 14(10):25–26.

USGA Green Section Staff. 1993. USGA recommendations for a method of putting greens construction. *USGA Green Section Record* March/April: 1–3.

Vanini, J.T., J.N. Rogers III, and J.R. Crum. 1999. Crumb rubber benefits trafficked turf. *Golf Course Management* April: 71–74.

Vittum, P.J. 1989. High pressure injection for white grub control. *Golf Course Management* Nov.:46–48.

Waddington, D.V. 1992. Soil, soil mixtures, and soil amendments. pp. 331–383. In D.V. Waddington, R.N. Carrow, and R.C. Shearman (Eds.). *Turfgrass.* Agron. Monograph 32. ASA-CSSA-SSSA, Madison, WI.

Watson, J.R., H.E. Kaerwer, and D.P. Martin. 1992. The turfgrass industry. pp. 29–88. In D.V. Waddington, R.N. Carrow, and R.C. Shearman (Eds.) *Turfgrass.* ASA-CSSA-SSSA Monograph 32, Madison, WI.

West, B. 1997. Standing PAT. *Lawn Landscape* August.

Wiecko, G., R.N. Carrow, and K.J. Karnok. 1993. Turfgrass cultivation methods: influence on soil physical, root/shoot, and water relationships. *Int'l Turfgrass Soc. Res. J.* 7:451–457.

Chapter 13. Lawn and Landscape Use

Christians, N. 1998. *Fundamentals of Turfgrass Management.* Ann Arbor Press, Chelsea, MI.

Duble, R.L. 1996. *Turfgrasses: Their Management and Use in the Southern Zone.* Texas A&M University Press, College Station, TX.

Knoop, W.E. (Ed.). 1997. *The Landscape Management Handbook.* GCSAA and Advanstar Commun. Inc., Duluth, MN.

Morton, J.F. 1973. Salt-tolerant siltgrass (*Paspalum vaginatum* Sw.). *Proc. FL State Hort. Soc.* 86: 482–490.

Watson, J.R., H.E. Kaerwer, and D.P. Martin. 1992. The turfgrass industry. pp. 29–88. In D.V. Waddington, R.N. Carrow, and R.C. Shearman (Eds.). *Turfgrass.* Agronomy Monograph No. 32, ASA-CSSA-SSSA, Madison, WI.

Chapter 14. Sod and Sprig Production

Anonymous. 1998. Pesticides registered for use on turfgrass sod farms. *TPI Turf News* 22(6):21–26.

Anonymous. 1999. RapidTurf and their licensing arrangements for turf growers. *TPI TurfNews* 23(1):29.

Carrow, R.N. and R.R. Duncan. 1998. *Salt-Affected Turfgrass Sites: Assessment and Management.* Ann Arbor Press, Chelsea, MI.

Christians, N. 1998. *Fundamentals of Turfgrass Management.* Ann Arbor Press, Chelsea, MI.

Krenisky, E.C., M.J. Carroll, R.H. Hill, and J.M. Krouse. 1998. Evaluation of natural and man-made erosion control materials. *Crop Sci.* 38(4):1042–1045. Also, *TPI TurfNews* 23(1):15–16, 1999.

Watson, J.R., H.E. Kaerwer, and D.P. Martin. 1992. The turfgrass industry. pp. 29–88. In D.V. Waddington, R.N. Carrow, and R.C. Shearman (Eds.). *Turfgrass.* Agronomy Monograph No. 32, ASA-CSSA-SSSA, Madison, WI.

Chapter 15. Influence of Irrigation Water Quality on Turfgrass Fertilization

Ayers, R.S. and D.W. Westcot. 1985. *Water Quality in Agriculture.* Irrigation & Drainage Paper #29, Rev. 1. FAD, Rome, Italy.

Carrow, R.N. and R.R. Duncan. 1998. *Salt-Affected Turfgrass Sites: Assessment and Management.* Ann Arbor Press, Chelsea, MI.

Eaton, F.M. 1950. Significance of carbonates in irrigation waters. *Soil Sci.* 69:123–133.

Gaussoin, R. 1999. Algae control in ponds with barley bales: On-site results in Nebraska. *Center for Grassland Studies* 5(2):3.

Harivandi, A. 1994. Wastewater quality and treatment plants. pp. 106–129. In J.T. Snow (Ed.) *Wastewater Reuse for Golf Course Irrigation.* Lewis Publishers, Boca Raton, FL.

Snow, J.T. (Ed.). 1994. *Wastewater Reuse for Golf Courses Irrigation.* Lewis Publishers, Boca Raton, FL.

Westcot, D.W. and R.S. Ayers. 1984. Irrigation water quality. In G.S. Pettygrove and T. Asano (Eds.). *Irrigation With Reclaimed Municipal Wastewater—A Guidance Manual.* Calif. State Water Resources Control Board. Sacramento, CA. (Republished 1985. Lewis Publishers, Boca Raton, FL.)

Chapter 16. Seawater Irrigation

California Coastal Commission. 1999. *Seawater Desalination in California.* Web site: www.Ceres, CA. gov/coastalcomm/desalrpt/dkeyfact.html.

Carrow, R.N., and R.R. Duncan. 1998. *Salt-Affected Turfgrass Sites: Assessment and Management.* Ann Arbor Press, Chelsea, MI.

Duncan, R.R. 1998. Keys to success with paspalum on golf courses. *Golf Course Management* 66(2):58–60.

Duncan, R.R. 1999. AP-10 (Sea Isle 2000) and FWY-1 (Sea Isle 1) Vegetative Release Documents. UGA, Crop and Soil Science. Sea Isle 2000 is a greens type and Sea Isle 1 is a tee/fairway type. Also Lee, G.J., R.R. Duncan, and R.N. Carrow. 1998. Diversity of salinity tolerance within *Paspalum vaginatum* and selected *Cynodon* spp. *Agron. Abstr.* p. 127.

Glenn, E.P., J.J. Brown, and J.W. O'Leary. 1998. Irrigating Crops With Seawater. *Scientific American* (August) 279(2):76–81..

Iyengar, E.R.R. and M.P. Ready. 1994. Crop response to salt stress: Seawater application and prospects. In M. Pessarakli (Ed.) *Handbook of Plant and Crop Stress.* Marcel Dekker, Inc., New York, NY.

Newport, B.P. 1977. *Salt Water Intrusion in the United States.* EPA-600/8-77-011. Environmental Protection Agency. Ada, OK.

Todd, D.K. 1997. Salt-water and its control. *Water Works Assoc.* 66(3).

Chapter 17. Excessively Acid Soil Fertilization

Foy, C.D. 1988. Plant adaptation to acid, aluminum toxic soils. *Commun. Soil Sci. Plant Anal.* 19:959–987.

Helyar, K.R. 1991. The management of acid soils. pp. 365–382. In R.J. Wright et al. (Eds). *Plant-Soil Interactions at Low pH.* Kluwer Academic Publishers, The Netherlands.

Sumner, M.E. 1995. Amelioration of subsoil acidity with minimum disturbance. pp. 147–185. In N.S. Jayawardane and B.A. Stewart (Eds.) *Subsoil Management Techniques.* Adv. Soil Science. Lewis Publishers/CRC Press Inc., Boca Raton, FL.

Chapter 18. Environmentally Sensitive Sites

Beard, J.H. 1998. Reducing pesticide and nutrient runoff using buffers. *Golf Course Management* Sept.:57–61.

Bowman, D.C. 1999. Buffers—Fact or fiction? *North Carolina Turfgrass* 16(7):18.

Cole, J.T., J.H. Beard, N.T. Basta, R.L. Huhnke, D.E. Storm, G.V. Johnson, M.E. Payton, M.D. Smolen, D.L. Martin, and J.C. Cole. 1997. Influence of buffers on pesticide and nutrient runoff from bermudagrass turf. *J. Environ. Quality* 26:1589–1598.

Hammer, D.A. 1989. *Constructed Wetlands for Wastewater Treatment.* Lewis Publishers, Boco Raton, FL.

Walker, W.J. and B. Branham. 1992. Environmental impacts of turfgrass fertilization. pp. 105–219. In J.C. Balogh and W.J. Walker (Eds.). *Golf Course Management and Construction: Environmental Issues.* Lewis Publishers, Boca Raton, FL.

Wood, S.L., E.F. Wheeler, R.D. Berghage, and R.E. Graves. 1999. Temperature effects on wastewater nitrate removal in laboratory-scale constructed wetlands. *Trans. Amer. Soc. Agric. Eng.* 42(1):185–190.

Chapter 19. Bioremediation and Reclamation

Anderson, T.A., E.A. Guthrie, and B.T. Walton. 1993. Bioremediation. *Environ. Sci. Technol.* 27:2630–2636.

Baldwin, A.H., K.L. McKee, and I.A. Mendelssohn. 1996. The influence of vegetation, salinity, and inundation on seed banks of oligohaline coastal marshes. *Amer. J. Bot.* 83:470–479.

Batianoff, G.N. and T.J. McDonald. 1980. *Capricorn Coast Sand Dune and Headland Vegetation*. Tech. Bulletin, Bot. Branch, Qld. Dept. Primary Industries No. 6., Indooroopilly, Qld. Australia.

Brown, S.L., R.L. Chaney, J.S. Angle, and A.J.M. Baker. 1995. Zinc and cadmium uptake by hyperaccumulator *Thlaspi caeruleacens* grown in nutrient solution. *Soil Sci. Soc. Amer. J.* 59:125–133.

Burvill, G.H. 1956. *Paspalum vaginatum* for salt land. *J. Dept. Agric. W. Austr.* 5:121–122.

Burvill G.H. and A.H. Marshall. 1951. *Paspalum vaginatum* or seashore paspalum. *J. Dept. Agric. W. Austr.* 28:191–194.

Cameron, D.G. 1954. New grasses for soil conservation in New South Wales. *J. Soil Conserv. N.S.W.* 10:116–126.

Cameron, D.G. 1959. Grasses tested for soil conservation. *J. Soil Conserv. Serv. N.S.W.* 15:189–202, 281–293.

Chaudhri, I.I., M.Y. Sheikh, and M.M. Alam. 1969. Halophytic flora of saline & waterlogged areas of West Pakistan plains. *Agric. Pakistan* 20:404–414. Also *Herb. Abstr.* 41:3007.

Colman, R.L. and G.P.M. Wilson. 1960. The effect of floods on pasture plants. *Agric. Gazette N.S.W.* 71:337–347.

Comis, D. 1995. Green remediation: letting the earth heal itself. *Agric. Res.* 43(11):2–9.

Craig, R.M. 1974. Coastal dune vegetation. *Proc. FL State Hort. Soc.* 87:548–552.

Craig, R.M. 1976. Grasses for coastal dune areas. *Proc. FL State Hort. Soc.* 89:353–355.

Department of Agriculture, Western Australia. 1961. Salinity investigations. *Rep. Dept. Agric. West. Austr.* pp. 36–38.

Dushenkov, V., P.B.A. Nanda Kumar, H. Motto, and I. Raskin. 1995. Rhizofiltration: The use of plants to remove heavy metals from aqueous streams. *Environ. Sci. Technol.* 29:1239–1245.

Ewusie, J.Y. 1974. Delimitation of ecological zones in strand vegetation at Elmira, Ghana. *Ghana J. Sci.* 14:59–67.

Ferguson, D.S. 1951. Construction of coastal bunds in Malaya. *Malay Agric. J.* 34:3–12.

Forti, M. 1986. Salt tolerant & halophytic plants in Israel. *Reclam. Reveg. Res.* 5:83–96.

Glenhill, D. 1963. The ecology of the Aberdeen Creek mangrove swamp (Sierra Leone). *J. Ecol.* 51:693–703.

Gross, F.C. 1952. Restoring salt-affected land to productiveness (in Australia). *J. Dept. Agric. South. Austral.* 55:401–405.

Hill, J.R.C. 1972. The mine dump problem in Rhodesia. *Rhodesia Agric. J.* 69:65–73.

Hill, J.C.R. 1978a. The use of range plants in the stabilization of phytotoxic mining wastes. pp. 707–711. In D.N. Hyder (Ed.) *Proc. 1st Int'l Rangeland Congress.* Denver, CO. 14–18 August 1978. Soc. Range Mgmt.

Hill, J.C.R. 1978b. A root growth study used to examine the suitability of two grasses for stabilizing toxic mine wastes *Proc. Grassland Soc. South. Africa.* 13: 129–133. Dept. Conserv. Exten., Salisbury, Zimbabwe.

Hoyt, G.D. and D.C. Adriano. 1979. Americium-241 uptake by bahiagrass as influenced by soil type, lime, and organic matter. *J. Environ. Qual.* 8:392–396.

Kumar, P.B.A. Nanda, V. Dushenkov, H. Motto, and I. Raskin. 1995. Phytoextraction: The use of plants to remove heavy metals from soils. *Environ. Sci. Technol.* 29:1232–1238.

Le Houerou, H.N. 1977. Biological recovery versus desertization. *Econ. Geogr.* 53:413–420.

Logan, J.M. 1958. Erosion problems on salt-affected areas. *J. Soil Conserv. Serv. N.S.W.* 14:229–242.

Malcolm, C.V. 1962. *Paspalum vaginatum* for salty seepages. *J. Dept. Agric. West. Austral.* 3:615–616.

Malcolm, C.V. 1977. Saltland and what to do about it. *J. Agric. West. Austral.* 18:127–133.

Malcolm, C.V. 1986. Production from salt-affected soils. *Reclam. Reveg. Res.* 5:343–361.

Malcolm, C.V. 1983. Wheatbelt salinity. A review of the salt land problem in SW Australia. *Tech. Bull. #52.* Dept. Agric. W. Australia, Perth.

Malcolm, C.V. and I.A.F. Laing. 1969. *Paspalum vaginatum*—for salty seepages and lawns. *J. Agric. W. Austral.* 10:474–475.

Malcolm, C.V. and I.A.F. Laing. 1976. *Paspalum distichum* for salty seepages and lawns. *Tech. Bull. #3696.* W. Austral. Dept. Agric. Perth.

McCutcheon, S.C. 1998. The environment: plants and microorganisms to control pollution. *PBI Bulletin* Sept: 1–4.

McCutcheon, S.C. and N.L. Wolfe. 1998. Phytoremediation: The vital role of plant biochemistry in cleaning up organic compounds. *PBI Bulletin* Sept.: 17–20

McPhie, G.L. 1973. Three successful salt tolerant plants. *J. Agric. South Austral.* 76:5–8.

Medina, V. and S.C. McCutcheon. 1996. Phytoremediation: modeling removal of TNT and its breakdown products. *Remediation* 6(4):31–45.

Miles, N. and N.M. Tainton. 1979. Establishing vegetation on kimberlite mine tailings. 1. Defining the problem and selecting the species. *Proc. Grassland Soc. South Africa* 14:37–41.

Millington, A.J. 1951. Soil salinity investigations. Salt tolerance, germination and growth tests under controlled salinity conditions. *J. Dept. Agric. W. Austr.* 28:198–210.

Mitchell, A. 1965. The role of grass for soil & water conservation in Australia. *Herb. Abstr.* 35:1914.

Paradis, G. 1976. Contribution to the study of the flora and the coastal vegetation of Dahomey. *Bull. du Museum National d' Histoire Naturelle, Botanique* 26:33–67.

Ragonese, A.E. and G. Covas. 1947. The halophilous flora of the south of the province of Santa Fe, Argentina Republic. *Darwiniana* 7:401–496. Also *Herb. Abstr.* 17:1811.

Rose, S.A. and M.D. Lorber. 1976. Sand dune stabilization and revegetation in Brevard county. *Proc. FL State Hort. Soc.* 89:346–348.

Salt land reclamation in W. Australia. 1967. *Chemy Ind.* 36:1518. Austr. News and Info. Bur. *Herb. Abstr.* 38:522.

Schnoor, J.L. 1998. Petroleum and other organic contamination: Vegetative remediation of volatile and semi-volatile organics. *PBI Bulletin* Sept.: 6–9.

Sigua, G.C. and W.H. Hudnall. 1991. Gypsum and water management interactions for revegetation and productivity improvement of brackish marsh in Louisiana. *Commun. Soil Sci. Plant Anal.* 22(15–16):1721–1739.

Sigua, G.C. and W.H. Hudnall. 1992. Nitrogen and gypsum: Management tools for revegetation and productivity improvement of brackish marsh in Southwest Louisiana. *Commun. Soil Sci. Plant Anal.* 23(3–4):283–299.

Soil Conservation Authority, Victoria. 1963. Fourteenth annual report for year ending 30 June 1963.

Steffens, J.C. 1990. The heavy metal-binding peptides of plants. *Ann. Rev. Plant Physical.* 41:553–575.

Straatmans, W. 1954. Reclamation of tidal mud flats in Tonga. Tech. Paper #53. South Pacific Commission. (*Herb. Abstr.* 25:874.)

Swaine, M.D, D.U.V. Okali, J.B. Hall, and J.M. Lock. 1979. Zonation of a coastal grassland in Ghana, West Africa. *Folia Geobotanica et Phytotaxonomica* 14:11–27.

Theron, E.P., R. Ludorf, and A. Jones. 1972. Notes on the value of *Paspalum vaginatum* Sw. as a pasture grass for saline and structureless soils. *Proc. Grassland Soc. South Africa* 7:126–129.

Vanden Berghen, C. 1982. Vegetation of the Djibonker sands in the Casamanse Basin (southern Senegal). *Bulletin du Jardin Botanique National de Belgique* 52:211–224.

Wong, M.H., W.M. Lau, S.W. Li, and C.K. Tang. 1983. Root growth of two grass species on iron ore tailings at elevated levels of manganese, iron, and copper. *Environ. Res.* 30:26–33.

★ ★

Miscellaneous References

Adam, J.-G. 1965. The vegetation of the Senegal delta in Mauretania. (The littoral strand and Thiong island.) *Bull. Inst. Fr. Africa* Noire 27:121–128. *Herb. Abstr.* 37:908.

Alberdi, M. and C. Rameriz. 1967. Studies on zonation of the higher vegetation of the littoral of Mehuin (Valdivia, Chile) on the basis of osmotic values. *Phyton, B. Aires* 24:77–83.

Aldous, D.E. and W.J. Scattini. 1999. Turfgrass to complement sunny coasts. *Turf Craft* 65:42–46.

Anonymous. 1994. Seashore paspalum gets around water restrictions. *Landscape Management* 33:40, 42.

Basto, M.F.P. 1987. Notes on the flora of the Cape Verde islands. *Boletim da Sociedade Borteriana* 60:179–186. *Herb. Abstr.* 58:2926.

Beehag, G.W. 1999. What's new in turfgrasses. *Turf Craft* 65:50–51.

Breakwell, E.J. 1923. *The grasses & fodder plants of New South Wales.* Sydney, Dept. Agric. Roseveare 1948.

Burson, B.L. 1985. Cytology of *Paspalum chacoense* and *P.durifolium* and their relationship to *P. dilatatum. Bot. Gaz.* 146:124–129.

Carrow, R.N. and G. Wiecko. 1989. Soil compaction and wear stresses on turfgrasses: future research directions. pp. 37–42. In H. Takotah (Ed.) *Proc. 6th Int'l Turf Res. Conf.,* Japanese Soc. Turf Sci., Tokyo, Japan.

Clayton, W.D. and S.A. Renvoize. 1986. Genera Graminum, grasses of the world. *Kew Bulletin,* Add. Ser. 13:1–389.

Danneberger, T.K. 1993. *Turfgrass Ecology and Management.* Franzak & Foster/G.I.E., Inc. Pub., Cleveland, OH.

de A. Lima, D. 1951. The flora of the seashore at Boa Viagem (Brazil). *Bol. Sec. Agric. Pernambaco* 18:121–125. *Herb. Abstr.* 22:1013.

de Granville, J.-J. 1976. A transect across the Sarcelle Savannah (Mana, French Guiana). *Cahiers OSTROM, Biologie* 11:3–21. *Herb. Abstr.* 47:1545.

Duble, R.L. 1988. Seashore paspalum. *Texas Turfgrass, Winter.* pp. 12–13.

Duble, R.L. 1989. Seashore paspalum. pp. 86–89. In *Southern Turfgrasses: Their Management and Use.* Tex Scape Inc., College Station, TX.

Duble, R.L. 1996. *Turfgrasses.* Texas A&M University Press, College Station, TX.

Filgueiras, T.S. 1994. Nomenclatural and critical notes on some Brazilian species of *Paspalum* (Poaceae, Paniceae). *Acta Amazon.* 23:147–161.

Gossweiler, J. and F.A. Mendonca. 1939. Phytogeographical map of Angola Memoir descriptive of the principal types of vegetation in the colony, determined by their physiographic aspects and ecological characters according to the nomenclature of Rubel. Lisbon, Portugal. *Herb. Abstr.* Suppl., pp. 61–65.

Hafliger, E. and H. Scholz. 1980. *Panicoid grass weeds.* Ciba-Geigy, Ltd. Basel, Switzerland.

Hall, J.B. 1973. Vegetational zones on the southern slopes of Mount Cameroon. *Vegetatio* 27:49–69.

Hall, T.D., D. Meredith, R.E. Altona, N.J. Mentz, A.B.M. Whitnall, and E.A. Lilford. 1959. Grasses for sporting purposes, parks, and aerodromes in South Africa. Ch. 13, pp. 724–745. In D. Meredith (Ed.) *The Grasses & Pastures of South Africa.* Central News Agency. Cape Times Ltd. Parow C.P., S. Africa.

Hansen, A. 1971. Floristic notes from the Canary Islands (mostly Tenerife). *Cuadernos de Botanica Canaria.* 13:1–7.

Haruvy, N. 1997. Agricultural reuse of wastewater: nationwide cost-benefit analysis. *Agric. Ecosyst. Environ.* 66:113–119.

Hayward, H.E. and L. Bernstein. 1958. Plant growth relationships on salt-affected soils. *The Botan. Rev.* 24:584–635.

Kleinschmidt, H.E. and R.W. Johnson. 1977. *Weeds of Queensland.* Brisbane Dept. Primary Industries, Victoria, Australia.

Lakanmi, O.O. and O.T. Okusanya. 1990. Comparative ecological studies of *Paspalum vaginatum* and *Paspalum orbiculare* in Nigeria. *J. Trop. Ecol.* 6:103–114.

Langkamp, P.J., G.K. Farnell, and M.J. Dalling. 1981. Acetylene reduction rates by selected leguminous and nonleguminous plants at Groote Eylandt, Northern Territory (Australia). *Austr. J. Bot.* 29:1–9.

Leithead, H.L., L.L. Yarlett, and T.N. Shiflet. 1971. One hundred native forage grasses in 11 southern states. *USDA Agric. Handbook #389.*

Lewis, J.P., N.J. Carnevale, E.F. Pire, S.I. Boccanelli, S.L. Stofella, and D.E. Prado. 1985. Halophilous communities of southeastern Santa Fe (Argentina). *Studia Oecologia* 4:57–73.

Linhart. Y.B. 1980. Local biogeography of plants on a Caribbean attoll. *J. Biogeography* 7:159–171.

Lubin, T. 1995. Controlling pH with irrigation water. *Golf Course Management* 63(11):56–60.

Luces de Febres, Z. 1964. The grasses of the Federal district (Venezuela). *Agronomia Trop.* 13:251–252.

Maas, E.V. 1994. Testing crops for salinity tolerance. pp. 117–132. In J.W. Maranville et al. (Eds). *Adaptation of Plants to Soil Stresses.* INTSORMIL Pub. 94-2. University of Nebraska Int'l Programs. Lincoln, NE.

Maitland, T.D. 1932. The grassland vegetation of the Cameroons mountains. *Kew Bull.* pp. 417–425. *Herb. Abstr.* 3:8c.

Malcolm, C.V. and S.T. Smith. 1971. Growing plants in salty water. *J. Agric. West. Austral.* 12:41–44.

Mesland, F., L.T. Ham, V. Boy, C. Van Wijck, and P. Grillas. 1993. Competition between an introduced & an indigenous species: The case of *Paspalum paspaloides* (Michx) Schribner & *Aeluropus littoralis* (Gouan) in the Camargue (southern France). *Oecologia* 94:204–209. *Grassland Forage Abstr.* 1994. 64(5):1333.

Pinto da Silva, A.R. 1940. The genus *Paspalum* in Portugal. *Agron. Lusitana* 2:5–23. *Herb. Abstr.* 11:335.

Pinto da Silva, A.R. 1942. *Paspalum* species from Portuguese Africa represented in the herbarium of the Colonial Garden, Lisbon (Portugal). *Rev. Agron., Lisboa* 30: 518–529.

Puente, E., M.J. Lopez-Pacheco, and T.E. Diaz. 1985. On the plants of Leon (Spain) Note III. *Acta Botanica Malacitana* 10:41–44.

Puhalla, J., J. Krans, and M. Goatley. 1999. *Sports Fields: A Manual for Design, Construction, and Maintenance.* Ann Arbor Press, Chelsea, MI.

Ramirez, G.C. and A.M. Romero. 1978. The Pacific as a transporting agent on the Chilean coast. *Ecologia* 3:19–30.

Rose-Innes, R. 1977. *A manual of Ghana grasses.* Surbiton, Surrey U.K., Min. Overseas Develop., Land Resources Division.

Schuman, G.L., P.J. Vittum, M.L. Elliott, and P.P. Cobb. 1998. *IPM Handbook for Golf Courses.* Ann Arbor Press, Chelsea, MI.

Swallen, J.R. 1967. New species of *Paspalum. Phytologia* 14:358–389.

Takayama, S.Y., P.M. Freitas, M.S. Pagliarini, and L.A.R. Batista. 1998. Chromosome number in germplasm accessions of *Paspalum* (Plicatula group) from different regions in Brazil. *Euphytica* 99:89–94.

Taylor, B.W. 1965. An outline of the vegetation of Nicaragua. *J. Ecol.* 51:27–54.

Trenholm, L.E., R.N. Carrow, R.R. Duncan. 1999 Relationship of multispectral radiometry data to qualitative data in turfgrass research. *Crop Sci.* 39:763–769.

Trochain, J. 1990. Contribution to the study of vegetation of Senegal. *Mem. Inst. Franc. Afr. Noire* #2:434

Verts, B.J. and R.H. Mohlenbrock. 1966. The Illinois taxa of *Paspalum. Trans. IL. St. Acad. Sci.* 59:29–38.

White, C.T. 1934. Queensland grasses. *Herb. Rev.* 2:5–7. And *Qld. Agric.* 41:54–58.

Index